Seven Golden Miles

The Fantastic Story of Blackpool

by

Kathleen Eyre

Dalesman Books
1975

The Dalesman Publishing Company Ltd.,
Clapham (via Lancaster), North Yorkshire.

First published 1961
(by Weaver & Youles (Printers) Ltd.)
This revised and enlarged edition 1975
© Kathleen Eyre, 1961, 1975

ISBN: 0 85206 306 7

"I have laboured honestly to transmit whatever I could ascertain from common report for the instruction of posterity."

BEDE A.D. 673-735

Printed in Great Britain
by Galava Printing Company Limited, Hallam Road,
Nelson, Lancashire.

Contents

The front cover painting and all uncredited line drawings are by Bruce Danz.

Photographs are on pages 49-56 and 105-112.

(Pages 52 (top), 106 (bottom) and 108 are by kind permission of Blackpool Central Library, and pages 110 and 112 by Frank Dean.)

Chronological summaries of notable events in Blackpool appear on pages 45, 58, 61, 64, 92, 115, 120, 124 and 127.

Raikes Hall Royal Palace Gardens, Blackpool (from a contemporary brochure).

Blackpool

Cottage life in early Blackpool

FOR several centuries after the Norman Conquest, the Butlers, a powerful and influential family, were the Lords of the Manor of Layton. William le Botiller was granted a charter for holding a market and fair in "Laton" and for free warren in his estates there, 1256-7. The market was held weekly on Wednesdays, and the three-day annual fair took place on the festival of St. Andrew the Apostle. Later in that century, an enquiry into these privileges, including the right to set up a gallows, to benefit from "wreck of the sea", and the regulation of assize of bread and beer, confirmed Wm. le Botiller's claim that his ancestors had enjoyed these concessions from the time of the Conquest. The jury found ... "that the memory of man ran not to the contrary and that these rights had been used in the manner alleged". During the 14th century Sir William Boteller held in Bispham, Laton and Warbreck a knight's fee of John of Gaunt, Duke of Lancaster, at that time the chief Lord of the Soil, by fealty and an annual rental of xxiijs. ivd.

On the Thursday after Easter 1416, by deed executed at Laton, the manors of Great and Little Laton, Magna Bispham, Norbrick, Le pull, and other lands, were granted to the use of William Boteller and Elizabeth his wife. This mention of Le pull (the pool—the word applied to running water, at that time) is probably our earliest record of the Blackpool we know to-day. The Butler family continued to hold Bispham, Norbreck and Layton until 1554 when Thomas Fleetwood of Rossall purchased the estate, part of which was sold in 1592 by his son, William Fleetwood, to Edward Rigby of Burgh; whereupon the Rigbys left the Chorley area and took up residence at Layton Hall which they occupied until about 1717 when Sir Alexander Rigby died in the Fleet for debts incurred in an overseas trading concern. The estates thereafter were managed by trustees for the benefit of the creditors. In 1842 Thomas Clifton of Lytham Hall purchased the Manor of Layton for £495.

From the beginning of the 17th century extracts from the Bispham Parish Registers, in which unfortunately there are gaps, lead us to believe that there was a small fishing community in existence near The Pool and the following are baptismal entries for the year 1602. At that early period it was not customary to enter the name of the mother.

1602.	viij July	Robte s. of Thomas Bamber de Poole.
	xxj Sept.	Ellen d. of Thomas Cowban de blackpoole.
	xxx October	William s. of Thomas Bamber Juni' de Poole.
	November	Richard s. of John Roskell de poole xxj.

Unfortunately from 1603-1632 there is a lapse in the records but from the entries which do appear less than twenty surnames can be found in the whole community of Blackpool in the hundred years between 1600-1700. In 1602 the first Blackpudlian pioneers were named Bamber, Butcher, Roskell and Cowban (sometimes written Coobine or Cooban). In 1633 we find Welche (Walsh) and Whiteside; 1635 Singleton; 1636 Jolise; 1640 Hodgson; 1643 Wilkins; 1645 Gotar (sometimes Gaulter or Galter); 1664 Warbreck; 1673 Salthouse; 1683 Parre; 1689 Baley; 1690 Thomason; 1691 Crookall; and 1696 Dobson. It is obvious that the number of surnames gradually increased when the daughter of a house looked further afield for her spouse and brought in a "foreigner" from distant Poulton or Bispham.

There was at this time only a thin splattering of cobble and clay huts perched in an exposed position on the cliffs looking out over the Irish Sea. For convenience, the community took its name from a sluggish dark-coloured stream which emptied out into the sea opposite the present Manchester Square. Two water outlets, one from Marton Mere and the other, Spen Dyke, bringing drainage water from Marton Moss, joined at Spen Dyke (Waterloo Road) corner, and the resultant stream, several feet wide, meandered between marshy meadows towards the sea where its peaty content stained the waters at that point. Wm. Hutton, 1788, tells us: "The water is of a chocolate or liver colour ... so that the place might, with as much propriety, bear the name of Liverpool as Blackpool".

Housebuilding methods in the early 1600s were primitive and likely to be a hundred years behind those of more progressive districts. The Fylde was geographically isolated and travellers would not come here except on specific business and that most rarely. Without traffic and new ideas the natives clung to their old traditional habits. They had never heard of progress, would certainly not have welcomed it, and they took the line that what had suited their grandfathers was good enough for them. Their amateur attempts at home-building provided them with only the barest accommodation necessary for existence. Their tiny homes were insanitary, foul-smelling, draughty and badly short of headroom. Often there was only one room with a hearth in the centre and a hole in the roof through which the sooty smoke might, or might not, eventually emerge and this served as a communal shelter and sleeping place for a man and his wife, their family, and the animals. The walls were crudely knocked up in clay and stone, both materials being free, plentiful and at hand. The floors were of clay or beaten earth which in the dry weather was well enough though a winter's rain churned them to a greasy mud. Strewn rushes might have made for greater comfort but they

6

were renewed infrequently and left lying until they became lice-ridden and foul.

None of these miserable shanties rose to the dignity of glazed windows and throughout the winter the family lived bedevilled by draughts and dampness and sighing lustily for some sign of spring in the air. Meantime there were long dark months when the rain dripped in dismally through the thatch and father sought out the offending leak and rammed in a clod of turf to keep out the weather. The housewife's was a toilsome lot. All the family washing, cooking, spinning by distaff and whorl and weaving having to be accomplished in one room overcrowded with bawling ailing children, elderly relatives and livestock.

Better cottages were built up on crucks, timbered arches prefabricated by the carpenter and notched with his marks (on the same principle as a modern dressmaking pattern) ready to be set up on the site and filled in. The two arches, joined by a sturdy ridge pole at the top and purlins halfway down, formed a wooden cage which was strengthened by shorter timbers pegged in with wooden pins. Once the framing was erected the daubers moved in. Spaces were left for windows and a door, and the daubers working one inside and one outside the building, threw puddled clay on to interlaced wattles set in between the timbers. Strangely enough, to our modern minds, the walls dried out as hard as concrete. Even so, draughts managed to creep in between the crevices around doors and windows. Shingles from the beach were used as decoration and reinforcement and cruck houses generally had two apartments. The "Hall", which was far less grand than it sounds, housed the family and the animals by day. Everyone slept communally in the "Bower" which again fell short of the romantic notions conjured up by the name. Furniture of any sort was a rare luxury and would be confined to a rough trestle table, a few stools and straw-filled pallets laid on the floor for sleeping.

For lighting, the old folk, women and children gathered rushes at full summer and having peeled off all the rind except for a narrow strip to hold the pith intact they dried them in the sun and soaked them in a grease pan containing melted mutton fat mixed, when possible, with beeswax. The greased rushes were laid in a strip of hollow bark which was fastened to the cottage wall with leather straps and burned with a clear light at the rate of approximately half an inch per minute. Two or three shillings-worth of fat gave a provident housewife a whole winter's illumination. Seated by the warmth of his turf fire and by rushlight or tallow dip, the cottager whiled away his winter's evenings carving wooden bowls, platters and spoons for family use and wondering, as food supplies ran low, how long the pig could be allowed to add his snoring contribution to the buzz of family conversation.

Parsnips, beans, peas boiled in the pod, home cured bacon and an occasional egg from the few scrawny hens, salted meat, barley and rye bread, formed the staple diet of the old natives. If there was a shortage of fruit in this area there was an abundance of sea-food, cockles, mussels, shrimps and so on. Now and again a pheasant, hare or pigeon poached from a neighbouring estate, added variety to the menu. Jannocks, a leavened oat bread, and throdkins made from oatmeal and bacon, were a popular labourer's dish. Leeks, onions and parsley masked the rancid flavour of tainted meat and wild honey was prized as a rare delicacy. Potatoes were rare enough for Thomas Tyldesley to mention them specifically in his diary ("potetows") as late as 1713-1715. Buttermilk or water carried from a distant fresh water spring made do when the ale cask ran dry and dried turf and driftwood stoked the family fire. A black stack of turfs stood on one side of the door and the family dunghill on the other, customs which prevailed long after Blackpool had become popular with visitors of fashion.

As the 17th century moved on, flagstone floors replaced the old beaten earth, and a firehood, sweeping down from the roof apex and forming a wide-spreading canopy over the hearth at one end of the hall, replaced the central fireplace and became the focal point of family life. The hood was commodious enough to allow Grandad and his old lady to take their chairs under its shelter and enjoy the full benefit of the fire. But it was still a draughty, smoke-laden and blood-chilling existence and until as late as 1730-1740 in these parts, the mullioned and shuttered cottage windows had seen no glass. A few of the cottages, but not many, would be graced with a porch. Usually the door opened directly opposite the firehood which was supported by a stout oaken beam running the full width of the room. A high-backed settle, called a "speere", diffused the draughts when some caller let in a full blast of chilling Atlantic ozone, for as Fuller wrote in 1662, "the ayre of Lancashire is subtil and piercing". During the 18th century the bower was frequently divided into a small parlour and lower chamber (pronounced "chommer") and ceilinged over to form sleeping quarters in the triangular roof space. A small flight of steps, or a ladder, led up to the bedroom out of the Hall. (There was an example of this at Smithy Cottage, Bispham, where in recent years the bed was set under the highest point and two tall young men had to kneel down on either side of it to get undressed!)

Home-spun flannel, or linsey woolsey, made up by the travelling tailor who boarded with his customers until their order was completed, kept the cottagers tolerably warm. Young and old slept in their every day clothes counting themselves fortunate indeed to possess an extra blanket or two for warmth. The Packman or Pedlar, with his shoulder pack or a horse pannier full of stock and a fund of breezy gossip, was a welcome sight to the housewife hard pressed for needles and thread and other items of haberdashery.

By 1750 it was something of an achievement to have planted half a bushel of potatoes and the cottager preened himself who still had a bushel of wheat in his oaken "kist" at Christmas. Merry indeed was the month of May "that doth inspire, mirth and youth and warm desire" (Milton). The prospect of soft warm days and the summer sun and food in plenty and months of health giving fresh air rejoiced the heart and banished the miseries of winter.

Yet, with all their poverty and rigorous conditions of living, the natives of the Fylde coast were notoriously healthy and long lived. Those who survived the perils of infancy more often than not achieved a ripe old age, worked vigorously and walked prodigiously to the very end of their days. They were hardy and independent, full of superstition and homely fun. They believed in their boggarts and witches; they enjoyed their card games at Christmas. A marriage, a christening, or even a funeral was an excuse for drinking and feasting and many a corpse arrived somewhat tipsily at the church on the unsteady shoulders of his nearest. Bull baiting and bear baiting were popular amusements, and until little more than a century ago cockfighting still reared its infamous head. Telling fortunes, casting spells and charms, and curing by magical formulae every kind of physical ill from nettle-sting, warts and the toothache, to ague, incessant bleeding or the rheumatics, kept the local wisewoman hard at work exercising her peculiar powers. Great store was set on the interpretation of dreams, of keeping watch on the Feast of St. Agnes for the sight of a future husband, of hanging a hag-stone on the stable door and a horse shoe on the one at the cottage, to keep away witches, of scoring a cross into the dough to drive away evil, of sowing onion seeds at the Feast of St. Gregory, and from the early 19th century, the solemn poring over the teacup! Our early natives were a "rude and homely people" all right but we can salute the pioneers of this, the most fabulous holiday resort in the world!

Foxhall and the Tyldesleys

THE spirit of the times can perhaps best be recaptured by looking into the story of the Tyldesley family and their connection with Blackpool. Sir Thomas Tyldesley, a country gentleman of Myerscough, met his death at the Battle of Wigan Lane in 1651 during the Civil War in Lancashire. Serving under him at that time was the youthful Alexander Rigby, a cornet in the royalist forces. Many years later (1679) when Alexander Rigby Esq. had been appointed High Sheriff of Lancashire, he raised a monument to his old commanding officer on the exact spot where Sir Thomas had fallen, then a quarter of a mile to the north of Wigan, but nowadays well within that town. The commemorative pillar was thus inscribed:

An high Act of Gratitude, which conveys the Memory of
SIR THOMAS TYLDESLEY
to posterity,
Who served King Charles the First as Lieutenant-Colonel at Edge-Hill
Battle
After raising regiments of Horse, Foot and Dragoons,
and for
The desperate storming of Burton on Trent, over a bridge of 36 arches,

He afterwards served in all the wars in great command,
Was Governor of Lichfield,
And followed the fortune of the Crown through the Three Kingdoms,
And never compounded with the Rebels though strongly invested;
And on the 25th August, A.D. 1651, was here slain,
Commanding as Major-General under the Earl of Derby,
To whom the grateful erector, Alexander Rigby, Esq., was Cornet;
And when he was High Sheriff of this county, A.D. 1679,
Placed the high obligation on the whole Family of the Tyldesleys,
To follow the noble example of their Loyal Ancestor.

The Tyldesleys, like many north-western gentry, were loyal supporters of the Stuart line and unswerving in their allegiance to Rome. Their ancient faith placed them in constant danger of persecution and after Sir Thomas Tyldesley's death, and possibly to ensure greater freedom and isolation, his son Edward came to this quiet coastal region, drained the marshy area around the black pool, and built for himself a hunting seat and summer residence. It was a sturdy but unpretentious place with three gables, a small look-out tower, and walls of a great thickness made out of sea-stones. The sea on the one side and the marshes on another left only the northerly aspect vulnerable to unwelcome visitors and thus secure from the attentions of Government spies, Edward Tyldesley settled into his quiet retreat in the years following 1651.

It was a pleasant life for the family living in the "little hall among huts". Roman Catholic priests came and went without detection. The humble cottagers would accord their betters a very proper respect. Within a pleasant morning's gallop there were families of similar fortune and standing, and around them a whole region sympathetic to the faith. Moreover, in recognition of the gallant services rendered to the Crown by his family, Edward Tyldesley confidently expected to be elevated to the proposed Order of Knights of the Royal Oak, but somehow, despite reminders, Charles II never got around to making good his intent. Lawton Hawes, a tract of common land which Edward Tyldesley had anticipated as a reward, did not pass into his hands. If there were disappointments, however, there were also compensations.

Layton Hawes, covering 1,800 acres from Division Lane to Manchester Square and bounded by Common Edge Lane, Hawes Side Lane and Ansdell Road, was common to the inhabitants of the Parish of Bispham and the Martonians in the Parish of Poulton. There every householder could pasture his cattle and sheep and cut turf for his own domestic use, entirely rent free. The broad flat acres of springy turf were an ideal setting for races and sports gatherings of all kinds and until an Act of Parliament of 1767, by which "Laton Hawes" was "inclosed, allotted and divided", the sporting gentry of the Fylde and crowds of pleasure-seeking rustics regularly flocked there on Holy Days and Sundays.

"Morality", says Thornber, "was at a low ebb. At a distance of three miles from any place of worship ... who can wonder, knowing what human nature is, that wickedness and sin abounded? ... Upon the unenclosed commons of Layton Hawes and Thornton Marsh, numbers were wont to spend their sabbath in the pursuit of their daily avocations, buying and selling, or in encouraging the young in games of amusement; in fact, that holy day was peculiarly devoted to business and pleasure, not to rest and holiness ... Here ... the injunctions of the notorious book of sports were religiously observed ... with all their host of enormities."

The Book of Sports was the product of King James I who, irritated by the Puritanical element which he encountered during his Lancashire travels did, "in his princely wisdom, publish a declaration to all his loving subjects concerning lawful sports to be used on Sundays and Festivals" (1618) and permitting dancing, games, archery, leaping, vaulting, Maypoles, May-games and Morris-dances to be enjoyed on the Sabbath Day after divine service. These privileges did not extend to papists and non-attenders at church. Nevertheless, whether Protestant or Catholic, rich or poor, the young and old of the district flocked to the Hawes on Sundays and all other days convenient for the purpose of having a jolly good time.

We gather a clear picture of this from the diary of Edward's son, Thomas Tyldesley who, during the three years 1712-1714, was scribbling an almost Pepys-ish account of the daily life in the household of a sporting country squire. Thomas Tyldesley was born on 3rd April, 1657 and was twice married. By 1712 we find him in his mid-fifties, a jolly, garrulous, sociable, sporting and somewhat intemperate character who seemed to divide his time between galloping all over the country and staying "in the house alday" purging himself with quantities of "phissick". The entries reveal a lovable hypochondriac with troublesome bowels and a tendency to gravel and the gout, a regular attender at the cock-pits, a socialite, a prodigious horseman, keen gardener, devout Catholic and an acute observer of the trivial but fascinating details of 18th century domestic life.

1712: 24th April. Gave Evan Williams, the Manx skipper, 8 double bottles to fill with brandy, gave him a piece of beef to take to the island. (A hint of smuggling here.)

10th May. Alday att Fox Hall, busy in my garden. Pd Will, the Maynes gardener, pro three days, 1s. 6d.; so I went to bedd.

31st May. Went to ye Hays (Layton Hawes) to see a race betwixt Mr. Harper's mare and Sanderson's; meet a greatt deall of good company but spend noe thing, my coz. W.W., with me, who had been all night with me; affter ye race went to Litham; stayed there two hours; thence backe to Fox Hall.

17th June. Alday at Fox Hall till the eivening, when sister and Mrs. about 4 went to wate on my Lady Peters (Mary Clifton married the 6th Lord Petre) and I went to Rogers to meet my Lord and company about messuring ye horses to run next day ... soe to Fox Hall; gave Mrs. 2s. to bye provision with.

18th June. Went to Litham to dinner; thence to the raice; won 10s. of Sir Francis Andrews, but Jem Singleton treated all, so I spent noething ... Will Hesketh and Mr. Whitingham went with mee to Fox Hall and stayed till 12.

11

7th August. Very bussy all morning in my hay; after dinner went with Mrs. to Thurnham; (the home of the Dalton family, near Cockerham) gave her 4s. to give two majds for ye Lady had made a shee child; soe home.

18th August. Bussy unloading the boatfull off turfe; spent 6d. at Bridge-end; pd. the boatman 10s., viz. : Wilkinson, his man and dum Jemmy; sent pro Mrs. 10s. to Mr. Jo : Lawson pro boatte hier.

3rd Sept. Pd. 2s. pro buttr to Sara; 6d. pro a day's thatching; gave Sara 6d. pro her boy to gett me crabes and 1s. pro her paines; thence to Lanr; meete the sheriff and went with him to meet ye judge; suped with him that night.

11th Sept. Almorning at Fox Hall with Samy Butler a ffowling; about noone Capn Veale came and dined with us, where we were very merry over one bottle claret and two off sherry.
8th Oct. Paid 2d. pro potetows.

22nd Oct. 2d. pro tobaco.
November primo. Went a hunting with Cos. Butler; meet a many com-pany; killed a brace of hares; went to ye White Bull (Preston) with Sany Butler, Young Lord Gabrel Hesketh and honest Tho Lucas, where Sany B . . . r and Gabr H. devoured all the pyes in the house but not one mouthful to us 3 poor pill garlickes—spent 4d. thence to Kirkland.

7th Nov. Went to Cos. Hesketh's a hunting and ffell lame off the goutt.

17th Nov. Very lame in both ffeet.

25th Nov. Outt of ordr; tuck man (Mannate—a laxative), and very sicke all day.

1713: 27th Jan. In muche paine occasioned by the bad wethr off angr winde and vast great snow wh ffell in great ffleakes, licke ye largest off goose quills, wch obligded my godson to afford us his acceptable com-pany an othr night.

15th Mar. Doctr Harden here and dined with us as did Cos. Carus; gave Ned Malley 5s. to goe to Preston ffaire with Ruby (a mare). I walked down to ye stables, with helpe. Cos Tom Carus and his lady suped with us on whilkes in the shell.

16th Mar. About 10 gott on horseback and calld att Mr. Beardsworth door where Cos. Sherson and Tom Tayr treated me with a noging off brandy.

17th Mar. Went to Cockerham and dined with Brothr ffrost.

21st Mar. Went to meet Bro ffrost and Sany Butler a ffowling at Condor Green, butt they came nott; went to Cockerham . . . stayd there till 4, soe home.

18th Sept. Gave ye postboy 2d. to carry a letter to Dicke Gorney and pd 4d. pro a London lettr; soe to beed.

9th Oct. Gave Hen. Hosfeild towards reparing the stone brooken, wch was the inscription on ye moniment ffor Sir Tho Tyldesley, 2s. 6d.

23rd Dec. In the morning went a-coursing with Sir W. G., Lawr. Rigby &c., to Ashton. Found Mr. Walker just come ffrom Scotland, Sir Will G. & I went to dinr to Thurnham. In ye eivening Bror Dalton returned home who tould us hee was apprehensive of beeing robed on Mirscough Planke by 3 well mounted. (Highwaymen lying in wait on the highroad.)

28th Dec. Gave Mrs. 1s. After diner went to Ye White Bull; Mr. Beards-worth ffollowed mee; Met ye tenents, spent 5s. on them . . . we had a hare & ffowle rosted and were very merry.

From the beginning of 1714 "poor Tom", as the diarist some-times refers to himself, suffered declining health, lameness, pains, the "gripes" and occasional depressions. When "a great deal of wimen came to see sister", he tells us, "they satt with mee till I was sicke with theyre chattle". Similarly, when his gentlemen friends came to bid him good cheer, he sourly notes how they "stick together, jolly and merry; I in paine alday". But as soon as he is fit to move out of doors, "I ventured to ye mill and stayd there half an howr", and in the spring we find him travelling to Myerscough, calling at Thurnham for a fishmeet, getting soused in a hail shower at Kirkland and having to "call for 2 hott potts to comfforth my stomake"; "ffox hunting to Sullam"; dining with the Lord of the Manor at Crooke Barne; Hunting at Claughton; and chivvying the "Mrs. ... to bye sugr, corkes hops etc." for a summer brew. Between the activities of summer and autumn, however, the diarist recites a mounting list of physical discomforts and his diary ceases abruptly on the 11th November, 1714. He died a few weeks later and was buried at Garstang towards the end of January, 1715. Not, however, without having left us a clear picture of a substantial home with stables, flower and vegetable gardens, beehives, meadows, fruit trees, a stone tablet over the gateway on which was carved a pelican feeding her young, and a stout cobble wall surrounding the whole.

By dying early in 1715, Thomas Tyldesley was spared the turmoils and stresses in which his son, Edward, was to become involved later in the same year in connection with the Jacobite Rebellion. Edward Tyldesley, who had raised a troop of men, joined the rebel forces at Preston, and had been seen dining with Jacobite officers and marching through the town with a drawn sword, was miraculously acquitted by the jury at his trial, despite the protests of the Judge and a mass of damning evidence. His friends were scarcely as fortunate. John Dalton of Thurnham Hall was extended the royal clemency after a spell in Newgate Gaol but his enormous fine crippled him for life. Richard Butler of Rawcliffe Hall died in prison and his father, the old Squire Henry Butler, who managed to escape by boat up the Wyre, was never heard of again. Lesser mortals were transported or brought to execution and thus ignominiously ended the Jacobite Rebellion of 1715 which brought death or ruin to those who had taken part.

In any case, by this time the Tyldesley family, beset by mortgages and debts, was rapidly on the decline and within two or three generations had dwindled into obscurity. Edward Tyldesley probably never lived at Fox Hall though his stepmother stayed on there for several years after her husband's death. Edward Tyldesley died in 1736 and some years later Fox Hall passed out of the family. Its grandness swiftly fled. Possibly it was divided between one or two tenants who would not hesitate to open their doors to summer visitors or serve thirsty travellers with home brewed ale. We know that it was being let furnished for the season in the early 19th century.

In 1838 George Caton held the Foxhall beershop, cottage, garden and bowling green. He was succeeded by his son, Richard Caton, who bought the place for £1,200. He retired in 1885 and it was bought by Mr. Tom Lockwood for £5,000 and, after the custom of the times, provided with a large room for singing and dancing. Within ten years Mr. Lockwood sold out to Seed's Breweries for £10,000 and removed to the Golden Ball at Poulton. Upon the death of Mr. Richard Seed the hotel was auctioned and withdrawn at £34,000. The Seed family had a great sentimental attachment to the old Foxhall and when their public houses were taken over by Dutton's Breweries the thought of this historic structure having to be pulled down and replaced in modern style prompted them to keep it in the family. The original cobble walls, though cemented over, were still there and indeed, behind the brick frontage, they still are! The downstairs rooms have been modernised but not enough to disguise the thickness of the walls, nor to destroy the picture of Thomas Tyldesley scratching away at his diary, looking out on a grey sea and "snow fflakes" as big as "ye goose quills", and shivering over the fire in his parlour feeling "uneassy at my stomacke".

It is worth calling at the Foxhall to see the two tiny parlours set one on either side of the front door; and the corner room, timbered in Tudor style, where the diarist's initials are set above the fireplace. On the opposite wall is a replica of the Tyldesleys' carved stone tablet showing a mother pelican feeding a nestful of young. The original tablet disappeared for a number of years but came to light eventually at Rawcliffe Hall. Mr. Seed had a plaster cast taken from it and the design has been faithfully reproduced at the Foxhall. Towards the end of last century crowds flocked to the singing room at the hotel, as much to be entertained as to be refreshed. Out of work music hall artistes were glad of a few weeks' work, waiting on the tables, cheering the customers with comic and sentimental songs. They arrived flat broke at the beginning of the week and had to "sub" their wages so frequently that there was often nothing to be collected by Saturday. Most famous of the singing waiters at the Foxhall was Wilkie Bard, the stuttering comic singer of "K–K–K–Katie!", but there were many others who later made their names on the halls.

Fox Hall in the late eighteenth century.

14

In the early years of this century a building contractor, Mr. Gregson, was called in to demolish an old cobble place a few yards away from the Foxhall and to build on its site a Working Men's Club. Under the clay at that point they discovered a well some 50 feet deep and capacious enough to provide all the houses in South Shore with fresh water. Its discovery provided a handy receptacle for the old surplus cobbles which otherwise could only have been removed by horse and cart and sold for a meagre 2s. 6d. per ton. It is not at all unlikely that this long covered well once supplied the Tyldesley family at Foxhall.

1720—1780
The first visitors arrive—Blackpool on the map

DURING the persecutions of Roman Catholics in England in the 16th and 17th centuries, the Fylde in general and the coastal plain in particular remained as a world apart, the stronghold of the old faith. Taking their lead from the landed and influential families, the Cliftons of Lytham, the Tyldesleys of Myerscough and Foxhall, Blackpool, the Veales of Whinney Heys, the Rigbys of Layton Hall and later of Poulton, the Westbys of Mowbreck, near Kirkham, and so on, the humbler classes clung to their Romish traditions secure enough in their remoteness to escape the more vigorous persecutions meted out in more accessible districts. Through many generations, Catholic priests had been harboured by the rich and powerful families, disguised sometimes as domestic servants or farm labourers. Their presence was an open secret amongst the sympathetic communities grouped around the great halls and all who had a mind could avail themselves of the facilities for secret worship afforded within these privately maintained chapels.

Travelling Jesuits moved about with comparative impunity. The gracious hospitality which they enjoyed, and the diversity of sporting entertainments in a green countryside where wealth provided the means and nature ensured an ideal setting for such enjoyable pastimes as shooting, coursing, otter-hunting, fishing, horse-racing and games, doubtless impressed the Fathers whose favourable reports would be passed by word of mouth to far off places. The penal days were by no means over in the years 1720-1780, but the worst had long since passed. The Toleration Acts, as well as the natural toleration of the people, had made things easier for Roman Catholics to follow their faith except in difficult years like 1715 and 1745 (the two Jacobite Rebellions).

Still, in the early years of the 18th century, only a few visitors had braved the journey and trickled into Blackpool. Until the 1730s no arrangements had been made for their accommodation. Blackpool was merely a straggle of hotch-potch hovels strung out intermittently along a stretch of desolate cliffs and numbering less than thirty. From the Lane End (Church Street and Promenade junction) to Fumbler's Hill (then on the cliffs north of the present Butlin's Metropole) there were perhaps less than ten lowly domestic shelters. In the Central Pier region, along cliffs long since crumbled into the sea, there were perhaps twenty or so dilapidated dwellings comprising Walsh's Row and Butcher's Cottages. These and an occasional labourer's shelter completed the hamlet. The few inhabitants lived in their tiny clay-floored dwellings, living and sleeping in close proximity and seeing nothing unusual in a hen perched on the back of a chair, a pig snoring in front of the turf fire, a duck with her young splashing about in a puddle collected into a hollow of the floor, or a huddle of children singing to forget their hunger.

The natives were ignorant, riddled with superstitions, poverty stricken and long lived. A man was considered to have been deprived of his just dues if he failed to reach his 80th birthday and many far exceeded this ripe old age. There can surely be no better testimony to the health giving properties of Blackpool's boisterous sea air, especially when one pictures the stinking family dunghill, to which offal from the day's catch of fish added its own pungent contribution, set immediately outside the door. Yet, the early visitor, clasping a handkerchief to his nose, would be glad to find shelter in one of these humble homes, thankful perhaps to share an already overcrowded bed, astonished if he managed to get a straw pallet to himself, and not in the least put out if he had to bed down in an outhouse. Indeed, communal sleeping was so customary a thing that, as visitors gradually became more choosy, one old Blackpudlian grand-dam declared she didn't know what people were coming to; in her young days they were glad to sleep twelve in a bed; nowadays they grumbled if they had to sleep five!

By 1735, sufficient visitors were arriving to encourage Ethart a-Whiteside to make over a cottage especially for their reception. This was an ordinary cobble and straw-thatch building, rectangular in shape and with no special amenities beyond a proximity to the cliffs and the shore, and a pleasant setting in fields now covered by General Street. The local tale runs that Whiteside had been lucky enough to wed a Welsh cook of no mean skill. Her excellent catering and hospitable manner, plus the rejuvenating air of Blackpool, drew a houseful of visitors for half a century. Having thus made his "fortune", Whiteside retired to Layton and died there at a ripe old age. He was succeeded at the cottage lodging house by a native called Tom the Cobbler. His methods, by contrast, were crude and haphazard for he approached the dinner table with fingers still blackened from his trade and proceeded to dole out portions of bread from the depths of his apron pocket. We can imagine the genteel shuddering with horror at these insanitary habits and when better houses became established visitors transferred their patronage and the cobbler lost his monopoly.

In 1750 the much travelled Bishop Pococke recorded: "At Black Pool near the sea are accommodations for people who come to bathe", and "Black Pool Town" was marked on Bowen's map of Lancashire in 1751 for the first time. Soon after this date Mr. Forshaw established his small white inn (site of Clifton

Hotel) which quickly rose to pre-eminence and became "the chief abode of the fashionables". At the Lane End Mr. Lewtas served refreshments at his little white cottage (site of Montague Burtons, Ltd.) and a former blacksmith's shop had been turned into a coffee room; and, if we can believe an advertisement of 1910 which refers to the "Oldest Hostelry in the Town", with a "Licence dating prior to 1750"!, the County and Lane Ends Hotel stood on the opposite corner.

Far to the south and isolated, many visitors sought refuge at Old Margery's, later Bonnys (site of King Edward VII, Chapel Street). The proprietress in this early period provided genteel accommodation for 10d. per day, but away to the distant north guests were boarded at the old Gynn for as little as 8d. The Rev. Wm. Thornber in his history records for us that at one time 74 horses belonging to visitors were quartered simultaneously at the Gynn. Fortunately there were vast open acres for grazing and the animals were turned out into a huge field and captured at the end of the stay. Saddles and bridles were thrown in a jumble into some convenient outbuilding and sorted out from amongst a massive pile in time for the return journey.

Further up what is now called Church Street, commencing at the site of Samuel's, Jewellers, there were three thatched cottages with gardens, and a little way up the rise was the No. 2, the demolished Adelphi public house. (This would perhaps be a good opportunity to settle once and for all the local arguments about which was the No. 2. Some of our old ones get very hot under the collar if you try to tell them it was the Adelphi in Church Street (listed under that name in the 1850's). "You're wrong, you're wrong", they will tell you, with a great deal of emphasis and a ruffling of feathers. "The No. 2 Hotel was The Grosvenor". A glance at the Tithe Map for Layton would show them that in 1838 the Adelphi was there in full flourish when the site of the Grosvenor was an unmarked spot in the midst of wide open fields!)

But back to 18th century Blackpool in which it was no easy matter to provide for the family, much less cater for a few dozen guests. Mr. Henry Banks, who kept the Lane Ends Hotel shortly after the visit of the Huttons, recalled some of those early difficulties in an after-dinner speech made at the age of more than 80. He could remember when there was but one sash window in the whole of Blackpool; all the rest were small and leaded. Every roof, with the exception of four which had been recently slated, was thatched in the old manner. There was no shop, and neither butcher nor baker in the hamlet. Supplies of every kind had to be carried in from Layton or Marton. Even in later years Mr. Banks recalled that "nothing came into Blackpool for sale, neither ducks, fowls, butter, eggs, nor any kind of vegetables. We had to send into the country three or four days a week to get what was wanted". Other hotelkeepers sent regularly as far as Poulton and when supplies ran low any unexpected visitors would have to nurse their hunger in patience and wait for a mounted messenger galloping back with extra provisions. The west side of the beach, extending to a considerable width, was green grassed from top to bottom. Starr-grassed sand-dunes came in very handy for the hiding of smuggled goods and wreck-plunder. The sea, except in times of storm, came in gently and rarely ventured beyond the gravel cast up into high ridges by successive tides and stretching along the beach as far as South Shore.

Except for the visitors, no-one thought of travelling beyond walking distance. Consequently there was "neither donkey, pony, gig, car, or any other kind of conveyance then kept" in the vicinity. It must have been a world-shattering event when the first stage-coach rumbled into the hamlet and the venerable Mr. Banks could recall the incident and remembered that the fare was then 7s. inside and 5s. outside. (He did not, however, stipulate the point of departure.) It is obvious that in the years before the building of the first good hotels the lower orders who frequented Blackpool during the summer were quite prepared to accept the rough and ready conditions of the times. Only better accommodation could hope to attract the wealthy, the fashionable and the proud.

18th century travel and accommodations

FYLDE roads, if a maze of pot-holed tracks meandering around farmers' fields could be graced by such a name, were as vile and bothersome as any in the kingdom. The King's Highway from Preston to Kirkham wandered like a sulky river around all the neighbouring hamlets; the road over Clifton and Lea Marshes was "frequently overflowed by the tides ... and sometimes impassable", and a brief stretch of toll road, privately con-structed in 1781 by landowners Thomas Clifton and Sir Henry Hoghton, was a bare twelve feet wide and bordered by capacious ditches floating with mud. From Kirkham, where a blacksmith plied his trade in the confident expectation of lively business occasioned through breakdowns, the harassed traveller, having no Blackpool Tower to lure him towards his goal, took his choice from a tangle of tracks and hopefully turned his horse's head into the teeth of a salt wind. There were neither signposts nor milestones, and inhabitants of whom he might have enquired his direction, were almost as scarce in this level countryside "sore destitute of wood".

At this time the clay cliffs of Blackpool rose to heights ranging between three and one hundred feet (highest point at Uncle Tom's Cabin), and there was neither hedge nor tree to soften a naked and wind-bitten coastline. About fifty hovels, as if tossed by some giant hand, without conformity or design, straggled to the extent of one mile along the sea bank. The shelters of the local families remained degenerate and unkempt, a jumble of wind-blown shanties without pretensions or comfort. A handful of new cottages with slated roofs and one or two well equipped hotels had made their appearance along the sea front by the 1780s. The proprietors never thought to name their houses but rather the houses were known by the names of their owners. Apart from the old-established Gynn which stood beside the cliff road leading to Bispham, the most northerly was Bailey's (later Metropole, now Butlin's) which appeared on an old print dated 1784. In 1785 its proprietor was endeavouring to attract the "Gentry and the Public" by advertising in the Manchester press:

1785. June 14. Lawrence Bailey takes the liberty of acquainting the Public that he has completely furnished and fitted up a commodious genteel house in an eligible situation and that he hopes by his accommodations to merit the encouragement of such ladies and gentlemen as may be pleased to favour him with their company. N.B. A bathing machine will be kept for the use of his friends.

Apparently the advertisements paid off. Bailey's which had a bowling green, a bathing house and a well, was soon established and remained for long years the principal resort of the elite. The daily tariff was 3s. 4d. per day, exclusive of liquors. Casual visitors paid 1s. 0d. for dinner or supper and 8d. bought tea or breakfast. These amounts may seem small but bed and board of an inferior sort could be had for eighteenpence a day and at some cottages beds cost as little as 6d. a night. Here are two other advertisements which appeared in the "Manchester Mercury":

1787. 1st May. John Bonney informs his friends and the public that he has built a very large dining room, with lodging room for 20 beds, in addition to the House lately occupied by his father-in-law, Mr. Bickerstaff, which has been fitted up in a neat and commodious manner for the reception of families during the bathing season. Ladies and gentlemen, 2s. 2d. per day each; Children 1s. 6d.; Servants, 1s. 6d. Table beer included. Horses, Hay and grass per night, 8 pence.

1787. 26th July. Mr. Sharples, Blackpool, begs to inform the public that he had fitted up his house in a very genteel manner for the reception of ladies and gentlemen who resort to Blackpool during the bathing season. The house is very pleasantly situated and contains 18 lodging rooms; a coach house, stabling for 16 horses and other conveniences. The terms are: For ladies and gentlemen, 2s. a day; Children and servants, 1s. 6d.

A few hundred yards in a southerly direction brought the visitor to Forshaw's (now Clifton Hotel), a pleasantly situated and well equipped tavern with terms similar to those at Bailey's, though with a less prideful air. The next establishment of note was the Lane Ends (County) Hotel, and on 23rd October, 1787, we find the following interesting announcement:

To be let for a term of years, by private contract, all that large and commodious and well established Inn at Blackpool, known as the LANE ENDS, with the barn, stabling and other out offices and conveniences thereto belonging, together with any quantity of land from 12 to 30 acres. N.B. The house is at present fitted up with 70 beds and all other necessary and proper furniture, which may be had on a fair valuation, and if more agreeable, paid for by instalments. Further particulars to be had of Mr. Thos. Lewtas on the premises, who may be treated with on good terms.

Obviously Mr. Hudson was not tardy in treating with Mr. Thomas Lewtas, for in the following summer The Lane Ends ("the house of 80") now referred to as Hudson's, was opening its doors and its heart to the Hutton family. Further south still, on the site of Woolworth's, was Hull's Tavern, later known as The Houndhill and then as The Royal. Bailey's, Forshaw's, Hudson's and Hull's, then, were the most prominent company houses in the centre of Blackpool. At the southern extremity of the hamlet was the old Foxhall, now toppled from its lofty status and reduced to taking in visitors. But first, the visitor would come upon Elston's tavern on the front whilst a few minutes' walk inland up the rising Bonny's Lane (Chapel Street) the sturdy shape of Bonny's-i' th'-fields, formerly known as Old Margery's, rose up out of the green.

Bonny's-i'-th'-Fields, formerly Old Margery's, a whitewashed farmhouse "far out in the country". Demolished in 1902, its site is now occupied by the King Edward VII, Chapel Street.

Despite its southerly and isolated location, Bonny's (site of King Edward VII) was extremely popular with visitors who, perhaps attracted in previous years to the Foxhall, had developed a fondness for this little bit of Blackpool-in-the-country. The Bonnys were an old farming family. Their land, covering nearly 50 acres, extended from the present railway bridge over Chapel Street through to the old Whitegate-lane. From their property, in a landward direction, a much used foot-track "Lovers' Walk", crossed the fields and connected with the old country lane leading to Marton (now Whitegate Drive). Except for Church Street and until Hornby Road was opened out in the 1870s, there was no other way through from the sea except by "Lovers' Walk" which came out almost opposite the old Belle Vue Gardens.

John Bonny built his wine-house on to the western side of the original cottages in 1787 and there were several reasons for his success so far inland, or so it would be considered at the time. His father-in-law, Mr. Bickerstaff, had catered for visitors for a number of years and the goodwill was inherited by his daughter Jenny, Mrs. John Bonny. John Bonny no doubt had learned the knack of anticipating his customers' needs from his parents who, from as far back as 1741, had kept the "gin" (Gynn). Despite the demands of a large family of 7 sons and 1 daughter, he succeeded in filling his house in the season. He had ready access to fresh farm and kitchen-garden produce. There was wisdom, too, in having placed the tavern high and out of the reach of the overflowing sea. The depression between Bonny's and the beach was frequently waterlogged by high tides and flooding from the main dyke. The dampness only evaporated in a long dry summer and plant life flourished and decayed, only to spring up anew.

In addition to these first class establishments, cottage tenants snatched at the opportunity to boost their family income by stuffing every cranny and outbuilding with paying guests.

By this time the fashionable George Cooke, who returned to England upon the outbreak of the War of Independence and settled in Blackpool about 1780, established a tavern and post office in the fields between Forshaw's and the Lane Ends, after spending several years in America. He originated the first postal service by having a mail bag carried to Kirkham several times a week. On 14th June, 1791, he advertised in the "Manchester Mercury":

George Cooke returns his respectful acknowledgments to the ladies and gentlemen who frequented the place the last two seasons for the great encouragement he received from them, and as he now flatters himself his place is generally approved of, no exertion in his power shall be wanting to merit the future approbation and support of the public. He has commenced business for the season and will dispose of, upon reasonable terms, Gunpowder, Hyson, Souchong and Congou teas of the first quality; White's Cocoa, coffee, chocolate, loaf and brown sugar, sago, tapioca, spices of all kinds and other groceries; Jewellery of the newest fashion from one of the first houses in London. An assortment of hosiery, millinery, linen, drapery, haberdashery, perfumery and stationery; turnery, confectionery, bathing caps and dresses, etc. ... The public room will be furnished with a library of books, a large collection of copper plate engravings ... newspapers and magazines, etc.; and in the billiard room is a handsome table and every thing necessary to render that genteel amusement agreeable to the company. Ladies may have anything made in the genteelest manner and at the shortest notice. He has also laid in a good assortment of all liquors and wines.

In 1789, or thereabouts, this enterprising man established the first lending library in Blackpool, requesting the subscribers to be so good as "to return those they take out of the room as soon as they are perused". His terms were: Week, 1s. 6d.; Fortnight, 2s. 6d.; Month, 5s.; Season, 10s. 6d. "The encouragement given to his undertaking", he states, "has far exceeded his most sanguine expectations". All these facilities, plus a little white cottage coffee house at the Lane Ends, were gradually making it easier for the innkeepers and more attractive to the visitors and natives. That Blackpool had become well established by the end of the 18th century is borne out by an article which appeared in the "Blackburn Mail" on 24th June, 1795:

We are happy to inform the public, the accommodation at Blackpool this season exceeds all the excellencies of former years. At Mr. Bailey's house they are most superb, and the hilarity and wit of the company are enlivened by the superiority of the viands and the wine. Mr. Hudson of the Centre-house has lately set up a new chariot for the use of the ladies, and for the devotees the Rev. Mr. Elstone delivers most excellent admonitions. To describe the sea prospects as seen from the cliffs of Egbert is impossible. The beauty of passing ships, and the grandeur of the ocean, can only be exceeded by the loveliness of the ladies on the sands, on horseback, in their walks, and in curricles and other carriages. A Company of Comedians is shortly expected: and in the meantime Mr. and Mrs. Cooke are extremely anxious to render their print and news-room agreeable to the company, and their circulating library is replete with novels, romances and every publication that the literary world affords—in short, we may justly call Blackpool the first watering place in the kingdom, whether we consider the salubrity of the air, the beauty of the scenery, the excellence of the accommodation, or the agreeable company of which it is the general resort. We can therefore safely recommend it either to the valetudinarian, the bon-vivant, or the lover, and we are happy to find the company is likely to be more numerous and general than in any former year.

Regular coach services operated in the 1780s. The Manchester and Blackpool Diligence departed at six o'clock in the morning, three times a week, from the Royal Oak Inn, Manchester, and connected with the Lancaster and Carlisle Diligences at Preston, about noon. A Halifax to Blackpool service, instituted in 1782, cost 18s. 6d. for a single journey which took over twelve hours. The discomforts and expense involved in such an undertaking were considerable; but nothing could stem the tide of visitors to this health giving coast.

Blackpool in 1788, as seen by William Hutton and his daughter

THE earliest descriptive account of a young and rising Blackpool is preserved to us through the efforts of her earliest historian, William Hutton, following a summer's visit in 1788. Seabathing, and the visiting of watering places, had by this time caught the national fancy, royalty setting the lead at such places as Bright-helmstone (Brighton) and Cheltenham, the nobility and gentry swiftly following suit, and the lesser orders being no less eager to follow the example set by fashionable society. During the previous summer, the Hutton family of Birmingham had ventured as far as Aberystwyth, but in July 1788 "we determined to change our watering place and this year made a visit to Blackpool".

William Hutton, son of a wool comber, was born at Derby on 30th September, 1723. At the age of seven he was apprenticed at a silk mill, and at fourteen he entered into another seven-year apprenticeship under his uncle at Nottingham, learning how to manufacture silk stockings. At the age of twenty-six, how-ever, he was sufficiently attracted to bookbinding to walk to London and back to purchase the tools of the trade. His first bookshop was opened at Southwell, twenty miles distant from Nottingham, and this involved him in forty miles daily of walk-ing to and fro. Twelve months of rising at 4 a.m., and arriving home at ten o'clock at night, proved more than enough. William Hutton moved to Birmingham in 1750, opened the first circulating library there in 1751, and after starting a warehouse, launching into the paper trade and prospering through land speculation, he published his "History of Birmingham" in 1782. Perhaps at last he had found his true bent and on arriving at Blackpool he tells us:

I was struck with the place, wrote its history, which was my fourth publication, price one shilling. The landlords met, agreed to take the whole edition, 720 copies and I agreed to sell them at prime cost, six-pence each. Hudson and Bailey (two Blackpool hotelkeepers) stood joint paymasters. These worthy gentlemen, stationed at a distance, which often tries a man's honesty, obliged me to stay four years for the money. Bailey, in the interim, broke. Hudson would pay only his own share of the nine pounds. The other I lost. We stayed here near three months. My poor wife was attacked with an alarming fever.

None of this, however, could have been in the mind of William Hutton, as he happily contemplated the pleasures of a visit to an up-and-coming little seaside village on the Lancashire coast. At home, meantime, at Bennett's Hill, Washwood Heath, Birming-ham, the ladies were caught up in all the domestic excitement of holiday preparations, and something of it is captured in a letter from Hutton's daughter, Catherine, to her friend, Mrs. Andre of Enfield:

I thank you for the description of the long gauze cloak which would have enabled me to make mine correctly if it had not been made before it arrived, but having waited a fortnight I considered your milliner was very uncertain, that my wanting to take the cloak to Blackpool was very sure, and that if I committed a trifling error there was probably no-one who could detect me. So I made it without a lesson from my good preceptress and have succeeded tolerably well. It is very full and elegant and when it appears it draws all eyes after the wearer. There is nothing to be seen like it in Birmingham. On Saturday we set out on our journey and on Monday evening expect to arrive at Blackpool where we shall pass two or three months if the place agrees with my mother.

Let Catherine herself take up the tale after what must have proved a protracted, bone-shaking, tedious and thoroughly un-comfortable three-day journey, in her first letter from Blackpool to the same friend:

You desire an account of Blackpool. You shall have it. Blackpool is situated on a level dreary moorish coast; the cliffs are of earth and not very high. It consists of a few houses ranged in line with the sea and four of these are for the reception of company. One accommodates 30, one 60, one 80 and the other 100 persons. We were strangers to all, and on the recommendation of the master of the Inn at Preston we drove to the house of 80 which is called Lane's End. The company now consisted of about 70 and I never found myself in such a mob. The people sat down to table behind their knives and forks to be ready for their dinner, while my mother, my father and myself, who did not choose to scramble, stood behind till someone more considerate than the rest made room for us. These people are, in general, of a species called Boltoners, that is, rich, rough, honest manufacturers of the town of Bolton, whose coarse-ness of manners is proverbial even among their countrymen. The other houses are frequented by better company, that is Lancashire gentry, Liverpool merchants, and Manchester manufacturers. I find here that I have no equals but the lawyers, for those who are my equals in fortune are distinguished by their vulgarity, and those who are my equals in manners are above me in situation. Fortunately for me, there is no lack of lawyers in Lancashire, Preston alone containing 50; and there are always at Blackpool some whom I like, and with these I laugh at the rest.

It is not difficult to picture poor dear Catherine, a spinster of 32, riddled with all the lamentable snobbery and class consciousness of her time, tittering behind a politely raised hand at the antics of the gruff and entirely unselfconscious Lancastrians. Our very genteel chronicler continued:

Good company, like good wine, needs no bush. The company of this house being in general not good, I am its bush. If any strangers of a better sort stray here by chance they are sure to find me out, and I have more than once been the occasion of their not seeking other quarters. The master of the house has been heard to declare that he would keep me for nothing and save the credit of his establishment rather than let me go. The general observations I have been enabled to make on the Lancastrians are that the Boltoners are sincere, good humoured and noisy. The Manchestrians reserved and purse proud; the Liverpoolians free and open as the ocean on which they get their riches. I know little of the gentry but I believe them to be generous, hospitable and rather given to intemperance.

All the same, she has to admit that "all ranks and both sexes are more robust than the people of the south. Hysterics and the long train of nervous disorders are unknown in the county". The vigorous north must have come as something of a shock to the gently-reared town-dwelling Catherine. Lancashire women were scarcely less loud and forthright than their menfolk and, having come to the seaside to enjoy themselves, they were unlikely to waste one precious moment on suchlike feminine foibles as fainting fits and the vapours. Even the wife of the Rector of Rochdale, a gentlewoman "in person and manner resembling a good fat housekeeper ... is excellently skilled in pickling shrimps, potting herrings, raising goose pies and flourishing in pastry" ... but, remarks Catherine with a hint of disapproval ... "I daresay never heard of curry in her life!" Despite all her criticisms of the "Boltoners", as she called them, these rough, honest, inland folk were extremely polite and thoughtful towards their fellow guest, and again she writes:

I was a great favourite with these people who would have done anything for me in their way. One thing they did, I should think, out of the common way. My mother and I slept over the dining room and one night after we were in bed they were so obstreperous below that the noise was insupportable and ringing for the chamber maid I sent her with my compliments to the gentlemen, begging that they should not make quite so much noise as we were immediately over their heads. Not another sound was heard and I believe they went to bed to oblige me. Next morning before I could apologise for the liberty I had taken, they were all around me expressing their sorrow for having disturbed us and their ignorance that they were doing so.

One other incident must surely have endeared Blackpool to Catherine Hutton as much as the financial set-back attendant upon the history must have impressed it upon the memory of her father:

I have had an offer here, and for the first time in my life I have not instantly refused such an offer, but I shall refuse it (she writes to her friend). The man is handsome, gentlemanly and agreeable enough, but he has been an officer in the army and a free liver, things totally out of my sober way. Your brother, who observed his attentions, says I am "saucy". I think I am not, but nothing should prevail on me to quit my mother during the time she has to live and if I had not the objection above mentioned how could I desire any man to wait for her death?

24

These sentiments, admirable if misguided, were upheld during the lifetime of Mrs. Hutton, and beyond. Catherine herself died at the age of ninety on 13th March, 1846, having acquired some literary recognition, but never a husband. On the other hand there was some comfort in the memory that she had been offered for during that summer of 1788 in far-off Blackpool. By 16th October, 1788, she was writing: "I am sorry to say that my mother has not received the benefit from Blackpool we expected".

The family's visit to the boisterous Lancashire coast, where occasionally "instead of sea breezes we have land breezes laden with smoke of turf" had come to an end. "The wintry blast howled on three sides" of the deserted boarding house and William Hutton had arrived to escort his beloved wife and daughter on their homeward journey. Truly our Catherine Hutton was extremely difficult to suit, but for her acute observations and candid comments on Blackpool in the days of its extreme youth, we cannot but be most thankful that she came.

Slights, delights and every modern inconvenience

THE better accommodation provided by Blackpool in the 1780s had begun to attract visitors who were richer, prouder and more elegant than in previous years. When the weather was favourable fashionable crowds paraded the grass promenade, some 200 yards long and less than 20 feet wide (between present Clifton and County Hotels) which was separated from the road by white wooden railings. Wm. Hutton laments that no attempt had been made to transform this natural parade into "one of the most beautiful walks in the island". It could, in his opinion, have been extended to the length of at least one mile and provided with shelters and benches. Instead, it was bounded at the northerly end by a single alcove and to the south it terminated abruptly with what Hutton describes as "a vile pit". This would be nothing more terrible than an old clay hole providing materials for hand-made bricks, but no doubt it was an untidy sight which ought not to have offended the eyes of genteel visitors.

Blackpool, however, was still in its infancy. One day it would get around to removing this and similar unsightly blots from its centre. Meantime, a number of lime kilns and brick crofts were still scattered along this popular stretch of cliffs in preparation for buildings already in hand and others about to be started. Despite all, however, in the height of the season visitors thronged the parade, flaunting their youth, their fortunes, or their beauty or, in the case of the "stale belle", offering her "fading charms upon easy terms".

In faithful detail, Wm. Hutton captures the spirit of early Blackpool where the hotelkeepers were friendly enough amongst each other but where their guests reserved their favours for those staying only under the same roof. Like members of hostile tribal groups the visitor at Forshaw's (Clifton) would exchange neither glance nor word with another who had elected to stay at Hull's (old Royal, now Woolworth's). Even out on the parade, where cliques foregathered and at times it must have been extremely difficult to find walking space, poor Wm. Hutton found himself "repelled" rather than drawn if he tried to strike up a conversation with someone staying in a rival house. Pride and prejudice, snobbery and insularity, were the order of the day and "even the miser", says Hutton, "stationed by frugality at an inferior house, dares not look up to his own daughter at Bailey's" (Butlin's Metropole) "while the pride of that house will scarcely permit her to follow him with a glance". As to the ladies, Hutton, who had grown up with the belief that all Lancashire women were surpassing fair, utterly irresistible and justifiably named the "Lancashire Witches", had to admit that on closer examination they seemed "a leetle below mediocrity"! Nevertheless, when the weather permitted, young and old paraded their fashions, eyed each other's bonnets with envy and, when the tide went out, amused themselves by watching the nobility and gentry sporting their smart equipages or taking their mounts for a canter, accompanied by their ladies, along a twenty mile length of tightly packed golden sand left behind by the receding waves.

On every second Sunday in the summer all the village lads and lassies within walking distance of Blackpool converged upon the Lane End and made their own amusements and diversions to crown a hardworking fortnight. This fair in miniature, with its stalls and simple fun, gave as much pleasure to the vigorous rustics as to the elegant visitors who looked on in affected amusement. John Gisborne, a Derbyshire visitor who brought his invalid wife here in 1812, and who settled in Blackpool three years later, frowned on these boisterous and sometimes drunken affairs and made a move to suppress them. Remonstrances and warnings were issued and from about 1815 the Sunday Fairs ceased.

In addition there was a limited amount of sailing which was not helped by the flatness of the shore and two small bowling greens, one of which, together with an archery ground and butts, was set on the cliffs between Bailey's and the sea. Dances were arranged at the hotels to a fiddle accompaniment and there was a primitive theatre set up on the threshing floor of a barn. Hutton recalls how the company of actors rolled up somewhat ignominiously on a cart laden with stage props to play to half filled houses and audiences seated on wooden forms. Admission was 2s. 0d. to the "pit" and 1s. 0d. to the "gallery", a nice distinction which again could only have had its roots in self esteem.

There were invigorating walks to be taken along the cliffs past Bailey's to the Gynn, or up Lane End-street (Church Street) to the Layton Raikes (rakes-slopes) to get a fine and unimpeded view over the green countryside of the Fylde. From this vantage point the visitor could see as far as Poulton on the one side and the little whitewashed Church of St. Cuthbert at Lytham, set in a cluster of trees, on the other. Far beyond, the rolling fells, the curling smoke of Preston, the toy-town buildings of North Meols (Churchtown) and the distant hills of Wales provided a panoramic scene to reward the uphill climb.

Descending the little country lane, with the smithy and a few whitewashed cottages on the left, and Raikes Hall Farm and the spacious grounds of Raikes Hall on the right, another gentle stroll brought the visitor to the Number Three, celebrated for its "fine ale". This old whitewashed cobble inn (now Old No. 3 and Didsbury, Devonshire Square) then stood in the midst of green fields at the beginning of Whitegate Lane leading into Marton. Its hospitality and quaint country atmosphere made it a great favourite with both visitors and locals and few spent a holiday in Blackpool in the 1780s without sampling its famous brew.

When the weather was rough the company stayed indoors amusing themselves at cards or backgammon, but it was no secret that visitors to Blackpool, rich or poor, young or old, had come to gain full benefit from the sea. Seabathing had become a national craze. For the preservation of modesty, horse-drawn bathing vans, resembling striped hen cabins on wheels, conveyed the fair and the bashful to an appropriate depth and enabled them to flop about in their sodden voluminous garments with the utmost decorum. Otherwise, assisted by their personal maids, ladies disrobed on the beach in boxes provided for that purpose, and a few of the more emancipated souls even walked from their lodgings dressed ready for their dip.

Formerly there had been some instances of immodest behaviour, for it was no uncommon thing for the 18th century bather to swim in the nude, to the fluttering confusion of passers by. By 1788, however, bathing arrangements were under control and there was a strict segregation of the sexes. Upon the ringing of the first bell the gentlemen were obliged to absent themselves from the vicinity. After the ladies' session, a second bell summoned the gentlemen bathers and by this time the fair sex had removed themselves to a considerate distance. The forfeit of a bottle of wine was extracted from any male person infringing the rules.

All the visitors were convinced of the extreme benefit to be derived from immersion in the sea. The more gullible characters were enthusiastic enough to drink it, like spa water, twenty-five gallons (a pint a time, of course) being the prescribed dosage. Despite the rebuffs from some of his fellow visitors, Wm. Hutton was successful in striking up conversations with some of the health-seekers at Blackpool. Many had trudged in over long distances not so much for enjoyment as for cure and restoration.

One of these, a Lancaster shoemaker still wearing his leather apron, was going down to the beach for a mug of sea water when he confided to Mr. Hutton that six weeks at Blackpool had cured not only his threatened blindness but a variety of physical disorders. An elderly Manchester gentleman, suffering from the paralytic effects of a stroke and having to be carried in and out of the water, had mended considerably and banished his

27

insomnia after only a few days at Blackpool. It was also said that many who had hobbled into the resort on crutches had so benefited from their stay that they were able to stride home briskly leaving those implements behind. "Ricketty and puny children find benefit from this friendly element", comments Hutton, bearing out the words of a wise old native: "A visit to Blackpool commonly restored health if health was restorable". Indeed, if enjoyment were the prime object of a visit, the search for health was only secondary to it.

Catherine Hutton regales us with an account of the medical facilities afforded to sufferers by a famous family of Lancashire amateur doctors. John Taylor, a talented blacksmith in his twenties, founded the "practice" about 1764 at Whitworth, near Rochdale, and was later joined by his brother, George. Their womenfolk helped out, sons and grandsons came into the business (latterly after an orthodox medical training) and the original "Dr. John" had the honour of being summoned to treat H.R.H. the Princess Elizabeth, one of the daughters of George III, in the 1780s. Catherine's account reads:

Surgery is practised in a curious manner by some individuals by the name of Taylor who are known by the appellation of the Whitworth Doctors. They were originally farriers and, by a transition easy in the county, they became bone-setters and surgeons, but it is said that they retain such partiality for their first patients that they frequently say to a human being: "Howd, mon; yo mon weat a bit; yon hoss has ben comm a lung while. I mon goo to it, so yo mun stop till E dun it". The success of the practitioner has rendered this village a collection of hospitals, almost every house lodging the maimed or diseased, and some being erected expressly for that purpose. No patient is visited in his lodgings if he is able to attend at the house of the doctor and there no attention is paid to rank or circumstance, the first comer being served first.

Glauber salts were bought by the hogshead; salves were boiled in large furnaces. In the shop stand 2 jars contining 4 gallons each, the one filled with a green digestive ointment, the other with a white cerate, and from one of these every patient who is able spreads his own plaister on paper, if he has not brought his own lint or rag. The doctors' wives compound the medicines by rule of thumb and finger. On an average the doctors dress 140 persons daily and on Sunday they bleed the patients gratuitously. This is conducted by 3 persons while the patients sit round the room. One opens the vein, one follows with a basin (presumably to catch the blood), and the third binds.

She also tells of a remarkable cancer cure effected by the Whitworth Doctors:

The cure was effected by the application of a powder which they call "keen" and of which they have two sorts, one red, one white. The pain occasioned by this powder was excruciating but it lasted no longer than the patient chose to bear it, for she was furnished with a plaister which relieved it instantly, but her cure was only going on while the "keen" was operating. The lady bore the pain for 1, 2 or 3 hours daily, and probably bore it better as it was in her own power to put an end to it. The cancer was totally eradicated and she married and has children but her constitution seems to have received a shock and perhaps she had acted wiser if she had taken a longer time to remove her disorder ... Her behaviour to her husband is complying and submissive yet she suffers him to retire to bed early and sits up late herself playing at cards ... I constantly see that her manner is affected yet I cannot help fancying that her real self is more amiable. Perhaps I am mistaken; perhaps she has vanity and no feeling.

Of the fare provided at the hotels, Hutton tells us that the food in 1788 was ample and excellently cooked by a woman employed for the season and paid the then princely sum of £40 and her keep. Yet he gives us an insight into the difficulties of running a large establishment by telling us that all the fresh water had to be carried, sometimes from half a mile distant, from the only public spring in the place. "It is well worth carrying", he says, "for I thought it the most pleasant I ever tasted". The servants who had the job of portering it, however, probably had their own strong ideas on the excessive use of this precious and burdensome commodity. Shrimps, Hutton tells us, were plentiful, but there was not the abundance of fish which an inlander might have expected at the seaside.

Amongst the eighteen-penny lodging houses Mr. Hutton discovered that there were many decent people who preferred quietness and privacy to the late-night laughter and revelries which had to be endured at the larger establishments. "Disturbance reigns at midnight", he tells us. "In a large and hollow-sounding house every noise operates with full effect and pervades the whole. Sounds are continually rising during the night which murder sleep and repose once lost cannot soon be recovered". Those of us who have spent summer holidays in noisy hotels know exactly what he means! Charges for liquors were collected at the table. Visitors paid the daily charge at their convenience or at the end of their stay.

There were no facilities in Blackpool for public worship. The nearest church lay several miles distant, at Bispham, and in 1788 no provisions had been made for divine service to be performed in any of the hotel rooms; nor had any Wesleyan preacher ventured into the territory during the summer months though a handful of young evangelists had attempted to open up the Fylde country during that decade. There was no school in Blackpool, but the hamlet had very few children. Even if schooling had been provided it is certain that even the youngest would have disdained anything as unproductive as mere book learning and would rather have turned their infant hands to the earning of money.

Though Mr. Hutton made light of the journey to Blackpool, admitting only that he got lost between Preston and the coast, it should be stressed that 18th century travel was toilsome and perilous and that even a journey from Manchester could not be undertaken without fortitude and determination. The following announcements appeared in "The Manchester Mercury":

1783: June 3rd. The Manchester and Blackpool Coach, from the Upper Royal Oak, Market Street Lane, Manchester, begins to run on Monday, the 9th of June, and every morning (Sunday excepted) at 6 o'clock, through Bolton, Chorley, Preston, etc. Performed by Math. Pickford, Pointon; Jas. Weights, Bolton; Thos. Cooper, Bull in Preston.

1784: 6th July. Lower Swan Inn, Market Street Lane. The Manchester and Black Pool Coach. Sets out from the above Inn every Monday, Wednesday and Friday morning, at 6 o'clock, dinner at Mr. Cooper, the Black Bull Inn, Preston, where it meets a diligence (a French, or Continental stage-coach) which proceeds to Black Pool the same eve. Inside from Manchester to Black Pool 14s. Performed by Mess. Dixon, Cooper and Co.

By the time the visitor cast up in Blackpool from Manchester, he had not only paid dearly, but had been rattled, shaken, imperilled and rendered thoroughly uncomfortable, for the best part of twelve hours! With a company of 400 in the flux of the season, it is obvious that the majority provided their own means of locomotion. The poor walked. The fortunate thumbed a lift in a carrier's cart. Gentlemen came on horseback, often with their plump wives perched up behind on the sociable pillion. The gentry and nobility rolled up in grand style in their own phaetons and carriages, counting themselves extremely fortunate to have avoided such serious mishaps as overthrows, shed wheels, broken axles and shattered limbs for which our atrocious lanes might have been specifically designed.

Yet, the 18th century visitors brushed all these obstacles and annoyances on one side and steadfastly pressed on towards our coast. The sea, the sands, the rejuvenating air, the cliffs, the Raikes, the fine views, the fashionable company, and the rising eminence of Hounds Hill from which many a day's coursing set out to rid Bonny's green acres (around Central Drive) of a multitudinous and destructive pest (the yelping hounds were brought from Raikes Hall, Layton Hall and Bailey's Hotel) ... were counted as sufficient reward.

Raikes Hall

THIS interesting hotel was originally a gentleman's residence of considerable dignity, set in the midst of a large, tree-girt, and beautifully maintained estate. Raikes Hall, a Georgian house, was built by a Mr. Butcher who, according to Vicar Thornber and the gossip rife in his day, had sprung from obscurity to wealth by somewhat dubious means. Mid-eighteenth century Blackpudlians, astonished no doubt by this grandiose building operation, put their own, and possibly quite erroneous, construction upon the situation. Who, for instance, had not noticed Mr. Butcher's frequent trips to the seashore? And wasn't it odd, to say the least of it, that Raikes Hall was commissioned shortly after a vessel containing the riches of three sisters had been cast up on this coast—especially as the reputed "treasure" had never come to light? Sourly, but probably not without envy, it was whispered that Mr. Butcher must have got there first. How otherwise could he have aspired to set himself up in such style? Porter gives little credence to the malicious rumours and tells us that Mr. Butcher, who died in 1769, achieved the ripe old age of eighty, and that his tombstone in Bispham churchyard bore the inscription:—

> "His pleasure was to give or lend
> He always stood a poor man's friend."

Mr. Thornber, on the other hand, was inclined to be less charitable. He took a grim satisfaction in recording that Mr.

Butcher's son lived for many years as a recluse, tormented by schizophrenic hallucinations. But the last word on the subject comes from Mr. Ernest Butcher, of London, a descendant of the builder of Raikes Hall. He writes: "That particular one had been a 'wrecker' and made his money by luring ships on to the sands. Then again, a Robert Butcher of about 1850-1870 was the most accomplished poacher in these parts. He could out-run and out-jump any of the keepers." Eventually, I can record, this tear-away was apprehended by two beaters after taking a flying leap over a stream. Not in the least discountenanced, "he shook hands with both and said—'Well caught, by God!'" —which leads us to think that there might have been something in the rumours after all!

In 1816 we hear of private apartments being let, and in the early 1820s Raikes Hall and its estate were bought by Wm. Hornby of Kirkham. On his death in 1824 the property passed to his brother, John Hornby, Esq., of Blackburn. John Hornby died in 1841 and his eldest son, Daniel, succeeded and lived at Raikes Hall until the early 1860s when the family left the district. Mr. Thornber tells us that the first carpet ever seen in Blackpool was brought there by one of the Hornby ladies. For about seven years after the Hornby family vacated, Raikes Hall became a convent occupied by the Sisters of the Holy Child Jesus. A Directory, 1866, tells us, "a polite literature, as well as a sound religious education, is imparted to the daughters of the upper and middle classes". The Sisters remained there until Layton Hill Convent had been made ready for their reception, and indeed long after these good ladies had departed, there still remained, in the corner of the best room, a cupboard, rarely opened, containing the seat and kneeler of a confessional. For long enough afterwards hotel customers of all persuasions cheerfully leaned against it, little realising how close they were to this relic of Roman Catholic occupation.

In 1868 it would appear that a family named Daggers were living, however briefly, or under what circumstances, at the hall. Recorded in the "Preston Pilot", I discovered two marriages in that name, the second, on 7th October, 1868, at Thornton, being that of Nannie, eldest daughter of Wm. Daggers, Esq., of Raikes Hall, nr. Blackpool, to Robert Porter, Esq., of Bourne Hall, nr. Fleetwood. As no previous historian has thought fit to mention the Daggers at Raikes Hall we can only assume that their sojourn there was brief and of little consequence, and in any case the whole estate was shortly to be developed and transformed beyond recognition.

Pennystone and a changing coast

DURING the 18th century the simple pleasures of the seashore were a prominent feature of a holiday visit. Walking for health, collecting seashells and pebbles, watching the shrimpers, or the carters and builders selecting pebbles to burn into lime or for the construction of walls and houses, and for the repairing of roads, all added to the diversions along the seashore where, as Hutton tells us, "the very cattle snuff up the sea breeze until driven back by the tide". In 1788 the cows were grazing as far out as the site of the North Pier. Fishing and sailing were not popular pastimes. The ladies had to be carried and gentlemen had to wade out to the available small boats.

Even though the promenade extended far west of its present line, some encroachment of the sea was clearly visible along the cliffs toward Bispham. The only road in that direction, perched perilously on the edge of the cliffs and with nothing to guard the traveller from a sheer drop of sixty feet, struck the historian as being "so extremely narrow as scarcely to admit one foot passenger with safety". We can imagine his horror when a wagon passed by that way with complete unconcern and only six inches' clearance. Shaken by what he had just witnessed, Mr. Hutton made it his business to enquire further and learned that half a century before, the tenant of the land had reserved the width of four roads before mounding his bank, "supposing that sufficient to last his time". He had reckoned, obviously, without the force of the waves which had already whittled away five road widths and was now biting viciously into the sixth. All within the space of fifty years!

Hutton's interest was next drawn to the curious stone which can still be seen at low tide opposite the slade at Redbank Road, Bispham. He was told that in the days when the coast stood far out, an inn plied its lonely trade where now the sea ebbed and flowed. Travellers tied their mounts to iron hooks fixed into the rock, then refreshed themselves with penny pots of ale before resuming their journey. How long ago this was, no-one could say, but in 1788 the local tradition was strong and "allowed by the whole country". Hooks, inn and all had disappeared, but the rock from long custom was known as the Penny Stone. Wm. Ashton in his "Battle of Land and Sea" tells us that a Mr. James Pearson of Blackpool positively testified to having seen an iron ring fixed into the rock, which was shaped as if it had steps on one side and was "black with mussels", as late as the 1870s.

The Rev. W. Thornber was intrigued by the tale but had searched without success for documentary substantiation of it. On the other hand, he had been told that a mid-18th century storm exposed enclosure walls which formerly had been covered by several feet of sand. But he was minded to think that any ring attached to the Penny Stone was little more than a leg-pull by some of the local fishermen. This is not in the least unlikely for in recent times one old character had so wearied his friends with the story that one of them privately declared: "I'll make sure the owd devil finds his ring if I have to put one there myself!" The Penny Stone, and similar masses of conglomerate—Higher Gingle, Lower Gingle, Carline and his Colts, Silkstone, the Bear and Staff, etc., had been washed out of the boulder-clay cliffs in earlier times by the encroaching sea. Some are still to be seen but Higher and Lower Gingle have disappeared. However, what the sea takes in one century it may think to give back in another and some future storm may yet enable archaeologists to probe the Penny Stone theory which, for the moment, must be left languishing in the realms of legend.

Obviously this coastal region has undergone a remarkable transformation from those far-off centuries when a thick woodland plain stretched out into the estuary of the Ribble. Wm. Hutton saw neither hedge nor tree and attributed it to man's indifference and want of energy. Yet, several years after his visit, there were tree trunks to be seen on the beach at Rossall. In the 1870s, Captain Bickerstaffe of Blackpool spoke of having seen tree trunks at the site of Central Pier entrance, and of others coming to light when foundations were being laid for modern buildings. Others have seen trees, laid in one direction as if swept down by some great storm, in the clay of the Manchester Square district, in front of the New Inn, and on the site of the Wellington Hotel extensions. When the present Woolworth's premises were being built on the site of the old Royal Hotel, the workmen found lumps of clay bearing the faithful imprint of long-buried leaf formations.

From the accumulated evidence, as Blackpool grew up and uncovered her secrets, it was obvious that a sturdy forest had flourished along the coast until, at some unknown date, the sea rose up in its anger destroying tree and field, livestock and homestead alike. Wm. Ashton even suggests that the restless Ribble at one time might have carved its course through the low-lying southern regions of Marton Moss to join up with the Wyre at Skippool, leaving the heights of northern Blackpool stranded into an island. Old Rossall Hall has long since fallen into the sea and Porter tells of a farm at Rossall which had to be set back four times in the fifty years following 1825, due to the inroads of the sea. On the beach at Rossall 400 Roman coins were unearthed and deposited in the Harris Museum at Preston.

Old-time visitors, whose memories ranged back to the 1830s and 1840s, recalled that the northern cliffs then extended far west of the site of the old original Uncle Tom's Cabin and would fix the distance at anything from half to one mile. By the 1860s there was still a large green field between Uncle Tom's and the cliff edge, but within thirty years only the barest safety margin stood between this popular holiday attraction and certain death. In 1911 the Coast Erosion Committee recorded a loss in the Bispham area of almost 25 yards in 17 years and in the region of Norbreck the sea was gaining almost 3 yards in every year.

Not only the Fylde coast suffered from the ravages of the sea. Wm. Ashton lists the terrible inundations, dating back to the 4th century, which notably changed the coasts of Wales, Lancashire and Cheshire. In 1279 Chester Bridge was carried away and the Cistercians of Stanlawe Abbey near Ince on the Lower Mersey, were flooded out. After this chastening experience, and following the death of Peter of Chester, the Rector of Whalley, all but a few of the brethren transferred their house to Whalley, preferring the distractions of a small neighbouring townlet, which

33

normally they tried to avoid, to the menace of a restless ocean.

In the 14th century, the ancient settlements of Aynesdale and Argarmeols, on the other side of the Ribble, and Ravensmeols, near Formby, were washed away, and between 1400-1500 Kilgrimol, on the St. Annes coast, was "worn into the sea" to the extent of two or three miles. In 1553/4 the Rossall coast was overflowed, and on the night of the 18th/19th December, 1720, the sea rose up in a tumult and hurled its full fury on the Lancashire coast. Cockerham, Pilling, Garstang, Lytham, Kirkham, Westby and Warton, north of the Ribble, and Hesketh, Tarleton and North Meols on the south of the estuary, took the full impact and in the final reckoning the sea had overflowed "6600 Aikers of land, had washed down 157 Houses, and damnifyed 200 more". This indicates the power of a high tide running before a driving wind, and the coast from Lytham to Fleetwood seems, throughout the centuries, to have had more than its fair share of erosion and inundation.

Mr. Thornber ventures into the realm of legend and folk-lore by telling us that in the 1553-54 inundation a whole village called "Singleton Thorp", off the Rossall coast, was swept away by the sea, so that "the inhabitants were obliged to flee from their ancient spot and erected their tents at a place called Singleton to this day". He conveniently overlooks, however, the fact that "Singletun, vi carucates" was recorded in the Domesday Survey compiled between 1080-6, and that this separate settlement of Singleton had existed for at least five centuries before the inundation!

Moreover, "thorp" (signifying a township), a word frequently employed in that connection in other counties, has never cropped up in any documents relating to this district. Diligent research has brought no "thorps" to light, yet Thornber would also have us believe that "Waddum Thorp", a village within the Lytham domain but reaching out to the Horse Bank (a corruption of "Hawes", meaning fields) was similarly devastated in 1601. Thornber claims to have gleaned the information from the Dodsworth Manuscripts, lodged in the Bodleian Library, Oxford. Yet, of this mass of papers compiled by 17th C. antiquary, Roger Dodsworth, no mention was made of chapter or page. Many have since combed the volumes but none has yet managed to verify the quotations and little credence, therefore, can be given to them. If the names, "Singleton Thorp" and "Waddum Thorp", emanated from the lively and sometimes misguided imagination of the historian, it is extremely probable that two settlements, and maybe others, were overwhelmed by the sea.

In 1893 an effort was made to unravel the mystery of "Singleton Thorp". Following a report by a Mr. Chew of Albert Road, Blackpool, Mr. A. Halstead, then Editor of the "Blackpool Times", accompanied by "a small party of adventurous spirits", took pickaxes, spades and other implements on a conveyance and set off to find the vanished village. The tide was the lowest for years and Pennystone stood well out of the water. The party struck out on the beach about 4 miles north of Uncle Tom's

Cabin and half a mile from Rossall, and within minutes were able to trace the fallen forest. Trees, still complete with their branches, twigs and leaves, were visible to the extent of one mile at low water mark though it was obvious that in the previous five years much had been covered by sand and shingle. Digging revealed half-buried trunks of giant oaks, elms and beech, lying as they had fallen before a sudden inrush. Picks and spades wielded at random hit enough woody and peaty matter to prove that the forest was not scattered but continuous. The wealth of leaves, twigs, ferns, branches and mosses which came to light formed an unbroken layer about two feet in depth. Beneath this vegetable mass was a peaty sub-soil, and beneath that a belt of clay perhaps four or five feet below the surface. The report states that the compressed ferns and leaves were in a beautiful state of preservation.

So far the exploration had proved the existence of a coastal forest. The amateur archaeologists now turned their energies to the question of "Singleton Thorp" and were eventually rewarded by the discovery of a straight piece of timber, measuring 17' 0" × 13" × 13" and notched with carpenters' marks. At first sight this could have come from some long forgotten wreck, but the party investigated further and presently, assuming that the beam was a roof rafter, discovered the foundations of a house wall. This followed a line some 22 feet in length and terminated in a right-angle formed by the gable-end. The rough lime and cobble stones of diminishing sizes were proof enough that this was a rubble wall foundation. 150 yards nearer the sea traces were found of other buildings. "That we were on the site of the ruined and wave-swept village there could be no doubt", records Mr. Halstead. As the incoming tide stole nearer we can picture the diggers loading up their tools and, with satisfaction, but no little regret, striking out for dry land. They were convinced that they had unearthed the lost village, and they probably had, even if its name was never "Singleton Thorp". The findings of the party were published in pamphlet form in 1893 and a copy of this valuable and interesting record, which made "no pretensions to any new discovery, except in the definite signs of the foundations of buildings", may be seen in the Reference Library at Blackpool.

1790—1820
Gradual expansion and the first regular stage coach service

SPEAKING OUT very bluntly against the immorality of these earlier times, Vicar Thornber tells us that drunkenness, profanity, atheism and blasphemy continually "met the eye and wounded the ear". The fortnightly fairs at the Lane Ends were the scene of public brawls, excessive drinking, loose behaviour and vice in all its "hideous forms". Smuggling was a local occupation. Boats went out under cover of darkness to relieve Irish vessels in the channel of contraband goods and spirits from the Isle of Man were brought ashore in hampers topped up with fish. Except in the Puritan areas sabbatarianism was never strong before Victorian times. Sundays had scant religious significance and were used, in the 18th and early 19th centuries, for merrymaking and noisy amusement. Eventually one of the hotel rooms was set aside for Sunday service, ministers from Poulton or Bispham, or even visiting clergy, leading the worship. But it often happened that no-one could be found to officiate.

The atmosphere of Blackpool in 1790 is captured in a poem written by a visitor about that time:

Of all the gay places of public resort,
At Chatham, or Scarbro', at Bath, or at Court,
There's none like sweet Blackpool, of which I can boast,
So charming the sands, so healthful the coast;

The houses are many, and all of them stor'd,
Not one but is able to spread a good board.
At Bonny's, and Hull's, there's plenty of meat,
Their rooms, and their beds, are both cleanly and neat;
My friend, Mr. Hudson, stands next in the row,
From Buxton he came, I would have you to know,
The next house is Forshaw's, a building enlarg'd,
Good doings, no doubt, but you're sure to be charged.
The next house is Bailey's, so new and so neat,
Much pains he has taken to make it complete.
It stands on the beach far detach'd from the rest,
And with a fine spring of good water is bless'd.
Old Ned and old Nanny, at Fumbler's Hill
Will board you and lodge you e'en just as you will.
The next house of fame, that I now do take in
Is fam'd Billy Snape's, "SURS", they call it the Ginn;
He keeps a good table and plenty to eat
With whey in abundance to drink to your meat:
His servants are civil, good-natur'd and mild,
You find none their like, if you search the whole Fylde.
Then who's like friend Billy? "Cum hither, I pray,
And sarvants remember when you go away".

"Old Ned and old Nanny" refers to a row of gabled cottages which stood on a green rise called Fumbler's Hill to the north of the present Butlin's Metropole and on what would now be the sea-side of the promenade, near Carleton Terrace. They turned their shoulders to the wind and faced south, as did all but the newest buildings in the resort. A Captain Fish of Fleetwood used to visit his grandparents who lived there about 1850, until erosion on the cliffs caused the gable end to fall over into the sea. "Cum, Surs, remember the sarvants" ... this was the custom at the Gynn when departing guests, settling their account with the landlord, were reminded to leave a gratuity for the staff.

Mr. Hudson who kept the Lane Ends at the time of the Huttons' visit was soon succeeded by the enterprising Thomas Lewtas whose white cottage on the opposite corner was run as a newsroom and who also had a coffee house (formerly a blacksmith's shop). Running two establishments on opposite sides of the road posed something of a problem. A dining room had been built on to the cottage. The kitchen was across the road at the hotel. For years the landlord scuttled between the two carrying trays of hot food, without covers!

During the year 1798 the very real threat of a Napoleonic invasion loomed large in the minds of the nation. Arms had been raised from Caithness in the north to Cornwall and Kent in the south and England had become "a nation of soldiers". There were rumours and counter-rumours in Blackpool, as everywhere else, and a beacon was ready to warn the inlanders in the possible event of a landing at the mouth of the Wyre. Mr. Thornber tells us that the Lord of the Manor, Squire Fleetwood, took the precaution of despatching his documents and valuables from Rossall Hall to a secluded place of safety among the hills. The poor, however, having but few possessions, went about their daily business untroubled by stirring international events and Lancastrian visitors, taking the same philosophical view, still poured into Blackpool in their hundreds. Many never found accommodation by the sea but had to fall back on Poulton and journey daily to and from the beach.

In 1799 a serious failure of the grain and potato harvests brought the threat of ruin and starvation to the natives along the coast. When prices for these two staple commodities rose to astronomical heights these poor people, who already lived from hand to mouth, were sorely put to it to keep body and soul in one piece. Never accustomed to luxuries, now suddenly there was a gnawing and rising hunger which could only be softened by the charity of less needy neighbours. The lives of a whole community were imperilled until a providential wreck cast a cargo of peas upon the shore. This bounty from a foundered foreign vessel was swiftly gathered and put to use. A monotonous diet of pea soup, pea bread, fried peas, boiled peas, or peas made into puddings, sustained not only the poor but many of the better off families who, along with the rest, were thereby saved from extinction.

In 1801 the sparsely populated Layton-with-Warbreck, of which Blackpool was a small part, contained only 473 souls, according to the first national census. Summer holidays by the sea had by this time become woven into the pattern of English life and many outside investors would have been happy to purchase plots of land and sink their money into expansion projects at the new resort. But as most of the land was already held by established innkeepers who were unminded to encourage competition, Blackpool stagnated for a number of years in the early 19th century and the investors took their capital and ideas to other places. It has always been thought that Southport grew while Blackpool stood still and at length the insular landowners came to realise that they were cutting their own throats by limiting expansion. People would go to the places which had the most to offer and after a few static years the landlords stood aside and even welcomed the builder and the investor. A number of pleasant furnished cottages were set up and let off during the season at rents varying between £5 and £7 per week. In 1801 coaches were beginning to come in from distant Yorkshire, making a tedious two-day journey entailing an overnight stay at Blackburn.

During the June of 1808 the Preston Volunteers encamped for two weeks at Blackpool, and for scores of years similar camps were set up on the northern cliffs or in the grounds of Raikes Hall. King George III celebrated his 70th birthday during their stay if, indeed, His Majesty, threatened with insanity and blindness, and grief-stricken by the death of his youngest daughter, was in a mind to celebrate anything. Still, the community around Blackpool, as doubtless throughout the kingdom, made light of the monarch's afflictions and the anniversary was celebrated in right royal style. Soon the gypsies were encamping regularly on the cliffs of northern Blackpool, attracting visitors by their picturesque way of life and their alleged gift of fore-telling the future.

The memorable year of 1816 saw the first regular public stage coach service set up between Blackpool and Preston. Antiquated travel by means of carts, packhorses and private equipages, was swiftly superseded by this lumbering method of locomotion. During that year we find a letter written by a visitor staying at Forshaw's (Clifton Hotel), telling in great detail his experiences on arriving in Blackpool. He had set out from the Star Inn, Deansgate, Manchester, at 8 o'clock in the morning. He arrived at Bolton at ten, Blackburn at twelve, Preston half-past one, and Blackpool at six thirty. A mere ten and a half hours for a journey now taking less than two! It was August, but he "fancied it as cold as winter", and no wonder. The full blast of a sea wind met him at the Lane End. By early evening, without British Summer Time, it was almost dark. The first impression was that there would be a sorry want of amusements but a little stock-taking soon convinced him otherwise. "So strong are the inducements", wrote he, "that to particularise them would be too tedious". He discovered that fellow guests from the great city had been coming to Blackpool for upwards of thirty years and, following the pattern set in Hutton's time, it was still the custom for the guests to "form themselves into a sort of (exclusive) social society", extending to each other "every possible politeness and the civility of a brother or sister". To be accepted, the new arrival was expected to acquaint the company with the details of his rank, his profession and his prospects.

Bailey's, or "Bailey Banks Hotel", as it was called by this time, had raised its tariff to 7s. a day. Forshaw's had meantime equipped itself with newsrooms and a shop selling useful and fancy goods and the charge here was 6s. 6d. a day. The Lane Ends (proprietor Henry Banks), an extensive and very respectable house much to be recommended, charged only 4s. 4d. Between these two hotels on the sea-front were four furnished cottages, two owned by Mr. Forshaw and the other two by Mr. Banks who also had two further cottages, beyond his hotel, let off by the season. A small shop in Lane Ends-street (Church Street) supplied such basic commodities as bread, milk, tea and sugar, but our visitor points out that "the best way is for a family to take those articles which are convenient to carry". On the site of Mr. Lewtas's cottage, Mr. Butcher's establishment drew the respectable type of visitor. John Bonny's (i' th' fields, further south) was extremely popular and regularly housed 40 guests on terms similar to the Lane Ends. On the beach near Chapel Street, the Yorkshire House, with bowling green, yards and outbuildings, made a smaller charge for slightly inferior accommodation. The green parade, which had considerably diminished in width even by Hutton's time, was "now wasting away to a gravelly footpath".

Surprisingly, we discover that Raikes Hall, hitherto a private gentleman's residence of standing, was prepared to rent off apartments to visitors catering for themselves, and this pleasant situation in spacious grounds sheltered from the harshness of the sea winds was strongly commended to the delicate and feeble. Mr. Riley, the proprietor of the Yorkshire House, had taken over the Foxhall and let it for the season to a Dr. Winstanley of Manchester. The coast road leading past the old hall had been gnawed by the sea to the extent of several feet and a former row of wayside trees had entirely disappeared. Behind Foxhall was a furnished cottage built by a Mr. Blundell out of the earnings of his wife who was a dab-hand at gingerbread making. Summer tenants provided their own "servants and meat" and while Mr. Blundell drew in the rent his wife followed her old occupation in a nearby cottage. This was demolished when Blundell Street was opened out.

In Bonny's Lane (Chapel Street) "there is a noted potted shrimp shop, which may be purchased by dozens, in pots, to any order, and where you may purchase whey, a good cooling drink". Without doubt, many Blackpool visitors would undertake this bracing walk to sample these wholesome fares. They would walk along South Beach (Golden Mile) and turn left at the cobble-built circular pinfold (site of Wellington Hotel) where stray animals were impounded until they were claimed by their owners.

On 22nd April, 1817, the dandified postal pioneer, librarian, shopkeeper and lodging house proprietor, George Cooke, died at the age of 77 and was buried at Bispham. His wife predeceased him in 1802, and their tombstone, in case anyone should misinterpret his American activities, carried the message: "Natives of this island".

The first Free School in Blackpool, 1817

BEFORE 1817 no arrangements had been made for educating the children of Blackpool and Layton. In any case, no child would have availed himself of the opportunity during the summer months when a few welcome pence might be earned. Similarly, a winter's education was discouraged by the long walks involved in getting to Marton (2 miles), Poulton (4) or

Bispham ($3\frac{1}{2}$). Lanes being what they were, and wintry weather what it is, very few children acquired even a smattering of formal education. It was a visitor, Mr. John Gisborne, who decided to remedy this regrettable state of affairs. For £50 he purchased from the executors of William Yates a plot of land bordering Poulton Road (now upper Church Street), then a pleasant country lane set between rolling green slopes (Layton Raikes). Friends and visitors were badgered for contributions to build a free school for the poor children of Blackpool and Layton-with-Warbreck, and the building was completed and opened with 40 scholars in 1817. A master and mistress were engaged at a joint salary of £50 p.a., which again was collected from visitors and residents by the indefatigable Mr. Gisborne. There were two distinct buildings for boys and girls, separated by the schoolmaster's house, and the rear outlines of these original buildings can still be picked out from inside the school yard though the frontages were turned into shops long ago.

On 22nd February, 1820, a Trust Deed referring to the "Blackpool Free Schools" was presented by the following: Robert Hesketh of Rossall; John Clifton of Lytham; Rev. Wm. Elston, Bispham; Rev. Thos. Bryer, Marton; Edward Hull, Marton; John Forshaw, Blackpool; Henry Banks, Robert Banks, Thos. Butcher and Robert Forshaw, Innkeepers of Blackpool; and Anthony Hodkinson, Schoolmaster. The school was set in a close called Great Field. Children from Layton-with-Warbreck could be educated, without recompense or reward from their parents, and others would be admitted if the Trustees thought fit. The original Trustees were the first nine gentlemen mentioned above, plus John Hornby of Raikes Hall, and these were to be succeeded by inheritance or appointment. Subscriptions totalled £621 17s. 8d., of which £50 was expended on land and £401 17s. 8d. on the buildings. The residue of £170 was invested.

The pupils were to be instructed in the reading of English, arithmetic, and the principles of the Christian religion, taught according to the monitorial method of teaching formulated by Dr. Andrew Bell, and made familiar enough with the catechism to be able to recite it once a year in the church at Bispham until another had been built at Blackpool. From March to November school hours were 8 a.m. to noon, and 1 p.m. to 5 p.m. In the dark months, November to March, 9 a.m. to noon, and 1 p.m. to 4 p.m. Holidays were three weeks at Christmas and three weeks in August or September (and no others), as directed by the Trustees of whom three were appointed in perpetuity, namely: (1) Patron of the Living of Bispham (Church Association); (2) Rector of Bispham; (3) Vicar of Marton.

In 1824 there were 30 scholars; in 1831 there were 40; in 1867 the average weekly attendance was 107; and in 1884 a total of 465 boys and girls, including infants from a separate department in Bank Hey Street (now R. H. O. Hills), opened 20th October, 1856, presented themselves for the annual inspection. Evening classes taught reading, writing and arithmetic. The Trustees of St. John's School (called so by common usage and having no connection with the church of the same name, but being properly styled "Blackpool National School") met annually, and still do, at a Blackpool inn or public house. There are nine of them at present, in addition to a Board of six Managers, and St. John's is now an aided school with 246 scholars between the ages of 5 and 11.

Some years ago, I talked with Mr. Leonard H. Hornby of Devonshire Road who celebrated his golden wedding on the 8th February, 1961. He had lived in this district, man and boy. Out came the family Bible with his pedigree entered on the fly leaf, beginning with great grandfather, Robt. Hornby, Poulton, 1787; grandfather Richard Hornby, August 1812; father, Leonard Hornby, born at Layton, November 1845; and Mr. Hornby himself, born 19th February, 1884. Labouring or fishing for cockles and mussels kept the first three generations active, but Mr. Hornby chose the building trade. First, however, he attended St. John's School, leaving at 13, but from 11 onwards putting in half time to education and the rest to earning.

An 85-years old friend of mine, who also attended St. John's School, tells me that all the eleven-year-olds of Blackpool had to present themselves for a Saturday morning examination at the Victoria School (now Employment Exchange, Tyldesley Road) to qualify for exemption from 1st May to 30th September. Those who failed had to attend school during the summer. The results were announced some time later and the successful candidates went to the Town's Yard to collect their certificates. As my old friend says: "You dudn't go to no more exams once you'd

St. John's National School, Blackpool.

passed; and even at eleven we was wanted at home to help out wi' th' visitors. We dursent but pass!" Mr. Hornby's parents had dolls and skittles stalls at Raikes Hall Gardens for nearly thirty years, and to his certain recollection at least three generations of his family had been daily customers at the old No. 3 Hotel. Naturally, this veteran Blackpudlian saw many changes. There were fields where now there are solid rows of houses in the Hornby Road district, and his mother could recall her younger days when she worked there in the old clay-hole alongside "Johnny" (later Sir John) Bickerstaffe.

In Mr. Hornby's childhood the road from the No. 3 up to the school still had a leisurely country air, and cows were driven up daily from their grazing in the Newton Drive fields to be milked in Ned Cardwell's shippons at the back of St. John's School. It would be interesting to see the poor bewildered beasts making the same journey to-day, what with the traffic lights and vehicles speeding in all directions. Even more arresting would be the sight of farm buildings, and green fields, and the whistling cowman clomping about the cobble yard, or clanking his buckets, in what is now the heart and centre of Blackpool! Naturally we cannot unmake the decisions of a previous generation. The Trust disposed of their frontage to shops, of which they own seven bordering Church Street. Building expansions have since left the school woefully short of playgrounds. St. John's is a good school, but so crammed in and obscured that one has to search diligently to find it. It is curious to find that the stranger and, presumably, the new scholar, can best be directed by being told to make for the Stanley Arms!

St. John's Parish Church

WHEN a building fund was launched on 22nd May, 1789, Thornber tells us, the response was half-hearted and produced only £100. Yet Blackpool urgently needed her own place of worship. Bispham Church was a long walk away and the Blackpudlian natives were rarely tempted to undertake it except on such necessary occasions as christenings, marriages and burials. Nearly thirty years after the first appeal, Derbyshire visitor, Mr. John Gisborne, who had already established Blackpool's first school, decided to press for the building of a church. A meeting was convened on 22nd August, 1818, to consider ways and means and contributions from leading citizens then amounted to a little over £800.

The first St. John's, an episcopal chapel attached to Bispham, was built during 1820 at a cost estimated at £1,072. Bricks from one of the cliff crofts near the present Butlin's Hotel went into the plain structure with a low embattled tower pinnacled at the corners. The interior, lit by oil lamps, was entirely without ornamentation. The consecration ceremony was performed on 6th July, 1821. The only item of interest in the original building was an old Roman Catholic font brought in from the chapel at

Singleton. Within a few years, however, the population of Blackpool had so increased that enlargements were necessary in 1832. An organ was purchased in 1834 at a cost of £100 and a side aisle was added in 1842. In 1851 a chancel was added with a stained glass window in memory of Henry Banks who died in 1847. (This window is now in the west gable of the church, over the gallery.) In 1860 St. John's was made the Parish Church of Blackpool, taking over a wide parochial area formerly under Bispham (between Spen Dyke and Talbot Road).

Further improvements were made to the building in 1862, including a new pulpit, reading desk and ground glass windows, and a pitch-pine domed roof in place of the old ceiling. The original cobble boundary wall round the churchyard was replaced with a heavy iron railing. The burial ground was also extended west of the church, up to the houses in Abingdon Street, and in 1866 a new larger tower, with a clock and eight bells, replaced the old. A new organ, worked by a gas engine, was installed in 1870 and a few years later, on 28th February, 1877, a memorandum of authority was issued for the pulling down and rebuilding of St. John's Church, incorporating the existing organ, tablets and mural monuments. The final service was held on the last Sunday in March, 1877, and in the same year the Mayor of Blackpool, Dr. W. H. Cocker, laid the foundation stone on 11th July. The consecration ceremony was performed by the Rt. Rev. Dr. Fraser, then Bishop of Manchester, on 25th June, 1878. (Services during the re-building period were held in the Talbot Road Octagon Room, and in the school in Bank Hey Street.) The public clock in the tower was lighted in 1890 and the heating apparatus was renewed in the following year. In 1915 there were a number of improvements, including the installation of electric lighting, oak choir stalls substituting the old ones made of pitch-pine, additional stained glass windows and a new organ.

The first burial in the churchyard was that of John Butcher, aged 3 days, on 14th October, 1822. The last was Eliza Foulkes, aged 2 months, on 31st May, 1873. By Act of Parliament, notice was served prohibiting any more burials, except in existing walled graves and family vaults, from 31st December, 1871, but there was some delay in preparing the cemetery at Layton, which was not ready until 1872, and a deferment was granted to 31st May, 1873. (Forty-two interments have taken place since that date, presumably in existing vaults, the last named being that of James Edward Scholefield on 3rd May, 1917.)

In 1895 the Corporation negotiated with the Lytham Charities for land in connection with proposed street improvements. Land leased to St. John's was to be taken over and ultimately the Corporation paid £1,250 for 250 square yards for which, much to their disappointment, the Church authorities received only £50 by way of compensation. In 1924 the Corporation proposed to widen the junction of Abingdon Street and Church Street, and, by agreement, 194 square yards of the burial ground were transferred at roughly £10 per square yard. This necessitated the disturbance of graves and a faculty was obtained for the removal of bodies to the cemetery. In 1927 (under the Open Spaces Act of 1908) the Corporation was granted the right and easement in perpetuity of converting the graveyard into an open space on condition that 334 names of bodies exhumed and re-interred were commemorated on a four-panelled stone. By 1929 St. John's old churchyard was still in an untidy state. Legal proceedings against the authority were under contemplation but cooler counsels prevailed and after a deputation had been sent to the Town Hall the work was put in hand without delay.

The church bells were re-pealed after renovation in May, 1923.

THE PARSONAGE

The original attractive parsonage house stood on a site bought in 1826, on the opposite side of Church Street and now part of the Winter Gardens site. The buildings which later sprang up around it spoiled its appearance and also interfered with the draught of the chimneys so that the parsonage folk found themselves literally smoked out. Part of the grounds were exchanged with the Winter Gardens Company for a neighbouring plot of land and £333 6s. 8d., invested in 2½% Consols in 1877 and in 1891 the Parsonage house and site were sold for £2,700 to Joseph Fielding & Son who shortly afterwards sold out to the Corporation for £4,200. Restrictive covenants prohibited such distractions as a "theatre, circus, concert hall, aquarium, menagerie or public dancing room" from being built on the site but in 1891 the Winter Gardens Company were released from these restrictions in consideration of the sum of £1,000 paid to Canon A. W. R. Little. A new parsonage house was built in Park Road in 1893 and after the first world war No. 19 Park Road was purchased for £1,650 for use by a curate or assistant clergyman.

1820—1840
The Victoria Promenade and other developments

BLACKPOOL changed but slowly in the first half of this period, and the 1821 population of Layton-with-Warbreck (749) rose by scarcely 200. Basically, except for the season when vast numbers of visitors were brought in by cart and coach from Lancashire and Yorkshire, Blackpool remained a homely community with a church and school of its own and a disposition to celebrate great events in the traditional village manner. At the coronation of George IV, on 19th July, 1821, the young made merry with tea and buns, spiced ale and coppers and, after receiving their coronation medals, paraded the town singing the national anthem to the accompaniment of two musicians. The costs of the celebrations were borne by voluntary subscriptions and after the children had been sent home the organisers treated more than 30 of Blackpool's aged to a dinner and a pint of strong ale.

During the next ten years Blackpool grew and improved, if in somewhat higgledy-piggledy fashion and with a marked lack of conformity. Whittle in his "Marina", published about 1830, tells us "that there are here frequently at the flux of the season from eight hundred to a thousand visitors". He finds no fault with the accommodation offered, stating that it is commodious and excellent. At Nickson's (Clifton Arms) there was even an orchestra in the ball and dining room. The company appears to have been fashionable and distinctive and "four assemblies have been known to take place in one week during the bathing season, extending from July to October".

A number of shops had appeared in the town, a handrail had been rigged up along the parade, and one or two hotelkeepers had placed seats outside their premises for the convenience of visitors. There was a daily post in the season (only thrice weekly in the winter), and the natives had been driven by stark necessity to uncover many fresh water springs below the surface. This was a great improvement on cisterns let into the marl. Old cottages improved and new ones erected gave Blackpool "when viewed from the sea a large and imposing appearance", says Whittle who bewails the absence of verandahs, trellis-work, climbing plants and such other ornamentation as he had noticed at Southport.

One great achievement of the 1830s was Dr. Cocker's Victoria Terrace and Promenade, opened on 24th May, 1837, in celebration of the coming of age of the Princess Victoria. This consisted of a block of shops stretching up Victoria Street from the north-west corner of Bank Hey Street, with a spacious assembly room overhead suitable for dances, public meetings and social gatherings. Blackpool had long needed some communal meeting place "to promote a more friendly intercourse amongst the strangers collected here from all quarters of the kingdom" and the billiard table, library and newsroom attached were sure to be appreciated by the visitors. Fifty-two gentlemen of Blackpool sat down to a sumptuous inaugural dinner in "the splendid Promenade room" under the chairmanship of Vicar Thornber. "No building could have been opened under happier auspices", he declared, referring doubtless to the excellent wine provided by Mr. C. Nickson, "nor any name be more admirably adapted to it than that of the Victoria Promenade". Meantime within the town 140 Sunday School children were treated to buns, coffee and coppers, and the old women were given packets of tea ... "the gift best adapted to increase their hilarity and garrulity". All in all, Victoria's 18th birthday "came off in a manner highly satisfactory ... cordiality and unanimity prevailing". Progress from 1837-40 was unspectacular but steady and by 1841 the population had risen to 1,968.

NOTABLE EVENTS IN THE 1820s and 1830s

1821. St. John's Church consecrated, 6th July.

1825. Small Independent Chapel in lower Chapel Street opened on 6th July by Dr. Raffles.

1827. Blackpool enjoys a prosperous season. August visitors finding lodgings in farm buildings and overflow into Layton and Poulton.

1828. The Albion Hotel goes up on Lane Ends Street (corner of Promenade). A grass walk with covered seats is laid out in the fields leading from the beach to St. John's Church (now Birley Street).

1835. A Wesleyan Chapel, with accommodation for approximately 300 worshippers, is erected in Bank Hey Street adjoining a group of whitewashed cottages (site of Queens Theatre). Adelaide Street has not yet been put through.

1836. Mr. Henry Banks of the Lane Ends builds a bath house adjoining his hotel on the promenade.
Sir Benjamin Heywood erects an imposing mansion, "West Hey", on the promenade (Palace site), with a spacious yard, coachhouse and stables (Sefton Street area).
There were about 40 houses at South Shore at this period.

The 1840s

THE most important single event of that decade was the opening of the Preston and Wyre Railway on 16th July, 1840. This was the creation of Sir Peter Hesketh Fleetwood of Rossall Hall, but for whose unwearied efforts to establish a railroad linking the new Fleetwood with Preston, the Fylde might have remained for many more years difficult of access. The opening of the line was celebrated with immense style and gusto. A train decorated with flags, drawn by two engines and packed with well-wishers and worthies, set off from Preston (50 minutes late) and proceeded "in a really majestic manner" towards Tulketh Viaduct where multitudes had assembled in the confident expectation that the bridge would collapse under the strain. Idle rumours had circulated, hinting at slipshod construction, but the train cleared the last of the fourteen arches with scarcely a vibration and headed for an enthusiastic welcome at Kirkham from "a great assembly of persons". From every church tower, from every house of consequence, flags flapped at full mast and cottage doorways were crammed with excited spectators. There were similar lively scenes at Poulton and a discharge of artillery greeted the train at Fleetwood where three steamers were waiting to take the guests on a short cruise round the lighthouse. Afterwards, the party ascended The Mount and solemnly viewed the infant town rising out of the newly drained marshland; and proceeded, after suitable congratulations, to the station buildings for a sumptuous cold collation, a glee band entertainment, speeches and toasts.

Four hours later, having raised their glasses to everybody from the Queen down to the "labourers on the line", the notables returned to the train which set off back to Preston at seven. A few minutes later it screeched to a halt when it was rumoured that someone had fallen off. Railway officials ran back to investigate and discovered William Dean of Butler's Court, Preston, lying between the rails with his head severed from his body. Dean, a young tailor, had muscled in on this historic occasion. Uninvited, he had boarded the celebration train and had twice been thrown off at Preston. Yet he travelled with the party, spent the day touring the taverns of Fleetwood and succeeded in climbing aboard, having twice again been ejected. His death, the first fatal accident on the Preston and Wyre line, was a shock to the revellers. The plight of his widow and three young children was brought to the sympathetic attention of the citizens of Preston.

The railway was a great convenience to visitors to Blackpool who could now alight at Poulton and find themselves a horse-drawn conveyance from that point to the coast. There were only three trains a day each way, except for an extra "stopping" train on Saturday afternoons for the benefit of outlying villages. Even so, this new mode of safe and comfortable travelling was responsible for bringing visitors in ever-increasing numbers to this coast. It was not until 1846 that Blackpool was linked by a branch line connecting with the main track at Poulton but within a very few years the rattling stage-coach had been elbowed out of business.

In 1841 Sir Peter H. Fleetwood sold to Thomas Clifton, Esq., of Lytham, the Manor of Layton which had been in his family since the mid-16th century and which Queen Mary ... "In consideration of the faithful services done by the said Thomas Fleetwood to her father (Henry VIII) did grant and confirm to the said Thomas Fleetwood, his heirs and assigns, the manor of Great Laton, with its rights and appurtenances, to hold for ever". (1554.) According to the gossip of the times, Mr. Clifton had "laid out £8,000 in the purchase of land at a penny a yard" and within a few years was selling it at 8s. 0d. a yard!

In 1842 a Scarlet Fever epidemic caused great alarm in the town and at a meeting held at the National School it was resolved that ... "the owners and occupiers of lands and houses within the town (be requested) to cause all nuisances connected with their property to be removed and that their cottages be thoroughly cleansed and whitewashed". Mr. Clifton was also to be warned of the "present unhealthy state of the town and respectfully requested that the large ditch which receives the wash of the town at the close gates, which, in the opinion of the medical men is highly prejudicial to the health of the inhabitants, be removed". (Lancs. Records: DDC1/1193/29.)

About this time Talbot Road (formerly New Road) was being opened out by Mr. Clifton. A letter to his Agent from a Mr. Ashworth of Turton, 9th Nov., 1843, indicates the condition of the times:

The New Road is a good improvement, and if you will make the road good and dry, both cart and foot ways ... it is the best and most pleasant walk out of Blackpool, but I observe the roads are wet and dirty for want of being properly drained ... This water, collected into one drain and turned into a Reservoir ... would serve all your premises in Blackpool with excellent water, was it mine I would make a good handsome Reservoir ... and make a Gravel Bed filtering drain from it into a cistern and from that cistern I would have lead pipes into the House and Stables, etc. The expense would be little and the acquisition would be very valuable during the season as good water is scarce and dear ...! (Lancs. Records: DDC1/1195/26.)

47

It would be interesting to know if that fragrant suggestion were ever acted upon, remembering that sanitation was negligible and all the traffic horse-drawn!

In the middle of Talbot Square stood a cottage and yard belonging to the proprietor of the adjoining hotel (Clifton). This was removed at the expense of Squire Clifton when the Square was opened out, and a drinking fountain was later erected on the site, in 1870.

Some interesting snippets of Blackpool in 1846 appear in the Blackpool Journal of a visiting Barrister, "J.B." (John Bell). On the 19th August he set off with his wife, three children and a nurse, from a town in Staffordshire, and after eleven and a half hours of travelling by carriage, horse omnibus and rail, arrived in Blackpool in the late afternoon, despite a half-hour's hold-up on Preston Station. "J.B." comments favourably on the trip compared with a previous one in 1809 when a one-horse covered cart called the "Blackpool Mail" took "eight mortal hours" to complete the journey from Preston to the coast. He tells us that "from Poulton to Blackpool there is only a single line of rails" and that the Blackpool terminus, "though very large and lofty ... was very uncomfortably crowded with spectators ... and idle people of all sorts and sizes", so that it was with difficulty that he retrieved his luggage, had it piled on to Dixon's omnibus and set off with his entourage for the hotel bearing the same name. It was full. The family then resorted to the Lane End Hotel, and Mrs. Richardson, and counted themselves fortunate to "procure good accommodations fronting the sea". Just like to-day, "J.B." discovered that he had come without his shaving brush and combs and he is presently sauntering to St. John's Market to buy these indispensable commodities.

Unlike to-day, our visitor was up next morning on the stroke of five and taking an early walk in "a misty sort of shower" in the direction of the "Gin". After breakfast he went up Church Street to Esau Carter's post office and passed the time, waiting for the mail to arrive, by playing billiards. In the afternoon, he set off on foot to the distant village of South Shore to look for lodgings and discovered that furnished houses were fetching as much as £3 10s. 0d. or £4 per week, plus an additional 4s. 0d. per week for linen. He returned to the Lane End to find a demonstration of "Mr. Carte's rocket apparatus, for effecting a communication with stranded vessels", by means of buoys, belts and rockets, in course of preparation. The performance took place in the evening and drew a good audience. By 21st August, "J.B." had settled for Mrs. Todd's cottage, No. 9, South Shore, at £4 per week, exclusive of plate, with an extra charge of 6s. 0d. per week for the services of a cook. In the afternoon an omnibus conveyed the party and all their belongings "to our new habitation". It transpired that No. 9 "is a favourite cottage" for which the owner drew "from five to ten shillings a week" in the winter. It was situated conveniently near to Moore's Baths into which sea water "being almost as pure as a bathe in the tide and well worthy the attention of the timid bather" was pumped by

Early Blackpool. Top: The Gynn Inn, showing the refreshment stall and the road to Bispham. Centre: Uncle Tom's Cabin. Bottom: Blackpool, about 1770.

The main entrance gate to Raikes Hall Gardens (site of the old Grammar School).

Stansfield's Patent Aerial Flight of 1887. Part of the placard reads: "Already patronised by 86,000 people. A delightful and thrilling sensation. Switchback eclipsed!"

Part of the gipsy encampment beside the future Pleasure Beach about 1905 (from a monochrome painting by Keith Wood).

The Pleasure Beach in embryo at the end of last century, approached by a boarded walk across the sands. Note the famous Flying Machine.

Talbot Square 1881.

Both pages:— Top. Talbot Square. In the 1886 photograph (left) the buildings on the right occupy the present site of the Town Hall. The monochrome painting by Keith Wood depicts the Square in 1881. Bottom: The construction of Princess Parade in 1911 — it was opened the following year.

Blackpool in the 1860s. Top: Carlton Terrace, North Shore. Centre: Assembly Room and Victoria Hotel. Bottom: Regent's Terrace and Brighton Parade.

Blackpool in the 1870s. Top: Bailey's Hotel. Centre: Queen's Square, Central Road. Bottom: North Pier.

Blackpool in the 1870s. Top: Imperial Hotel, Terrace and Lansdown Street. Centre: Imperial Terrace. Bottom: Lansdown Crescent.

engine from the beach. They were not reckoned to be the best baths in the place, but they were handy. On 23rd August, "J.B." watched a guest from the "Manchester House" meet his death by drowning after being stranded and almost rescued from the Horse Bank.

During his eight-day stay he took several walks into the country around "Martin", rode on a pony or drove "upon the sands ... in a pair-horse phaeton in the direction of Fleetwood", looked through telescopes, attended services at South Shore Church, "Martin" Church, and St. John's where there was an organ and "frightful factory windows". (At the first two, he described the musical arrangements as being ... "only vocal and yet hardly equalling the melody of the nightingale"!) He took his family to the bazaar, bumped into old friends, combed the rabbit-ridden sand-dunes, made a day excursion to Liverpool by rail, drove to Lytham, bought soles for 5d. a lb., and "fresh flukes at threepence", ... "rose at four, and taking a towel, bathed in the sea from the sands", and enjoyed all the crowds and changing scenes at "the great Babylon of Blackpool" which, "though long well known is, I apprehend, comparatively still in its infancy, having only cut its eye-teeth". Some teeth!

On 10th April, 1847, we find a letter from a South Shore resident, Mr. Dean, to the Clifton Agent (Lancs. Records: DDC1/1201/19) referring to the insanitary conditions of the times:

... the fever spreads and cock-fighting has re-appeared. I gave information to the Police and if they had done their duty the persons engaged might have been caught and two days' drinking spared. There seems to be sufficient cause for the fever in the want of sanitary regulations. I believe (and you can perhaps inform yourself by facts being compared with the theory) that early in the Spring the manure heaps which lie close to the dwellings are turned or removed and a most noxious gas escapes. This is drawn through the door towards the fire and the stream of course passes through the midst of the family. Besides, some houses require privys and many bedrooms are open to the shippon. Can you do anything to compel the regular whitewashing of the houses quarterly or cause the dirty holes round the houses to be filled up and the manure placed at least 10 yards from the doors in proper places. I am sure that cleanliness would do much to raise the moral condition of the poor.

In the previous year, 23rd Oct., 1843, similar complaints had been made about the centre of Blackpool (Lancs. Records: DDC1/1201/44) where, it was said:

... the nuisance is intolerable and if it continues will drive the visitors from Faint's, Nixon's and Bennett's lodgings. The complaints are great and the walk in front of their houses is deserted and when the wind blows in from the sea, which should be the best, the stench is past bearing, even in the houses, if the doors and windows are open.

Nevertheless, visitors of fashion continued to come into Blackpool and on 31st July, 1847, we find a letter from "B. P. Parker", of the Browsholme family, writing to her "very dear Mamma". (Lancs. Records: DDB. 72/1159.):

I think I shall not require a shawl. If you would promise me a cloak suitable for October ... as well as for the remainder of the summer, I should prefer it. I find it expensive work visiting, but I intend to be as economical as I can. Washing has already cost me more than 10s. 0d. We hope you and Papa continue to improve and are in sufficient health to enjoy the amusements Buxton affords, you are very fortunate in possessing a theatre, I wish we had one here, if it were a pretty good one, for there are so few amusements. Tonight fireworks are exhibited on the sands, which I shall most certainly sit up to look at.

During the 1840s a number of excellent hotels made their appearance along the front, including "The Manchester House", then isolated in the midst of open fields. Porter tells us that in 1847 the "first meeting of the Blackpool Agricultural Society was held in the grounds of ... the Manchester Hotel; the attendance was both numerous and respectable, including many of the most influential gentlemen, yeomen and farmers ... from the remoter localities of the Fylde. Cows, horses and pigs appear to have been the only stocks to which prizes were awarded". In the same year ... "the first Lodge of Freemasons held their initiatory meeting ... at the Beach Hotel ... which had risen shortly before, on the site of some furnished cottages facing the beach."

This was a decade when the astute sank their money into the land and the building of property and the faint-hearted shrank from paying 6d. a yard freehold for plots round Oddfellow Street and spent the rest of their lives regretting their timidity.

For many years in the early 19th century the Banks brothers were notable pioneers. New names, like James Caunce, John, James and William Cragg, and John Bonny, now came to the fore. The building fever was raging, Blackpool was growing fast, but her development was outstripping the arrangements for her good rule and government.

NOTABLE EVENTS IN THE 1840s

The Fylde's first newspaper—"The Fleetwood Chronicle and General Advertiser for Blackpool, Poulton, Kirkham, Lytham, Ulverston and Lonsdale North of the Sands", launched by Wm. Porter in 1843. Price 3d. per copy including a penny duty stamp. (The proprietor's son, John Porter, published his "History of the Fylde in Lancashire" in 1876 and a few years later was drowned in a canal at Antwerp.)

St. John's Market, described as of "16th century style", was built in 1844. A number of good class houses made their appearance on the Central Promenade and South Beach.

The Talbot Hotel in Church Street was built in 1845, and the Adelphi & Post Office Hotel, the original "No. 2" built in the 1830s (now demolished), was raised by one storey and improved.

The New Inn was built by James Butcher adjoining the first cottage along South Beach (Golden Mile). His daughter, Sarah, took over. She married James Barlow and it became known as Barlow's New Inn. When James Barlow died, his widow married James Duke. The name was changed to Duke's New Inn. Subsequent landlords were Thomas Cookson, Robert Mather, and his son, Ald. R. B. Mather, J.P., who bought the adjoining cottage for £450, demolished it, and rebuilt the New Inn and Central Hotel (since demolished). A salvaged ship's cannon which stood on the forecourt for many years and was a favourite perch for sailor-suited small lads having their photographs taken, is now preserved in the grounds of Grundy House, Lytham Road, S.S.

John Bonny (son of John and Jenny of "Bonny's i' th' fields") bought up fields between Chapel Street and the New Inn and built cottage properties in Bonny Street and Oddfellow Street, of which, after redevelopment, little if anything original can now be seen. This area quickly became the most populous part of the town. In 1847 he built the Victoria Hotel (now Ripley's Odditorium) which, though liable to flooding, proved an instant success. James Cragg was the first landlord, assisted by his wife Bessie and their daughters. He erected a camera obscura on the seaside of the promenade and boats were moored nearby for the use of guests. His brother, William Cragg, had bathing vans, stationed in the stabling at the rear (now Naventi's, Brunswick Street). These were drawn up at the side door so that the lady bathers could be conveyed directly to and from the water.

A New Independent Chapel was opened in Victoria Street (1849), replacing the small building which was built in Chapel Street in 1825.

Since the coming of the railway, more people were using coal for domestic fires. Previously they had used mostly peat, or turf. Such coal as came into Blackpool was transported by sea. The shallow vessels grounded on the shingle along the promenade and the coal was then unloaded into carts and delivered.

Mid-19th century Blackpool, by gaslight

BLACKPOOL was by this time a flourishing town with a resident population of more than 2,000 which swelled to an estimated 4,000 during the season. According to the Lancashire Directory of 1851:

None here need complain of lassitude or ennui—there is amusement and employment for all. The horseman, pedestrian, the geologist, the conchologist and zoologist may ever find occupation on the shore and the herbalist on the land ... The laying out of streets and walks, the erection of handsome houses and shops on every side, the establishment of elegant hotels and billiards, news and coffee rooms, lounges, bazaars, etc. ... and the opening and enlargement of places of worship, bespeak the rising importance of the town and the anxiety of the inhabitants to render the sojourn of their visitors pleasant and comfortable ... The months of September and October are considered the genteel season.

Steps were urgently needed to ensure the government and supervision of the fast growing resort. Pioneer John Bonny and Mr. James Heywood, M.P., pressed for the formation of the Layton-with-Warbreck Local Board of Health to administer the public affairs of Blackpool and in December, 1851, the ratepayers cast their votes for the appointment of 9 Commissioners, as follow:

John Bonny (Chairman), Robert Nickson, James Caunce, Robert Rawcliffe, John Cocker, Thos. Topping, Richard Banks, John Pool and William Shaw.

The Blackpool Improvement Act received the royal assent in 1853 and the Board operated with 9 members until 1871 when the number was increased to 18. Their early work earned favourable comment in the Directory & Gazeteer, 1857:

Great praise, we are glad to say, is due to the Commissioners of Blackpool who have done all in their power to sewer the town and cleanse it from all impurities, so that the most refined visitor may be pleased with its purity and sweetness ...

The Baths are very neatly fitted up, especially Mr. Banks', Hygiene Terrace and Mr. Moor's, South Shore, who has got an engine to pump the water from the sea. (In addition there were John Cragg's baths, "Rose Cottage", Church Street, and James Wylie's on South Beach.)

The sands, which are very hard, extend to 5 or 6 miles ... truly Blackpool may be called the Brighton of the North.

Stage-coaches, grimly competing with the increasingly popular railway, still gave a hint of the old days as they rumbled away from the New Inn twice daily to Lytham or departed every morning from the Clifton Arms for Preston and Rochdale. There were 9 livery stable keepers and coach proprietors in Blackpool and 13 local characters had bathing vans for hire. Mary Crookall's were in Bank Hey Street. John Moon of Bridge House and John Moore of Britannia Place operated from South Shore. The rest were centred on the South Beach (Golden Mile) area, around Brunswick Street, Oddfellow Street and Chapel Street. Along Cragg Street and Bonny Street, even to-day, there are yards and storage depots where once the fishermen, boatmen and van proprietors stabled their horses and stationed their cabs and horse "sharries".

Of all the districts in Blackpool perhaps this alone retains an atmosphere reminiscent of the old days. In little houses tucked away you can still find the descendants of the old fishing and lifeboat families—the Cornalls, Parrs, Rimmers, Stanhopes, the Salthouses, Swarbricks ... and many others. And you can still see the traditional peak-caps and navy blue jerseys beloved of these study sons of the sea, whose names have rippled through the pages of the lifeboat history, and whose ancestors stepped in at this crucial period of Blackpool's early development and ensured that holidays at Blackpool were enjoyed to the full. Beyond the pinfold site (now Wellington) there were two cottages with gardens leading down to the sea (the first occupied by "Bob's" father, Edward Bickerstaffe), and a cottage, shop and garden owned by John Wylie. From there to the Foxhall the land and foreshore belonged to the Yorkshire House (later York Hotel, now demolished and absorbed into the "Wonderland" site), which had a bowling green and extensive yards and out-buildings.

Foxhall and beyond was known as Lower Blackpool and South Shore was considered a distinct and "pretty village about 1 mile south from Blackpool, situated on a low sandy tract of land called the "Hawes", and consisting chiefly of a range of neat cottages fronting the sea. Through the enterprise of the late Mr. T. Moore, who in 1819 erected the first house, it has gradually progressed in attraction and extent and is now nearly joined with the south end of Blackpool".

Cornelius Bagot's "Dog and Partridge" was operating in 1834 and across the road (Royal Oak site) was another small beer-house. The vast acres of Layton Hawes were still a blank expanse on the map, punctuated only by isolated farmsteads which could almost be counted on the fingers of both hands. All the new South Shore building was centred on the junction of Waterloo Road and the promenade and it is not surprising that Mr. Moore's contemporaries exchanged sly grins when he built his house in the wilds of a sandy wilderness!—or that their derision turned into respect within very few years.

One of the first improvements effected by the Commissioners was the construction of a Gas Works to ensure the proper light-ing of the town. The first properties were lit by this medium in

1852 and by 1863 there were 650 consumers on the list. What with sewers and gas mains, two posts week-daily and one on Sundays, there was no-one who could accuse Blackpool of lagging behind other resorts by the mid-19th century!

NOTABLE EVENTS IN THE 1850s

1851. Layton-with-Warbreck population—2,564.
Robert Bickerstaffe, a Blackpool boatman, bought the pinfold site for a cottage and boatyard. He decided instead to build a hotel, "The Wellington", which cost £1,700 and was a great favourite with the fishing fraternity.

1852. Gas Works built.

1853. Fylde Waterworks Company provisionally registered. Apathetic response.

1856. Infants' School opened in Bank Hey Street (20th October), on site of R. H. O. Hills.
Schooner "British Token" wrecked with cargo of oatmeal opposite Star Inn, South Shore. Cabin boy washed up at Rossall, buried at Fleetwood.

1857. Sloops "Rose" and "The Thomas" wrecked (1st September). Schooner "Pride" (22nd November) off South Shore.
First Roman Catholic Church in Blackpool, dedicated to the Sacred Hearts of Jesus and Mary. Designed by Pugin. Previously the Roman Catholics had met in a room in Talbot Road. (Peal of bells added in 1866, and an organ some ten years later.)
The Baptists take over the room vacated by the Roman Catholics. (Foundation stone for a Union Baptist Chapel, Abingdon Street, laid 9th April, 1860.)

1861. Layton-with-Warbreck population—3,907.

12 Schools were listed in Blackpool and South Shore in the 1850s, including boarding, preparatory, private and free day schools.
There were 2 carriers to Preston. (1) Wm. Cragg, thrice weekly from his house on South Beach; (2) Nicholas Bamber, South Shore, daily in the summer and thrice weekly in the winter.

The 1860s, fresh piped water, two new piers, Charles Dickens, Old Uncle Tom's Cabin and all!

THIS was a period of outstanding development in which the population almost doubled that of the previous decade. (1861— 3,907; 1871—7,092.)

Victorian holiday-makers were addicted to their piers and at the beginning of 1862 a capital of £12,000 was raised for the construction of North Pier at Blackpool. It was to be more than 1,000 feet long, 28 feet wide, lit by gas lamps, and fitted up with octagonal shelters and refreshment rooms. The original tender was £11,540 but an October storm and the damage incurred during construction caused a revision of the plans. The decking was raised by an additional 3 feet at an extra cost of £2,000. The opening ceremony was performed on 31st May, 1863, by Captain Preston. The structure which was plain to the point of austerity nevertheless greatly added to the pleasures of a seaside visit, and it served as a nucleus for the present North Pier attractions. A jetty was added in 1869 and since that time widenings, extensions and improvements have changed the original beyond recognition. Nowadays the jetty is a favourite haunt of the anglers and such are the summer crowds of promenaders and sun-seekers that one would never be in the least surprised to see North Pier quietly submerge beneath its burden of massed humanity.

In 1867 work commenced on the South (Central) Pier and Jetty, having a total length of more than 1,500 feet, toll-houses, waiting and refreshment rooms, shops, seats and shelters. Obviously some of the novelty of pier building had evaporated by this time, for the "Preston Pilot" records:

The new pier on South Beach was opened last Saturday (30th May, 1868) but the proceedings passed off tamely, there not being any attempt at a public ceremony.

The most pressing need at this stage of development was the provision of good piped water. The population was increasing by leaps and bounds and those few inhabitants with access to abundant and reliable well water were fleecing their neighbours by charging exorbitant prices for barrelsful of this precious commodity. The Fylde Water Works had been provisionally registered as early as 1853 but lapsed through lack of financial support. By 1860, when Manchester Solicitor, Mr. E. C. Milne came to live at Warton Hall, near Lytham, it was imperative that urgent steps be taken "to provide a supply of pure water for the inhabitants of the Fylde district, the urgent need of which in the rapidly increasing towns of Lytham, Blackpool and Fleetwood, has been long and seriously felt". Through the promptings of Mr. Milne, and by general concern, examinations and analyses of the Brock and Grizedale Brook resulted in the Grizedale scheme being adopted by the Fylde Waterworks Company whose Act received the royal assent on 22nd July, 1861. It was estimated that an average of 15 people lived in every house in Blackpool at this time.

By the end of 1862 contracts had been let for the laying of pipes from Grizedale to the Weeton Reservoir and from thence to Kirkham, Lytham and Blackpool. On 1st July, 1864, before the reservoir was completed, piped water was brought into Blackpool and one of the first houses to be supplied was that of Mr. and Mrs. Masheter in Market Street. By the end of that year a total of 699 dwellinghouses and several public institutions within the area of operations had had the service laid on. Applications at the rate of more than twenty per week were flowing into the Company's offices. Thus, in very short years, the wide-boys of the water trade were put out of business. Some interesting reminiscences are recorded in "The History of the Fylde Water Works, 1861-1911" by C. Arthur, of the days before piped water came through:

Some visitors to Blackpool were very particular about the water they drank and sent for it from a pump at Layton Hall at Layton, said to be very good water.

Old Billy Dagger, a gardener at Raikes Hall, used to live in a farmhouse (on Raikes Hill, corner of Church Street and Park Road) ... and there was a pump not far away ... from which Dagger used to sell water at 1s. 6d. a barrel, and he made scores of pounds out of it.

When I lived in West Street I kept a confectioner's and grocer's shop and in the summer time we had no water and used to send a tub to my father's house at 11 Queen's Square, to be filled from a pump fixed in the kitchen, and we had to fetch it for all the baking. I went myself many a time to a pump behind Doidge's (West Street) to beg a pint of water.

The difficulties of maintaining catering and retail establishments, with staff and perhaps well over 100 visitors but without adequate supplies of fresh water can only too well be imagined. The services laid on by the Fylde Water Works Company must rank as the greatest single boon to Blackpool during the whole of her evolution.

On the northern cliffs, during the 'sixties, stood Uncle Tom's Cabin, developed from a small refreshment stall which had stood there for a number of years near the old gypsy encampment. The gypsies, the Smiths, Lees, Coopers and Boswells, arrived in Blackpool and set up their blanket tents here about 1810. It resembled a scene straight out of the Bible and drew crowds of visitors who were mildly afraid and pleasantly intrigued by the handsome dark-skinned campers. Aged crones seated at open tent flaps puffing on clay pipes before fires made of faggots did well out of the second-sight business and every Gorgio woman with curiosity in her heart and a mite in her pocket hurried north to consult the Gypsy palmists. A few caravan dwellers rumbled in during the summer to vie with the tent folk, generations of whom were born, lived out their lives, and died in their blackening shelters. The popularity of the gypsy settlement attracted other diversions for the entertainment of the crowds. Eventually an open-air dancing platform, wooden hut and pavilion, were built there and the proprietor, cashing in on the popularity of Harriet Beecher Stowe's best selling novel, placed wooden images of the three principal characters on top of his buildings and adopted the title for this long established holiday attraction. A visit to Uncle Tom's was an indispensable part of a visit to Blackpool. There were swings, hobby horses, a camera obscura and, of course, the inevitable photographers! Unfortunately the sea was encroaching at a rapid pace and with the passage of years the original Uncle Tom's Cabin was undermined and destroyed.

In April, 1869, Charles Dickens stayed at the Beach Hotel (part of Tower buildings) in connection with one of his famous Readings due to take place at the Guild Hall, Preston, on 22nd April. The event had been widely publicised and people from all over the Fylde and Lancashire had reserved their seats. Special trains were laid on for the convenience of patrons in the Lytham area. Feeling far from well, Mr. Dickens arrived in Preston, but was advised by his physician, summoned from London, to cancel the performance on account of the state of his heart and voice and general fatigue induced by excessive travelling. The Reading was stopped but too late to warn ticketholders who rolled up in full evening dress and by the elegant carriage-load only to have their money refunded. Nevertheless the novelist wrote of Blackpool in these terms:

I have had a delicious walk by the sea, I sleep soundly, and have picked up amazingly in appetite.

Another outstanding national figure visited Blackpool during this decade. On 22nd August, 1868, the "Preston Pilot" records:

We understand that Mr. Bright, M.P., has been staying for a few days at the Imperial Hotel. It must have been a good thing for the hotel as numbers of people paid a visit in hopes of seeing the celebrated M.P.

NOTABLE EVENTS IN THE 1860s

1861. Union Baptist Chapel, Abingdon Street, opened Good Friday. (Sold for G.P.O. site 1903.) A brick building, 80 ft. long x 49 ft. wide, with red pine open pews, two end galleries, and accommodation for 650. A Sunday School and organ were added in 1874.
Sod cut for the single line railway linking Blackpool with Lytham.
Schooner "William Henry" capsized off South Shore. Cargo of flour and lard confiscated by local inhabitants, despite official warnings.
Christ Church iron mission opened in Queen Street. (Replaced with permanent building and consecrated 1870.)
Read's Baths, Market Arcade and Assembly Rooms, South Beach.
Gas Works taken over by the Local Board.

1862. Police Station and Court House with offices and cells, Abingdon Street.
Lytham—Blackpool single line railway commences (April). 35,000 passengers used the service in 3 months.
New Wesleyan Chapel, accommodating 750, replaces smaller one on same site.

1863. Opening of North Pier.
Shard Bridge, linking Over-Wyre district, under construction (completed November, 1864).
Blackpool Land Building & Hotel Co. Ltd., bought 60 acres (from Carleton Terrace to the Gynn) and began developing Claremont Park, a private enclosure with walks, flower beds and shrubberies. Tolls were charged and people often paid their penny sooner than risk walking northwards along the crumbling cliffs.
Carleton Terrace was built.
The marriage of Prince of Wales and Princess Alexandra celebrated by massed assembly of school children in Talbot Square, parades, tea and buns.
Brig "Lemnos" sprang a leak and capsized near North Pier. Crew of 11 rescued by Will and James Parr, Thos. Salthouse, Will and Jim Stanhope, in their fishing smack "Faith".
Jas. Stanhope, Sam Rimmer, Wm. Jolly and "Bob" Bickerstaffe in his boat "Civility" rescued 2 men from a capsized boat.

1864. Fylde Water Works bring in first piped water (July).
Blackpool gets its first lifeboat, "Robert William" (named after Robert Wm. Hopkins whose widow donated £250 towards the cost). Crew: Bob Bickerstaffe (Cox); Jno. Swarbrick (Sub-Cox); Wm. Parr (Bowman); Rich. and Jno. Parkinson; Jas. Parr; Will and S. Jolly; Tom Maudsley; Rich. Gaskell; Wm. Stanhope; Samuel Rimmer; Thos Fish. Launched with a bottle of wine from slade opposite Manchester Hotel.
First rescue, Brig "St. Michael" (18th September). Cox Bickerstaffe's note: "The lifeboat's first time out in a strong wind and sea. She rowed well and under sail went like a steamer."
Old Lane Ends (County) Hotel demolished and rebuilt within 2 years.

1865. Clifton Arms Hotel demolished and rebuilt (1866).
Act of Parliament passed for the development of the new promenade.
Great shoal of herring passed under North Pier.

64

1866. Christ Church, permanent structure opened (consecrated 1870).

1867. Prince of Wales Arcade, Central Beach. Imperial Hotel.
Lifeboat called to three wrecks. Many lives saved.

1868. South (Central) Pier and jetty opened (30th May).
Blackpool Club Day. Benefit Societies, Oddfellows and Druids parade.
Lancashire Rifle Volunteers camp at Raikes Hall (June).
Pinder's Circus visits Blackpool (June).
Temperance Hall, Coronation Street (1st July).
Talbot Road Arcade and Assembly Rooms (Theatre Royal, now Tivoli).
Black Dyke Halifax Band wins £50 first prize at Blackpool Band Contest (1st September).

1869. High tides and great storm damage (Jan., Feb. and March).
Charles Dickens stayed at Beach Hotel (21st April).
South Shore Wesleyan Church (2nd September).

A late 18th century cottage and stable which stood at the west end of Cocker Street on the site of Middle Walk. The buildings were demolished in 1860.

"This shoal of death"—storms, wrecks and the sea in ugly mood

FROM medieval times the priors of Lytham and the Lords of the Manor of Layton established their "rights of wreck of the sea" and kept a calculating eye on this valuable source of revenue. There was keen competition between the two domains which were severed by Division Lane, running seawards from

Marton Moss and dissolving in the sand-dunes immediately south of Squire's Gate Camp. In 1338 we discover Widow Sybil Butler of Layton sneaking over the Lytham border and dragging a wrecked anchor to within her own Manor in order to lay claim to the salvage. Tricks of this nature fanned a smouldering hostility between the neighbouring landowners who, in any case, had to be pretty quick off the mark to beat the natives to the pickings. Time and again we hear of the lords' agents being outwitted and the locals openly parading their sly-gotten gains.

The boot was on the other foot in 1702, however, when an English vessel, "Employment", was captured by a Frenchman, held to a £1,000 ransom, and eventually "embayed under the Red Banks, behind Rossall". There she lay "in a very foul strong place, where she beat till she was full of water" but the natives were outsmarted when horses and carts "with empty casks to put the damaged sugars in" came roaring in from Lancaster and brought the cargo safely to shore. "We got the sugar into Esquire Fleetwood's barn, at Rossall, and the cotton wool into Bispham chapel", runs the account of William Stout of Lancaster's Journal. Salvage attempts were unsuccessful and the "Employment" was beaten to fragments. "The cotton wool was sent to Manchester and sold for £200", and there must have been some sour faces in Blackpool!

Thornber tells of a Traver Indiaman, laden with silks and lace, which sank with all hands but one in 1775. Squire Fleetwood salvaged two beautiful vases and put them in his drawing room, and the Blackpudlians plundered the wreck and flaunted Traver lace on their mob caps until well into the 19th century. In the early 19th century memories of a half-forgotten wreck were revived when local fishermen uncovered her cargo of porter in a sandbank off Norbreck. "A few of these, incrusted with sand and containing porter still fresh and of the best quality, were brought to Simpson's Hotel. The novelty of liquor, taken from such a cellar as the bed of the ocean, after having lain there thirty years, soon collected customers to consume it", says Thornber.

The year 1833 was disastrous for mariners and landlubbers alike. On 11th June a summer storm swept eleven vessels to their doom on the Blackpool coast and morning light revealed several other wrecks either floating waterlogged or sunk a little way off shore. During that doomful night a Lerwick sloop was miraculously saved when a candle light at the old Gynn hostelry enabled the master to cast up safely on the slade, the only opening in the cliffs at that point. The sloop's crew gave public thanks at Blackpool church on the following sabbath, in contrast to a rescued Irish crew who spent their time fighting and drinking and eventually moved off without thanks and with no offer to pay for their hospitality. On 31st December of that same year (1833) there occurred an inrush of the sea which had no parallel within living memory. The tide swept over lower Blackpool, razing dwellings, hurling down walls and inundating field and meadow alike. Roofs became airborne, spray shot up to the heavens and the Parade resembled a turbulent seascape. On the reflux of the tide the damage was counted in broken embankments, shattered roads and a vast heartbreaking litter of domestic paraphernalia, bricks, sticks, broken pots, cracked slates, lumps of turf and scattered cobbles. Great damage was also sustained by Squire Fleetwood and his tenants at Rossall.

In January, 1839, the tale of violent destruction was repeated. The roofs were bodily removed from three of the principal hotels (Dickson's, Nickson's and the Yorkshire House), exhausted sea-birds were cast up in their hundreds, and more than twenty vessels were crippled or sunk off this Lancashire coast. Included in them was the "Crusader", a Liverpool—Bombay vessel laden with valuable silks, cottons and Government despatches. Her crew of 26 were rescued and succoured at the old Britannia Inn, South Shore, but her cargo was energetically plundered and secreted by the Martonians, in pig-styes and outhouses, dangling down wells or buried under the old apple tree in the orchard. Five local men were charged with theft and sent to the House of Correction at Preston. (In 1867 the remainder of the cargo broke loose from the hulk when the Ribble shifted her course, and was washed ashore at Blackpool.) After this heavy toll of life, Blackpool's Vicar-Historian pressed hard for a lifeboat at Blackpool, but to little avail. If there was plenty of public sympathy there was scant financial support, and it was not until 1864 that the "Robert William" commenced her service at Blackpool.

By that time the Blackpool and Bispham registers had recorded for posterity how many an unfortunate stranger came to rest in these parts; of whole crews, and single victims; of fishing expeditions and pleasure trips that ended in tragedy; of unknown mariners, and of eager emigrants like Alice Wrigley (28) of Bury who now lies quietly sleeping in the churchyard at Bispham. She was one of the 360 souls aboard the "Ocean Monarch" which left the Mersey early on the 20th August, 1848. Within short hours the vessel was afire and the flames could be seen from Blackpool promenade. Perhaps 170 victims came to a watery grave and 9 of them were washed up and interred at Bispham. Truly, of major and minor tragedies, Blackpool has had more than her fair share.

1868-9 were years of tremendous devastation. Hotels, roads, cottages and low-lying lands were inundated by high tides running before great gales. North Pier was damaged, hulkings were battered, the Central Promenade and Golden Mile were several feet deep in water; the Foxhall, Manchester Hotel, New Inn and old Royal Hotel were waterlogged, and the work on the 1870 promenade was in many places almost destroyed. The façade of one house on the front was ripped down from attic to cellar, and not a single gate nor a garden wall remained. Lamp-posts keeled over, the roadway had been cracked up like toffee and gouged out to a depth of several feet exposing the gas pipes far below the surface and shingle had been cast up, window high, in front of the houses. No wonder that Lancastrian visitors flocked here in their thousands and counted their trouble well rewarded by this freak exhibition laid on by nature.

By this time all the big newspapers were making a regular feature of Blackpool's nautical trials and tribulations. The merest hint of a high sea evoked lurid paragraphs of disaster and destruction and in February, 1871, following the usual dramatic accounts of yet another storm, we find one irritated Blackpudlian pointing out to the "Preston Pilot": "No such damage ... has taken place ... it is gross exaggeration in every respect. The total amount of damage to the three miles of sea fencing is less than £10." This deflating statement put the "Considerable Storm Damage at South Shore" in its proper perspective and blunted the edge of an otherwise exciting story.

In contrast to all these tales of watery ferocity, that beloved Lancashire poet, Edwin Waugh, who often visited this way and, along with Ben Brierley, gave readings at the Crystal Palace in the 1860s, recalled an amusing incident which occurred over a hundred years ago. It was 5th March, 1860. Tides higher than for a century were expected at Blackpool and hordes of Lancashire mill workers forsook their looms and took the day off to see their favourite resort in "March-mony-weathers". They expected to find the Fylde under water, with roof-top rescues and all the sensational happenings which had been written of so graphically, and so often. Instead, on a windless day, the sea was a sheet of sparkling glass and, to add insult to injury, the sun blared forth from a sky of cloudless blue. The tide rose scarcely higher than usual and the thwarted inlanders went home convinced they were the victims of a hoax. One ancient Boltoner declared that he wouldn't come to Blackpool again "for th' next fifty year, sink or swim. Their great tide were nowt i' th' world but an arrant sell, getten up by lodgin' heawse keepers, an' railway chaps, an' newspapper folk, an' sich like wastril devils, a-purpose to bring country folk to th' wayter-side and hook brass eawt o' their pockets. But they'd done their do wi' him ... he'd come no moore a-seein' their tides, nor owt else ... He coom fra Bowton, an' he're beawn back to Bowton by th' next train; an' iv onybody ever see'd him i' Blackpool again, they met tell him on't at th' time, an' he'd ston a bottle o' wine for 'em, as who they were!"

The reply to that outburst must come from "Owd England", a fishing farmer of Norbreck. "Th' idea of a whol teawn o' fooak comin' to t' seea for this. Pssho! I've no patience wi' 'em ... Tide! Silly divuls, there'll be no tide worth speykin' on ... But some fooak knaw nowt o' th' natur o' things!" Neptune's little prank, which brought a welcome burst of trade out of season could not have been bettered by an astute publicity manager! And there was an extra bonus, a few years after this disaster that never was, when a huge shoal of herring came inshore in such profusion that Blackpudlians waded in and threw them on to the sand, or dunked their pinnies and came up with a lapful. They sold for as little as 9d. for the 100 and hundreds of Fylde coast fishing boats followed the shoal which passed under North Pier.

The Blackpudlians, from long, and often bitter, experience have known their restless ocean in all its moods, from beneficence to belligerence. At summer's end they locked their front doors, boarded up their front gates and kept buckets of clay, rags and sacks handy to seal up the chinks. All too often they saw the waves cascading up Chapel Street, sweeping up Bonny Street and Oddfellow Street. There were carpets hung out to dry, kitchen furniture afloat, housewives thigh-deep commiserating with each other, and wry-grinned workmen returning home in small boats. Nowadays these full-scale disasters are rare, thanks to our sturdy marine defences and their imaginative planning which, at last, have rendered the homes of Blackpool secure.

Upper Church Street and district

DURING the 1860s, building developments were encroaching upon the wide open fields surrounding upper Church Street. Topping Street and Edward Street were being opened out and built upon in 1866. James Caunce, a Prestonian living at the Villa, Hoo Hill, died about this time, leaving his executors to sell off for building all his fields on which the ABC Theatre, King Street, Cookson Street and others as far as Buchanan Street now stand. This resulted in a big burst of building operations. A Mr. Edward Lomax bought up some of the plots and began building in Caunce Street, Cookson Street and King Street, and eventually he was putting up neat dwelling houses with small front gardens on Church Street, opposite the school, and offering them for sale at £250 apiece. Schoolmaster Brown would dearly have liked one of these houses but decided that the price was too high. A short-sighted policy, as it turned out. The Corporation paid out almost £3,000 each for the properties before half a century had gone by.

Again, during the 1860s, a row of houses was being put up near the school (Stanley Terrace), and the corner building was being erected by a Mr. Bond who intended to apply for a licence. At the same time the Neptune (now absorbed into the Grosvenor) was going up and there was keen competition to see which house would get the licence first. Mr. Bond won the race and his son, Whittaker Bond, who celebrated his Diamond Wedding on 4th April, 1923, was granted a temporary permit covering six months. When this expired a permanent licence was issued by Charlie Moore, the Excise Officer at Poulton, and this being the year of a General Election (1868), and Fred Stanley, afterwards Earl of Derby, being a candidate, that historic name was adopted at the christening of the new pub which has been known ever since as the Stanley Arms.

During the succeeding decade, the whole country atmosphere of that healthful and wide open district was entirely swept away by new buildings on Caunce's estate. Descending the lane leading to the No. 3 there was Mr. Masheter, the butcher's house, Parker's smithy, now a ladies' and gents' clothing shop, and a

69

ginnel at the side of it leading by a cobble path to an open court-yard bounded by a row of cottages and Mr. Masheter's old slaughter house. These still remain. Across the road, on Raikes Hill, was Daggers Farm and the descending estate around Raikes Hall. Between Elizabeth Street and Durham Road was a range of ancient cottages which have since disappeared. Within a score of years, upper Church Street had acquired an entirely new look. Licensed and private houses, shops and offices, had stepped up the population, and the green of Layton Raikes was fast being swallowed by the builder.

Raikes Hall Pleasure Gardens

THE Raikes Hall Park, Gardens and Aquarium Company, was formed in 1871 with the express intention of turning the estate, amounting to the best part of 40 acres, into an entertainments and super-pleasure centre. Indeed, why not? There was no opposition. The Tower and Winter Gardens had not been thought of; and who would not take advantage of this sheltered reserve, with trees, which you could find nowhere else, with distractions galore, and with seventeen bars operating at full tilt in the season (the licence extended to any part of the grounds) all within a short walk or a pleasant drive in a landau!

The scheme was bold and imaginative in conception. A large conservatory was built, terraces, footpaths and flower beds were laid out, and customers were being admitted during that first season. About 1875 a vast boating and fishing lake was formed in the dip towards Whitegate Drive and the higher ground nearer the sea became a splendid racing track where trotting and other contests and shows were held. There was a dancing platform, a monkey house (never an aquarium), and aviaries flanking the drive immediately inside the four-arched main gates (near the old Grammar School site).

In the year before his death in March, 1962, I spent much time with Reuben Davis, a gentle, courteous 82-year old honorary Blackpudlian with needle-sharp recollections of Victorian Black-pool and particularly of the Raikes Hall Royal Palace Gardens where his father, an ex-lion-tamer in a circus, who had turned to cameo-cutting, had taken a stall. On leaving school at 14, Reuben went as office-boy to the General Manager of the Company, worked his way up and stayed until the closure of the Gardens. Then, at 21, he became a commercial artist and was painting posters for the Tower Company for over 60 years.

The first manager was Mr. R. Rushton. The second was Mr. George Bart Taylor who died, in his thirties, in 1890. From that time the former secretary, Mr. Charles Iddeson, took over as man-ager and he quickly instituted a variety theatre. Which was only natural. Variety was at the height of its popularity. England re-echoed to the songs made famous by the immortals of the music hall world.

Contrary to beliefs, Marie Lloyd never appeared at the Raikes.

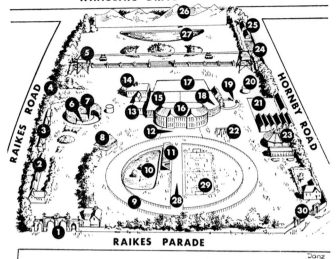

WHITEGATE DRIVE

RAIKES ROAD

HORNBY ROAD

RAIKES PARADE

Danz

Bird's-eye view of Raikes Hall Royal Palace Gardens.

1. Main entrance
2. Switchback railway
3. Monkey houses
4. Turnstile (now Liverpool Road)
5. Stansfield's Aerial Flight
6. Conservatory
7. Roller skating rink
8. Aviary
9. Trotting and race track
10. Boating lake
11. Grandstand
12. Paddock
13. Small theatre
14. Raikes Hall Hotel
15. Indian Lounge
16. Large theatre
17. Open-air dancing platform
18. Ballroom pavilion
19. Taylor's Railway
20. Camera Obscura
21. Bicycle track/ Hobby horses
22. Swings
23. Niagara
24. Hot house/ kitchen gardens
25. Fireworks stores
26. Fireworks scenic backcloths
27. Ornamental lake
28. Running track
29. Football pitch
30. Tollhouse (Hornby road)

She performed at the old Empire (Hippodrome) but the legendary Marie was far too costly for the Raikes whose directors could never have risen to her three-figure salary. But Katie Lawrence ("On a bicycle made for two") performed at the gardens, and so did Gus Elen ("Never introduce your donah to a pal" and "It's a great big shame!"). Gus Elen, whose name is perhaps less well remembered, was in every way equal to Albert Chevalier. Each excelled in the delineation of Cockney character, both made names as singers of coster songs. The difference was that Albert Chevalier, a former actor, shrank from the vulgarity of the whole thing and remained always a "bit of a toff", whilst Gus Elen, who was the genuine article, revelled in his work. He had started his career singing on the sands at Brighton and he was content to earn £12 per week at the Raikes. Mr. Davis remembers him well as an excellent and clean performer who never resorted to innuendo but stuck to the songs with a message and a moral. Eventually, of course, Coster Elen leapt to the top and when next invited to the Raikes he demanded £80 per week which the company could not afford.

The ballroom (common boards only, no parquet floors) was originally Cooke and Byers' Circus. In 1888 the company purchased the Manchester Golden Jubilee Exhibition building and erected it over the dancing platform, turning it into "The Indian Lounge" filled with seats and stalls.

Another indoor attraction was "The Niagara". This was an enormous panoramic picture painted by a French artist, Phillipoteaux, whose works had been exhibited in London, Paris and all parts of America. It was to be housed in a special octagonal building, some 80 ft. wide and about 60 ft. high, built by a Mr. Harris (or Harrison). For this purpose the bowling green was removed from its original site. Unfortunately for the proprietor, when the skeleton of the building got up, his money began to run out. He disappeared and the picture lay for three years still packed in its wooden box, about 30 ft. long. Eventually the Company lost patience, seized the picture and completed the building themselves. What should have proved a money spinner, however, turned out an absolute flop. Admission was 6d. a time. On the first day, August Bank Holiday, young Reuben Davis, seated in the pay box, took precisely 3s. 6d. Next day 4s. 6d. On the third day the admission charge was reduced to 3d., but the Niagara failed to make good.

At the outset, a Captain Clancy was engaged as a guide but the poor takings brought his career to an abrupt end. Having quickly picked up the patter, young Reuben took over, escorting small parties up the spiral staircase and pointing out the wonders and delights of the panoramic Niagara. But it was not very long before the "attraction" was sold, lock, stock and barrel, for £80, and the building was moved to the site of the Tyldesley Road 'Bus Station. It was used for the Royal Italian Circus, Bostock and Wombwell's Menagerie and Circus, and later by Bamburger whose troupe of 30 or 40 natives from French West Africa put on a performance against a backcloth of grass huts and jungle. Finally it became Blackpool's first cinema, The Colosseum, in 1906. It operated in primitive fashion, heated by coke-stoves. Penny matinees were put on by the proprietor, Mr. A. Blacker who eventually built, and transferred to, the Royal Pavilion. As time passed, the old Niagara building, which stood on the site of the Coliseum Coach Station, rotted away and was forgotten.

For those who craved outdoor amusements, the Gardens had everything to offer—acrobatic displays, agricultural shows and parades of beef cattle, contests of all kinds, and particularly the ambitious firework displays, built up on poles with a background of canvas scenery, in front of the trees bordering Whitegate Drive, Sometimes 200 youths were employed, put into uniform and paid 1s. 0d. a night, to heighten the reality of these mammoth performances which stretched from Devonshire Square to Hornby Road corner. Unfortunately, about 1895, there was a tremendous storm which did great damage to the firework stands. The cost of replacing, plus the fact that roofs of residences in Whitegate Drive were being pierced by falling rockets, resulting in complaints from the owners and court injunctions, brought the ambitious grand-scale displays to an end. Ground fireworks, however, continued for long enough.

Best remembered of all the performers must surely be the world famous Blondin. He came to the Raikes only once, for three weeks in 1895, though a coloured man, referred to as "The African Blondin" had performed there during the 80s. Blondin, then in his seventies, executed his daring tight-rope act on the old firework site. He spoke poor English, but understood it well, and Mr. Davis was always willing to act as interpreter. One of the highlights of Blondin's performance was the carrying of his middle-aged son on his back across the rope. In hoisting him up to the pole at the final Raikes show, the artiste strained his back, fell off the rope and had to be nursed for a while at the Station Hotel by the chambermaid whom he took for his second wife. He did very little performing after his experience at Raikes Gardens, appearing for the last time in Belfast in 1896 and dying on 19th February, 1897 in his digs at Ealing.

Thus, for more than twenty years, Raikes Hall, or Royal Palace Gardens, held pride of place in the list of Blackpool's attractions. During the 90s, however, the wind of change was beginning to blow and the promenade and town centre were becoming the focal point of interest. The common boards and crimson coconut matting at the Raikes could not compete with the plush carpets and parquet floors at the Winter Gardens. There were already two piers—North Pier, opened 1863; Central Pier in 1868. In 1893 Victoria (South) Pier was opened to the public, and with three piers, a fine promenade, the Empire Theatre (Hippodrome), 1895, and The Alhambra (later Palace) 1899, visitors were becoming less inclined to make even this short journey in search of amusement.

The opening of the Tower in 1894 and the building of the Big Wheel in 1896 heralded the beginning of the end for the Raikes. In 1896 it was decided to liquidate the Company and auction off the estate. A syndicate of local gentlemen, under the Chairmanship of John Bickerstaffe, acquired the company's possessions for little more than £80,000. The old shareholders who throughout had enjoyed a comfortable 5% on their investments, were paid out at £9s. 10s. 0d. per share. The syndicate soon discovered that the opposition put up by the Tower and other attractions was going to prove too great. During the great Diamond Jubilee Celebrations young and old flocked to the Gardens in their thousands, bands played, and the hobby horses, sideshows and swings operated at full blast giving no hint of despair and failure to follow; but the Gardens functioned as such for the last time about 1898. Maintenance work went by the board and the estate became progressively derelict.

For one season, in depressing surroundings, Gus Levaine, a travelling concertina player, made what he could out of a second-rate al fresco entertainment and "doing a bottle" (a theatrical expression meaning whipping around with a hat). In 1900 there was a slight revival of interest when Frank Fillis, a noted circus manager and showman, brought his "Savage South Africa" troupe of more than 100 Zulus and Matabele, Boers and English South Africans. They came to the Raikes fresh from Earl's Court in London and unfortunately, while they were in England, the Boer War broke out. Under the terms of the contract, the natives, with the exception of perhaps a dozen or so steady-going Zulus, were shipped back home and their places were filled by substitutes picked up from all over England. There were coloured dockers from Liverpool, Malays, Jamaicans, and at least one Aztec Indian. No-one enquired too closely so long as they were black!

Amongst the original remaining natives, most notable was Prince Lobengula, a chieftain whose people had been provoked into the Matabele War in the early 90s, and a highlight of the repertoire was a spirited enactment of the gallant last stand of Major Alan Wilson and his 32 men. They were ambushed and killed to a man by the Matebele and the climax of the show, with Frank Fillis blazing away with two revolvers in a circle of prostrate horses and "dead" heroes, brought Victorian audiences to their feet, overcome with patriotic emotion. The show always ended with a full throated rendering of "God Save the Queen" and even the Boers, who were not rebels, but loyal Cape Colony subjects of the Queen Empress, always joined in.

The "Savage South Africa" show went to enormous lengths to entertain the patrons. There was some mightily impressive sharp-shooting by the Annie Oakley of the day, and where Lincoln Road is now there were very convincing lion hunts (a real lion with its harness hidden by papier mâché rocks), chariot races, bull throwing acts, war dances, the original ambushed stage-coach which triggered off the Matabele war, and so on. Blackpool on the whole, however, was not sorry to see the last of this coloured two-month show. There had been scuffles in Blackpool pubs, full-scale clashes in the streets, and it was noticed that they had "left a trail of little black 'uns behind them".

In 1901 a bustling American showman decided to organise A World Fair on the Raikes Hall estate. A circus came down and a big variety show. A host of sideshows and Leonie Clarke's boxing kangaroos joined what should have proved a great and successful attraction. Unfortunately the event had been timed to open in June. The American had miscalculated the trends and Blackpool was as dead as a doornail. There were just not enough people to support such a mammoth venture and the fitters and riggers had no idea that the proprietor was depending on the first week's takings to meet his commitments. On the Saturday night, however, as they queued up to be paid, it became obvious that something was badly amiss. With nothing in the kitty, the organiser had gone off to London to raise funds. He was never seen again.

The private show companies, without too much hardship, were able to fold up their tents and move off. The contractors, some of whom went bankrupt, never got paid for the specially built grandstands, and the labourers dared not return to their lodgings without cash. They camped out in gangs at the Raikes, threatening to burn everything down until calmer counsels prevailed. At length they hung around glumly for a week, fed by the good ladies of Blackpool who hastily organised soup kitchens, and eventually the police cleared them away. After that fiasco, the whole of the estate was auctioned off piecemeal in the space of two days, and building operations commenced which soon wiped out all traces of the Raikes Hall, Royal Pleasure Gardens.

Now in that area there are hundreds of private houses and many of the inhabitants may be entirely unaware of the history beneath their foundations. For that reason the Raikes story has been told in full. Raikes Hall is now a hotel with a bowling green attached. It offers all the charm, hospitality and interest of a good 18th century house with lofty rooms and a fine staircase ("the best in Blackpool for getting a coffin down", declares a local undertaker with professional approval).

The story of Blackpool's famous Promenade

1760s. A wide grassy bank sloping gently down to the shingle at the water's edge.

1788. A grassy parade, diminished by this time to a width of approximately 20 feet and terminating at the cliff edge.

1816. Wearing away to a gravelly footpath.

BY 1828 the grass verge had almost entirely disappeared. Wooden stumps were driven in by private individuals for the protection of their promenade properties and to combat erosion. The grass path was replaced by a wide gravel walk. In preparation for the construction of the Poulton—Blackpool Railway (1846) large quantities of protective shingle were removed and used for ballast. Without this barrier Blackpool's promenade suffered great damage. The Rev. Wm. Thornber wrote to the Clifton Agent (Lancashire Records Ref.: DDC1/1197/28), in September, 1844, complaining that his embankment, opposite the Lane Ends, was badly affected ... "so much that the foundation of clay being torn up I was afraid the whole of it would sink down, but by attention we preserved it". By 1856 it was necessary to pay stricter attention to the maintenance of the promenade and to make preparations for its extension northwards from Talbot Square. In 1860 the Central Beach portion was asphalted over and decorated with fine white spar.

In 1865 the Local Board of Health sought powers for improving and extending the promenade and by Act of Parliament levied an extra Parade Rate on owners of properties bordering the front. The new promenade was to be two miles in length stretching from Carleton Terrace on the north to South Shore. Work started in 1868 and the first (southern) portion had barely been commenced when storms in January and February, 1869, washed out much of the construction. (See "Sea in Ugly Mood".) 21,000 cubic yards of embankment were broken up and 600 lineal yards of sea fence, carriage drive and promenade had to be renewed, at considerable expense. In March, 1870, the foundation stone for the new drinking fountain in Talbot Square was laid by Wm. Henry Cocker, Esq., Surgeon and then Chairman of the Blackpool Board of Health. Large crowds heard him declare that "the beautiful new entrance to the North Pier was nearing its completion and the new esplanade ... amounting to £100,000, would not fail to elevate the prominent position in which Blackpool has been placed by nature".

Meantime, the finishing touches were being added to this mammoth project of making Blackpool's front both attractive and secure. The sea-fence consisted of a one-in-four sloping breastwork of granite sets laid on a thick bed of puddled clay. It was bordered by a seven yard asphalt walk and a carriage drive twelve yards in width, and three rows of wooden sleepers, set in like ranks of soldiers and just about as effective at keeping back the tide! Especially during the winter the sea swept over, surrounding hotels and properties, bringing traffic to a halt, and leaving in its wake a vast tract of dirty coloured foam covering the promenade, often to two feet in depth. As a boy, Mr. Peter C. Miller, the well known Fylde artist, remembers losing one of his clogs under this blanket of salty bubbles. Not daring to return home without it, he hobbled to his grandfather's house in Victoria Street, borrowed a broom, and swept the promenade until his lost footwear was located.

On Easter Monday, 18th April, 1870, all the neighbouring residents and thousands of visitors flocked into Blackpool for the grand opening ceremony performed by Col. Wilson-Patten, M.P. (later Lord Winmarleigh). According to the "Preston Pilot" ... "great preparations had been made ... the town was profusely decorated in every street with flags and banners and triumphal arches spanned the roads". In brilliant weather a grand procession, with not less than twelve Lancashire Mayors, gentry, tradesmen, schoolchildren, benefit societies, volunteers and military bands, made for Talbot Square where the ceremonial opening took place. The Rt. Hon. Col. Wilson-Patten congratulated Blackpool on her magnificent achievement which was fully reported in leading newspapers. During that evening a grand ball was held and the town was illuminated in honour of the occasion. This fine promenade boosted Blackpool's already established popularity. Vacant plots of land were snapped up for the building of shops, and property owners were at pains to smarten up their houses and put elegant railings in place of the old wooden fences.

North Shore promenade was laid out between 1893-1899 at a cost of more than £144,000. But it was becoming obvious that the promenade laid out in 1870 would shortly become quite inadequate to cope with the ever-increasing holiday crowds. The brains of Blackpool began to wrestle with the problem of increasing the area, and the safety, of the sea-front. At first it was decided to extend the promenade seawards by an additional 60 feet but, on further consideration and on the prompting of the Borough Surveyor, Mr. J. S. Brodie, the more ambitious figure of 100 feet was finally adopted. Parliamentary sanction was obtained and in 1903 the work was commenced at the South Shore end. To complete this visionary undertaking, 22 acres of land were reclaimed from the sea, 20,000 tons of Basalt stone were used in the sea wall, and 1,000,000 tons of sand were brought from the South Shore area and used for filling in. A track was laid along the promenade along which "The Sands Express", a small engine drawing a string of trucks, chugged back and forth with supplies. The new promenade was 3,100 yards in length; 120,000 cubic yards of concrete went into the construction of the sea wall; and 700 workmen had been engaged on this gigantic scheme, at a cost of £300,000.

The opening ceremony was performed on 25th July, 1905, by the Mayor, Alderman Joseph Brodie, J.P. Thousands of visitors came in to watch the event which was marked by street decorations, floodlit buildings, a procession of 200 carriages, a reception at the Palace, and a banquet for 500 guests. In formally opening the promenade the Mayor pointed out that "we have not built for ourselves alone. The Blackpool Promenade is one of the greatest and grandest recreations in the kingdom. We have established a national asset, we have given the people a roomy space where they may exercise or rest at a spot exceptionally favoured in health giving properties". The scheme had not been completed without an immense show of determination and faith which had necessitated going down deep in search of a solid "bottom", of taming unmanageable quicksands, and of daring to match the sea with an upright wall against all the predictions of the wiseacres who had declared it impossible.

Schoolchildren in Blackpool were presented with commemorative pictorial handkerchiefs and a humorous situation arose in the striking of a souvenir medal to be presented to the prominent citizens of the town. Apparently there were a few would-be medal designers who submitted drawings to the organising committee. Among them was Cleansing Superintendent, Mr. Fred Rundall who, along with a draughtsman from the Borough Surveyor's Department, knocked up and submitted his design. It was turned down. Eventually the committee made their choice of a trefoil pattern bearing the word "Progress", the town's coat of arms, and commemorating "The Inauguration of the New Sea Defences and Marine Promenade, 1905". The finished product was shown to Mr. Rundall and at first glance it looked most attractive. "But where's the name?" asked Mr. Rundall, for there was no mention of "Blackpool" and the souvenir might have referred to sea defences and promenades at Brighton, Margate, or anywhere under the sun! It was one of those obvious omissions which no-one had spotted. The committee were thrown into a flurry and, with red faces all round, the medals were hastily recovered and roughly inscribed on the back with a longhand version of "Blackpool". For once, this vigorous, publicity-conscious, trumpet blowing town had forgotten to plug its own name!

The narrow foot-walk, supported on pillars, to the sea-side of the Metropole, disappeared when Princess Parade was laid out. This extended from North Pier to Cocker Street and was opened on Mayday, 1912, by H.R.H. The Princess Louise. There were further extensions to both north and south in 1923 and the last extension was opened by H.R.H. the late Duke of Kent in 1937. This consisted of 1½ miles of North Promenade, called Prince's Way. On the same day His Royal Highness opened the £165,000 Victoria Hospital at Whinney Heys, opened the new lifeboat house, launched the new lifeboat, switched on "The Lights" at the Town Hall, and toured the promenade in an illuminated tram. 15,000 people jammed the Central Promenade.

Maybe its evolution was slow and costly but Blackpool can feel justly proud of her seven golden miles which have been described as "the finest promenade in the world".

Victorian families flock to Blackpool

THE Victorian family, in the main, was as large as the average weekly pay packet was small. £1 per week supported a man and his household. Yet, with rigid economy, he contrived to bring his family regularly to the seaside. Beds could be had for as little as 1s. 0d. a night. When that was beyond the family's means they could still come in for the day, by railway excursion, and enjoy Blackpool at little cost. It was usual to see Victorian mamas, surrounded by sailor suited small sons, and daughters ringletted and bestarched, carrying all the food for the day in a round tin hat box with a handle on the lid. Boarding houses along the front bore notices "Hot Water 2d.", which meant that the landlady was prepared to provide seating and table accommo-dation, brew their tea and afterwards clear away and wash up, all for 2d. per head.

There was scant attention paid to hygiene as we know it. Flies were a great menace. Along with the cruet, the landlady regularly set on the table a horrifying glass contraption called a fly bottle, standing on three glass feet and baited with stale beer. Attracted by this delicacy the flies took a one-way trip up the central hollow spout and fell amongst a disintegrating mass of fellow victims. No-one ever thought to clean out the glass trap until it was packed almost solid with dead insects. Arsenical fly papers were in popular use, set in saucers in strategic positions, on side-boards, dinner tables, and window sills, and left until blackened with dead flies. No-one disapproved, nor was it considered odd when boarding house servants, from Albert Road and beyond, came down to the shore with basketsful of washing and began stringing the sheets out to dry on the wooden sleepers bordering the promenade, or laying them flat out on the hulkings, battened down with cobbles.

There was fierce competition in those days between the Black-pudlian landladies who used to hang around the station approaches, touting for business. The most enterprising of them snatched the newly-arrived visitor from under the noses of her rivals and hustled him off to loud protestations of the superior merits of her own establishment. When Mr. Reuben Davis was a shy teenager, he was sent by his old Guv'nor, Mr. Iddeson of the Raikes Hall Gardens, to meet a niece who was arriving at Central Station. This in itself was a trial to an easily blushing youth but, obediently, he met the young lady, picked up her bag and escorted her from the station. They were immediately mistaken for a honeymoon couple and seized by two rival harpies, both tugging, and each insisting that her house had the best accommodation to offer. There were two scarlet faces before the young pair managed to extricate themselves from an embarrassing predicament. This practice became such a nuisance that finally it was stopped by the police.

Still, once the visitor had arrived, whether for the day or for the week, there was plenty to be had in the way of entertainment. At the edge of the promenade three rows of pit props, like soldiers on parade, broke the force of the waves at high tide. Beyond was a sloping hulking of thick granite sets leading down to the sands. Opposite the New Inn and the Tower were two wooden breakwaters reaching some 150 feet out and the portion between was the most popular part of the beach. At this point all the entertainers, buskers, acrobats, concertina players, ventriloquists, out-of-work music hall artistes, fortune tellers, corn curers, bump-readers, and patent medicine and pill pedlars, congregated alongside the traditional Punch and Judy show, the pie stalls, rock stalls and donkeys. There was vigorous competition between the performers who paid nothing for their pitches but occupied them by determination and sheer force of character. When the tide came in they were driven out of business and into the Wellington where the proceeds of the last shift were quickly disposed of. As the tide turned, they flocked back to the water's edge and waded in after it to set their stalls up afresh. Some of these seaside performers were first-rate artistes who had fallen temporarily on hard times. Others came year after year to this veritable Tom Tiddler's Ground of entertainment where there was plenty to be seen, enjoyed, eaten, licked or laughed over, tide permitting, between six in the morning and midnight.

The oyster vendor, armed with a round basket, a bottle of vinegar and a dirty towel for the wiping of customers' hands, hawked his wares along the sands at sixpence a dozen. The Peeney Brothers and the Pye family sold ice-cream from hand-carts along the water's edge. Everywhere there were the booths of the photographers (every syllable accorded a terrifying emphasis!), and the middle of the 'eighties saw the forerunner of the modern quick-print machine. Customers queued up at a van laden with equipment where a Daguerrotype picture could be obtained, framed in gilt, for sixpence. The other day I was shown one of those somewhat rigid Victorian family groups taken by this method. After 90 years it looked remarkably fresh and clear.

Another well known character, in top hat, corduroys and clogs, was Billy Muggins, a seller of Blackpool rock. "One for you ... and you ... and you", he used to shout, flinging bars of rock into a quickly collecting crowd. This was a curtain-raiser to the serious business of selling his wares. There was Charlie Sennett, an ex-army doctor who, so he asserted, had been struck off the rolls. He used to boast that the only thing he couldn't cure was his own fat head (induced by frequent trips to the Wellington). He was a splendid entertainer with a loud abrupt voice. "What's the matter with you?", he used to roar, "Spots before the eyes? Want to remain in bed? Disinclination to work? Well, medicine won't do you any good. You want to go down to the water's edge and drink in God's clean fresh air. Still, if it's medicine you want, I can write you a prescription. Here, take this along to the chemist and get it made up. He'll charge you twopence. And that'll be sixpence please."

"Do you want hair like mine?" This was the everlasting cry of Professor Toole, a hair-restorer salesman with an abundant and frizzy thatch. Many a bald-headed hopeful paid up and went home clasping a bottleful of optimistic dreams. Another pseudo-professor, called Wells, astonished audiences with his mathematical calculations. "Tell me your birthdate and I'll tell you the day of the week you were born", was his promise, and he never failed.

Amidst all this glamour and excitement, the pupils from the Wesleyan Day School in Adelaide Street were sent down to the sands for the play-break. Listed in the Directory of 1851, this school, which had accommodation for 266 pupils, was badly short of playgrounds and sanction had been given for the scholars to repair to the beach twice a day so long as they avoided the popular stretch of beach between the breakwaters. In those days they were rewarded for good work or exemplary behaviour by a system of tin tallies which were hoarded until the end of term. The one with the most got the prize. Conversely, the pupil forfeited the number of tallies appropriate to any lapse in behaviour, including infringement of the breakwater rule. Unfortunately the temptation proved too strong for the more venturesome youngsters. When the master appeared on the beach and blew his whistle to re-summon the flock, they walked back to face a stony-faced teacher whose outstretched palm was waiting to collect the forfeits.

When the visitor tired of the sands he could spend an hour in the Coffee Palace Ballroom, the tall building opposite Central Station and adjoining the Palatine buildings. In one of the shops below, a Mr. Blackburn, a bookseller from Blackburn, was one of the early pioneers of the popular paperbacks. A salesman who tried to interest him in the current best seller was told to put it between flimsy covers and bring it back at a low price. This opened up a whole new market.

Between the Royal Hotel (now Woolworth's) and the present Tower buildings was a new market, called the Royal Arcade Market, linking Bank Hey Street with Central Beach. It cost £2,000 to lay out and included stalls of every kind. Here the children could be kept quiet with a halfpenny lucky bag fillled with sweetmeat fragments and pieces of broken rock. The Wesleyan school pupils were regular and appreciative customers. Next to it was the Blackpool Aquarium and Menagerie (1874) with all kinds of animals, bears, seals, birds and fishes on view, an orchestrion, bazaar and gardens. It was originally the imposing residence of banker, Sir Benjamin Heywood, who came to Blackpool earlier in the century for health reasons. It later belonged to Sir Percival Heywood, and then to a Mr. Lowe. It was subsequently acquired by Dr. W. H. Cocker, along with the adjoining Beach Hotel, and in 1880 floated as "The Blackpool Central Property Company".

Next along the front was the Prince of Wales' Baths and Theatre (1877 or thereabouts) where travelling companies gave some fine theatrical performances, and ambitious aquatic displays, with comic turns, were a regular feature. (Swimming only, however. There was no speciality diving in Blackpool until a Norwegian group performed from Central Pier early in the 1900s.) During the winter months, evening classes were held at the Prince of Wales' for school leavers and adults seeking further education in art and other subjects. In 1899 this popular place of entertainment was pulled down and The Alhambra went up in its place. It was described as a sumptuous building with a variety theatre seating 3,000, a circus holding 2,500, and a fine ballroom. The Alhambra fell into the hands of a Receiver in 1902, was acquired by the Tower Company in 1903 and re-opened under the name of The Palace in 1904.

Almost every public house of any size had a singing room attached for the entertainment of its patrons, and dancing, musical items and comic turns were laid on non-stop from 9-30 in the morning until 11 at night.

The visitor would certainly not leave without visiting St. John's Market (built on the site of Boots, Chemists, in 1844, at a cost of £1,200; St. John's New Market, for the selling of fruit, completed by 1895); or Read's Baths (Luna Park) which was a sea water bath with a bazaar attached. In those days tradesmen stuck to their own lines. There were no "mixed" shops, and none dealing exclusively in "Presents from Blackpool". Yet it was unthinkable to return home without one of these souvenirs, stamped with Blackpool's coat of arms, which could only be bought at St. John's, or at Read's where the prospective customer was liable to be torn apart by rival stallholders selling the same kind of wares.

Read's Baths, or rather "The New Market Hall or Arcade, in South Beach", was built by Mr. Wm. Read in 1861, and was described as an imposing stone structure containing 30 stalls for the sale of various commodities, including meat, drapery, fancy goods, footwear, greengroceries, fish, books, stationery, etc. To supply the "hot, cold and shower baths", sea water was pumped from the beach by steam power. Over the market was a large room, suitable for theatrical performances or public meetings, and capable of accommodating 1,000 persons. The exterior was embellished with an illuminated clock.

At that time there were no shops in Clifton Street and others now given over exclusively to the retail trade. All the properties were select boarding houses with private gardens. There were livery stables and coach houses in every part of the town and many of the prominent sites now occupied by important commercial establishments were then ragged plots rendered the more ugly by ramshackle wooden hoardings with tattered posters flapping in the breeze.

The Theatre Royal (Tivoli), part of the Talbot Road Arcade and Assembly Rooms, was opened in 1868. The Empire (later Hippodrome, now ABC Theatre), a variety theatre which employed all the top talent, including Marie Lloyd, Albert Chevalier and other fabulous immortals of the music hall world, was opened in 1895. It changed hands two years later and was operated for a period as part variety show and moving pictures. Ohmy's Circus was pitched on the site of the Grand Theatre until it was opened in 1894.

Naturally, as one would expect from a seaside resort, there were pleasure trips by paddle steamers departing from the piers for all parts. The "Wellington" and "Bickerstaffe" were operating from the 1870s and for many a year were a familiar sight, moored alongside the Blackpool piers, picking up passengers at St. Annes Pier, or conveniently anchored in the deep water of the North Channel nearby. In addition to these two were the "Renown", "Wasp", "Dandy" and "Nelson" and a whole flotilla of smaller, privately owned, boats of the "pull and sail" type operated by the old fishing families centred around Chapel Street, Blackpool. In the 'nineties, two cross-channel vessels, "Queen of the North" (from Central Pier) and "The Greyhound" (North Pier) began to operate between Blackpool and Douglas. The voyage of more than 60 miles was completed in three hours and there was intense competition between the two rival captains, each of whom tried to reach the Isle of Man first. These, and the "S.S. Deerhound" sailed regularly between Liverpool, Barrow, Llandudno, Lytham, Morecambe Bay, Southport and other convenient points, and operated without loss or serious mishap, despite the treacherous and broken waters of the Irish Sea. Occasionally a sudden storm upset the calculations, prevented a landing at Blackpool and obliged a captain to make for the safe shelter of Fleetwood, from which point, with the last train chugging away in the distance, a boatload of stranded passengers returned to the bosoms of their landladies by whatever means they could muster. These services came to an end on the outbreak of the 1914 war.

Apart from all the theatrical and nautical entertainments, there were trips by "wagonette" and "horse sharries" into the quiet green countryside all around Blackpool; or to the Belle Vue Hotel and Strawberry Gardens (open from 6 a.m. to 11 p.m.); to Raikes Hall Gardens, or the Oxford Pleasure Gardens beside the Oxford Hotel at Great Marton.

To the south of Blackpool, up to 1894 the promenade terminated at the Victoria (South) Pier. Beyond it lay wild acres of undeveloped sand-dunes. The North Shore gypsies, who, for generations, had encamped and made a living near Uncle Tom's Cabin, had been driven from their old site to new quarters near the Star Inn, drawn there possibly by a fresh water spring which bubbled up in the sand-dunes near Harrowside. These flamboyant folk, with their smouldering, almost sinister beauty, their gift of foretelling the future, and their ramshackle tents made from wattle hurdles slung over with rags and old blankets, attracted crowds of curious visitors to this pleasure beach in miniature. Mother Herring was a famous seer at South Shore, and the gypsy family Smith were renowned for their flashing good looks which won them many a prize in beauty competitions. In between customers, Gypsy Sarah Boswell sat puffing at a pipe in front of her tent, but in the season, at any rate, there was precious little rest for the black-locked dame, for "they hadn't been to Blackpool if they hadn't had their fortunes told at sixpence a time". In addition to these curious and colourful folk, there were the hobby horses of "Old Dan", a nigger minstrels' show, ice-cream stalls, games, a skittle alley, the inevitable pho-to-graph-ers and a switchback railway which was dismantled and set up on the site of the present Pleasure Beach when buildings began to creep over the southern wastes of Blackpool.

But it was still the central part of Blackpool which drew the heaviest crowds. Apart from the dominating Tower (opened 1894), and the scarcely less arresting Big Wheel (1896), there were bowling greens (one on the site of the present Public Library), skating rinks, camerae obscurae, public telescopes, eating houses, orchestras, and all the "modern" entertainments ever devised by Victorian fun-pedlars. Whatever the visitor wanted, Blackpool had it, and probably bigger and better than anywhere else in the kingdom. Blackpool had long since chosen her motto "Progress" and, by golly, she was going to live up to it or break her neck in the attempt!

The Winter Gardens

DOCTOR Cocker's house, "Bank Hey", facing the sea down Victoria Street, was purchased, along with 18,000 square yards of land, by the Winter Gardens Company in 1875. During the following summer the Gardens, including an open-air skating rink entered from Leopold Grove, were opened to the public.

Eventually the Grand Pavilion was opened by the Lord Mayor of London and from an account in the "Preston Pilot" dated 13th July, 1878, we recapture the brilliance of that occasion. The

Lord Mayor and his Sheriffs arrived in great style on Wednesday, 10th July, staying at the Imperial Hotel. Flags and streamers fluttered from the houses and, after a night of heavy rain, a sunny morning greeted thousands of people who had travelled to join in the celebrations. The procession assembled at Claremont Park on Thursday, 11th July, and I think nothing quite like it can ever have been seen in Blackpool. Following the three state carriages, the Mayors and Mayoresses, and, in many cases, the Town Clerks, from at least 63 English towns formed a landau cavalcade stretching far into the distance. There was no lady in the procession below the rank of Mayoress.

Supported by four bands, a Volunteer Corps, mounted police, marshals and a full body of foot-slogging shareholders well in the rear, the Lord Mayor formally opened the Pavilion in the presence of a brilliant company. Madame Antoinette Sterling sang "The Lost Chord" at the grand musical concert held in the evening and there were fireworks and illuminations on both piers. A torchlight procession, headed by "John Bull" and representations of all nations, and with the lifeboat carrying Old Neptune at the bow, wended through the streets until one o'clock in the morning. The Lord Mayor and his officers made the most of their three-day visit. On Friday morning they and 200 invited guests took a short trip on the packet steamer "Earl of Ulster", returning to a special morning concert in the North Pier Pavilion. Luncheon at Raikes Hall was followed by alfresco entertainments and another visit to the Winter Gardens. After a celebration dinner at the Imperial Hotel, 700 invited guests attended a Grand Ball at the Winter Gardens. By removing a partition it was said that 6,000—7,000 persons could be accommodated in this magnificent building.

In those days the Winter Gardens catered chiefly for select visitors. There was a skating rink beneath the floor of the building, but no ballroom. During the 1880s a fairyland grotto with papier mâché rocks and stalactites, scenes from the ruby mines of Burma, the Burmese wall, and suchlike, was set out in the cellars now used for beer storage. On the Olympia site were rockeries, gardens and walks and a switchback railway. In 1883 there was an orchestra composed of "thirty-six eminent instrumentalists" and the most illustrious companies, including D'Oyly Carte's and Carl Rosa's, came in the season.

Pretty much at this stage the Gardens remained until Mr. Bill Holland came as Manager in 1887. He was a genial man, mountainous and bewhiskered. This great impressario revolutionised the place, anticipating the needs of his customers and giving them the best. The Empress Ballroom was his idea, though it only opened (1896) some time after his death. It was Mr. Holland who made the Gardens famous for fine variety shows followed by half an evening's ballet. The scenic effects and choreography were of the highest order and the old ones who remember the superb artistry of these performances will tell us that we see nothing like it to-day. Bill Holland's name cannot be passed by without reference to his legendary carpet. When he mentioned to a friend that he was about to pay 100 guineas for a carpet for his pavilion there was an immediate and horrified reaction. "For the trippers!! Why, they'll spit on it!!" That tickled Mr. Holland's sense of humour and presented him with an advertising gimmick. "Come to the Winter Gardens and spit on Bill Holland's 100-Guinea Carpet!", ran the advertisements. They came, sure enough, but they were too impressed with all this grandeur and luxury to spit. No-one knew his customers better than Bill Holland.

On summer Sundays the most fabulous personalities in the world of music came to the Winter Gardens. Tettrazini, Patti, Kreisler and Madame Melba came, and, of course, the inimitable Caruso. Caruso couldn't get off the stage but was recalled again and again by an insatiable public. After ten or a dozen encores he only managed to tear himself away by singing his last song dressed in his outdoor clothes, ready to leave the theatre. He got nearly £1,000 for his performance in 1909.

The first Opera House was built for less than £9,500 and opened in June, 1889, with "The Yeoman of the Guard" by the D'Oyly Carte Company. Charles Chaplin played there in 1904 and there has been an awe-inspiring catalogue of talent since that time. The present Opera House, built in 1939, is the largest and most sumptuous theatre outside the capital, and I well remember the glittering spectacle of the Royal Command Performance held there a few years ago in the presence of H.M. The Queen and H.R.H. Duke of Edinburgh.

In 1928 talks between the Tower Company and the Winter Gardens Company resulted in an amalgamation of the two concerns. The Big Wheel came down in that year and in 1929 proposals were considered for a £150,000 building project, including the new Olympia. In 1931 notable extensions to the Winter Gardens included the Baronial Hall, Spanish Galleon and Courtyard, Tudor Room, etc.

Publicity-conscious Blackpool

DURING the 19th century, rough seas and storm damage ensured that Blackpool was mentioned regularly and dramatically in the larger newspapers. Each account, every column inch, pounded home the name which was rapidly assuming the familiarity of a household word. Blackpool was regularly featured in song, sketch and story, by such eminent Lancashire writers as Edwin Waugh, Ben Brierley, Samuel Laycock, Trafford Clegg and, of course, her own adopted Teddy Ashton (Allen Clarke). The opening of the promenade at Easter, 1870, released a tremendous burst of publicity but Blackpool was not yet geared up to the policy of advertising on a national scale. Indeed, there were no funds, on that occasion, to pay for the decorating of the town, the entertainment of guests, or for the presentation of a souvenir to the opener. The costs were borne by voluntary subscriptions from local residents, a state of affairs which pinpointed the need for organisation and action.

Following the success of the Easter festivities, it was felt that the campaign to draw visitors to the resort should not be slackened. At a meeting on 1st June, 1870, the Blackpool Trade Council was formed for the purpose of publicising Blackpool. Railway posters, costing 15s. 0d. each, were to be displayed on stations in Lancashire and Yorkshire. The Railway Companies asked £1,000 rental for a period of five years and this was to be met by voluntary subscriptions, plus charges made to hotelkeepers and entertainments companies for poster space. By this bold and experimental move Blackpool early proved that "It pays to advertise!" Still, in 1878, when the Lord Mayor of London and his retinue descended upon Blackpool for the opening of the Winter Gardens Pavilion, no moneys had been set aside for their entertainment and hospitality. Dr. W. H. Cocker personally bore the costs arising out of an event which covered Blackpool with glory and ensured full-scale write-ups in the leading newspapers of the day.

The need for spirited action was urgent if Blackpool were to maintain her lead in the race to attract seaside visitors. In September, 1877, Macclesfield Solicitor, Mr. Henry P. May, was appointed Town Clerk. His initial task was to draft a Parliamentary Bill providing for improvements to the borough, including the laying out of Whitegate Drive, new arterial roads from north to south, the straightening and widening of thoroughfares, acquisition of control of the foreshore, and new regulations concerning public health, building and sanitation. The subject of the Bill, which was supported by the majority of the ratepayers, was ventilated at public and private discussions and given widespread publicity in the press. One of the provisions ensured that "The Corporation may from time to time pay or contribute towards the payment of a public band or music for the Borough, and also the cost of maintaining at railway stations and other public places advertisements stating the attractions and amusements of the town; provided that the amount of such payments or contributions do not in any year exceed the rate of twopence in the pound on the rateable value of the Borough."

This novel idea of charging ratepayers with the costs of publicity campaigns evidently startled Government officials in far away London. Lord Redesdale, considered by himself and the House of Lords as something of an authority on such matters, raised an objection to the granting of powers to spend good ratepayers' money to such purpose. Fortunately the Town Clerk had an opportunity of discussing the matter privately with his Lordship who, country-lover and ardent sportsman, was possibly swayed by glowing tales of Raikes Hall Park and its beauties and the intention of the authority to develop the old Whitegate-lane into a gracious, tree-lined drive. At any rate he was finally convinced that this unprecedented move to levy a rate to pay for a promenade band and to advertise Blackpool was a good thing, and accordingly, in August, 1879, the Royal Assent was given to the Act of Parliament by which foreshore control and the better government of the town were assured. Once again, as often since, Blackpool had set the lead!

This vigorous, thrusting resort has come a long way from the days when a cart-load of broken-down actors, or the "Musical Society of Gentlemen of Preston" entertained a handful of visitors in a barn. From small beginnings Blackpool gradually emerged as the great holiday playground of the north, drawing Wakes Weeks crowds from Lancashire and the miners from over the Pennines. They thronged, jostled and poured into Blackpool as if by some age-old ritual, with a whole year's savings jingling in their pockets, and bent on having themselves "a reet good do". Whole streets, whole towns, arrived here en masse, and neighbours, looking slightly self-conscious with their lobster-coloured faces, peeling foreheads and new holiday cottons, nodded to each other across a sea of interlocked deck chairs on a beach crammed with robust humanity. A hundred years ago the visitor was satisfied with simpler amusements, the travelling circus, the dancing platform, the Band. Fifty years later his tastes had changed and enterprising Blackpool gave him full value for his "brass". Managements took extreme pleasure in presenting the most scintillating artistes of the day (and also in reminding the customers that "No Expense has been Spared").

During the '90s, one of the best known local characters was the Corporation's Advertising Manager, Mr. Noden, whose ingenious ideas for putting the resort on the map earned him the affectionate title of "Mr. Blackpool". This genial soul, short and stocky, with a mass of white hair and a vandyke beard, invariably dressed in a yachting cap and square cut reefer coat and looked like an old sea captain on shore leave. Wherever it could be seen by people in the mass he splashed the name of Blackpool. He advertised the place and its attractions until it almost hurt, but he got results. His motto was: "We cater for quantity and we give them quality!" When Nelson's old flagship, "The Foudroyant" was wrecked in 1897, it was "Mr. Blackpool" who flashed the news by telegraph all over England with the result that trainloads of trippers came in to watch. By arrangement, he sent telegrams all over the north informing individuals of high tides coupled with storms, and the announcement that "The Storm Cone is hoisted at Blackpool" ensured a welcome influx of visitors.

Another of his exploits still raises a chuckle in a few quarters. It concerned the battlefield of Waterloo where Napoleon was defeated by Wellington in 1815. During the third week in June of that year, Wellington and Blucher met at a post called La Belle Alliance in preparation for the final onslaught. The French Army was routed with 40,000 losses and allied casualties were 15,000 English and over 7,000 Prussian. In an area of three square miles it was estimated that some 45,000 killed and wounded lay putrefying or suffering under a summer sky. This scene of our costly victory became almost as sacred ground and for scores of years English visitors, escorted by guides, made a solemn tour of the battlefield of Waterloo. So, apparently, did the astute Charlie Noden who promptly rented the gable end of a white-washed farmhouse at La Belle Alliance and by this medium reminded tourists to "Visit Blackpool". This saucy stunt evoked a national hullabaloo, storms of adverse criticism, and yards of free publicity in the national press. It was long enough before the Advertising Manager lived it down.

Before the First World War Blackpool had its first Illuminations on an organised scale, but in 1925 "The Lights" went on in earnest, extending the summer season by several weeks and providing a fine excuse for another nostalgic peep at "Blackpoo'," before the winter. Thanks to Hitler, the Illuminations were suspended in 1939 but re-introduced on an even grander scale in 1949. It is estimated that eight million visitors and trippers from all parts of the British Isles make an annual pilgrimage to this six-mile stretch of winking, multi-coloured lights and illuminated tableaux.

Nowadays, Blackpool spends something like £200,000 a year on advertising and publicity in addition to vast free coverage of her principal events by press, radio and television. This largest and liveliest of British resorts, which has 4,500 hotels, guest houses and holiday flats, can sleep 250,000 at any given time and draws 16½m. annually, made up of 13m. day trippers; 3¼m. holiday makers; and ¼m. who attend conferences at Blackpool. In the variety and quality of her entertainments, Blackpool is second to nowhere. Three thousand people can dance simultaneously and in comfort in the Winter Gardens Empress Ballroom and almost the same number can enjoy a show at the Opera House, the largest theatre in England outside London. There are eight live shows, 10 cinemas, 13 cabaret lounges and taverns, discos galore, an open air zoo and a model village. In this year (1975) of international economic gloom, when recession and contraction create a dismal prospect for the years immediately ahead, a £1m. Star Entertainment complex with 4 cinemas, disco, beer keller with cabaret, and a public bar, proudly opens for business, opposite North Pier; and the new Space Tower, a bold and startling enterprise, adds a new dimension to the Pleasure Beach and affords magnificent views of the coast, the old Blackpool Tower and multi-coloured multitudes enjoying relaxation below.

At Blackpool, great gusts of Atlantic ozone catch up the scent of oysters, shrimps, fish and chips, and onions. You can enjoy a superlative view from the top of the world famous Tower; take a stroll along three piers and seven miles of promenade; watch international artistes of the circus; gape and laugh with the crowds along the fabulous Golden Mile; have yourself hurled, whirled and entertained, at the Pleasure Beach; swim indoors, or out; ride, fish, skate, sail, play golf, tennis or bowls; travel by road, rail and air; stroll in Stanley Park, see the best shops in Lancashire, eat candy floss and Blackpool rock, and wear mink or a Kiss-me-Quick hat, without looking odd. "The Most! ... The

Greatest! ... The Biggest! ... and The Best!" Whatever it is, Blackpool has it.

Meantime, Conferences, Festivals, Fairs, Rallies and Reunions, fill the resort in the winter, and one of these days Blackpool will be the only place in England where you can still ride by electric tram. At present, it is probably the only holiday resort to merit the construction of a special Motorway Link, opened 3rd July, 1975, and already known as "The Holiday Highway".

At the end of the season the shutters slam, the tradesmen rest their aching feet and reckon up their takings in terms of pounds, pence and profit. The noise of summer dies away to a gentle hum and the residents look forward to doing their shopping in comfort. But if the streets are quiet and the promenade looks deserted, Blackpool is not asleep. She has switched over to her winter tempo, to a social and cultural life that is rich indeed! Blackpool in every way lives up to her motto — "Progress". In other words, "You name it! It's here!"

Blackpool's famous Tower

IN 1889 several promenade properties, including the New Market, Menagerie and Aquarium, and Beach Hotel acquired by Dr. Cocker's company, were bought out by a London syndicate called the Standard Debenture Corporation, Ltd., who wanted to duplicate the Parisian Eiffel Tower in some place of national prominence. By this time there was no place more prominent, more vigorous, or more versatile, than Blackpool. Within months the negotiators were whispering persuasively in the ears of the Mayor, Alderman John Bickerstaffe, and other leading citizens, in the hope of gaining material support for the scheme.

They were not unsuccessful. On 19th February, 1891, the Blackpool Tower Company was formally registered and the properties mentioned above were acquired for £72,800. On 29th September, 1891, a huge crowd assembled round a boarded enclosure to watch Sir Matthew White Ridley, M.P., perform the stone-laying ceremony in the company of the Mayors of Blackpool and many other northern towns, civic dignitaries and notables from the county. It was a momentous occasion. Blackpool, which had encouraged many developments and changes, had foreseen nothing half so ambitious as this scheme to send a great iron finger thrusting 518 feet up into the sky! Indeed, but for the clever manoeuvring of Ald. John Bickerstaffe, this project might well have foundered at the blue print stage. For his outstanding services to the company he was appointed its first Chairman. The first Company Secretary was Mr. George Harrop.

The building, which took three years, proved a hair-raising job for the workers, at least one of whom fell to his death before its completion. One gang of labourers walked in daily from Weeton, calling at the Eagle and Child at five o'clock in the morning for the first pint of the day. The return journey was enlivened by calls at the Grosvenor, the No. 3, the No. 4 at

Layton, a trudge across the fields to the Plough Inn at Staining, and another stretch of the legs to the homely doorstep of the Eagle and Child.

More than 5,000,000 bricks, nearly 2,500 tons of steel and 93 tons of cast iron were used in the building of the Tower, taking no account of the lifts. The Circus, with seating for 3,000 spectators, was set between the four "legs" and thousands more could be accommodated in the pavilion. The whole plan was ambitiously conceived, spaciously designed and brilliantly contrived. From now on no other place in the kingdom had the faintest hope of catching up on this famous resort teeming with a million ideas and the courage to brandish her identity by means of a landmark visible for fifty miles all around.

On Whit Monday, 14th May, 1894, the Tower was thrown upon to the public. When rainspots splashed the pavements, the gloom-mongers shook their heads, but the wise ones knew better. "Let it rain. Let it pour", they said. "It's worth a guinea a drop". So it proved. When the weather turned sour the turnstiles clicked and the customers poured in by their thousands and tens of thousands. They have been doing just that ever since. The top of the Tower caught fire shortly after Queen Victoria's Diamond Jubilee (1897). The platform and stalls could be seen blazing merrily for miles, before being brought under control. Fortunately there were no serious casualties but by coincidence seven sudden deaths took place within the borough after the event.

But nothing could halt the progress of what can be regarded as one of the most powerful entertainments groups in the whole of the North. In the 'nineties, the old Prince of Wales' Theatre was taken down and in its place rose The Alhambra (1899) which, during its time, housed a circus, skating rink, ballroom, variety theatre, waxworks and other attractions. Unfortunately The Alhambra foundered within short years and the property was bought by the Tower Company and re-opened on 4th July, 1904, under the new name of The Palace. In March, 1961, it was announced that the Palace buildings, including five adjoining shops and the County (old Lane Ends) Hotel, had been purchased by Messrs. Lewis who intended to demolish the property and replace it with a £2,500,000 multi-storey emporium and shopping centre by 1963. This gigantic scheme commenced in the autumn of 1961.

Scores of thousands of visitors took a last farewell of the old Palace, enjoying modern and old-tyme dancing, or queuing up to watch pop-singer Frankie Vaughan who topped the bill at the last summer show. The last film screened at the Palace was the great cinema epic "Ben Hur". It was one of the greatest entertainments centres in the North of England, built of the finest materials to last a thousand years; and the magical names of the variety theatre were strung like sparkling beads across its history. Here, at the Palace Varieties, Ted and Barbara Andrews introduced a little girl in a frilly frock, ankle socks and hair ribbons, who sang most beautifully and captivated the audience.

That was the young Julie Andrews, now a film actress of international repute. Top of the bill artistes included George Robey, Lily Langtry, Sir Harry Lauder, Vesta Tilley, Florrie Forde, Nellie Wallace, Little Tich, Stan Laurel and Oliver Hardy, G. H. Elliott, George Formby Senior, Tom Mix, the hard-riding hero of the silent screen, the ex-Foxhall singing waiter, Wilkie Bard, and many others. The post-war parade of talent—Arthur Askey, Tommy Steele, Norman Wisdom, George Formby Junior, Vera Lynn, Alma Cogan ... and so many others, was no less imposing. Many remember the Palace with affection and watched its passing with regret, none more so than a few who remembered helping to build it. The traditionalists among us were particularly sad to see the old Lane Ends (County) Hotel go down (Hudson's "house of 80"), but it was acquired by the Tower Company in 1959 and it fell before the mammoth rebuilding scheme.

The Grand Theatre opened in July, 1894, with Wilson Barrett's "Hamlet". It was acquired and greatly improved by the Tower Company in 1909. The most brilliant theatrical artistes of this century have played in this cosy theatre, with its extravagant ceilings, ornate plaster work, lashings of gilt and red velvet, and an intimate atmosphere which makes an evening's entertainment there a memorable experience. Sadly, too, its fate hangs in the balance. Site values have increased and it has become all too tempting to cash in on the situation, even if it calls for the destruction of a theatre as outstanding and attractive as the Grand. There have been protests and public meetings and propositions, to little avail, so far! And it may yet be that the interests of Big Business will have their way. It will be a sad day for Blackpool.

The Tower and Winter Gardens companies amalgamated in 1928.

The Big Wheel

NEXT TO the Tower, this was Blackpool's most outstanding landmark for more than thirty years. This massive structure, rising some 220 feet into the air and weighing the best part of 1,000 tons, was erected over a former bowling green and opened to the public in August, 1896. The axle, weighing 36 tons, rested on eight columns set in 9 feet of concrete. There were 30 carriages, each capable of holding 30 or more passengers. Crowds flocked to the opening and in just over two hours 4,000 customers had queued up at the turnstiles.

Millions of passengers enjoyed this aerial trip which afforded a fine bird's eye view over the Fylde coast and country before "The Gigantic Wheel", to give it its proper title, was dismantled in 1928. The decision was taken by the Winter Gardens Company on 31st May; the contracts were let for the demolition on 12th October, and on 20th October The Big Wheel made its last trip. The carriages were sold by public auction on 29th October, 1928, fetching up to £20 apiece. They were snapped up for use as garden sheds, sports pavilions and living accommodation; and one of them, formerly used as a holiday centre by a Blackpool Orphanage, was converted into the Wild Boar Café on the road from Cartford Bridge to St. Michael's-on-Wyre.

NOTABLE EVENTS IN THE 1870s

1870. Opening ceremony of Blackpool's new promenade (Easter Monday).
Foundation stone laid by Wm. H. Cocker, Esq., for the new drinking fountain, Talbot Square (March).

1871. Raikes Hall Park, Gardens & Aquarium Company formed.
Blackpool's first paddle steamer, "The Wellington".
Robert Bickerstaffe appointed manager of South (Central) Pier Jetty Company.

1872. Blackpool Sea Water Company registered. The Company's intentions were to supply sea water to private houses and shops and also to bottle it and despatch it for health purposes throughout the north.

1873. Cemetery opened at Layton.
Talbot Bowling Tournament.
"The Blackpool Gazette" published by John Grime, "Gazette" Steam Printing Works, Church Street, price 1 penny, appears for the first time (3rd April).

1874. Aquarium (now part of Tower) formed by Wm. H. Cocker and opened 1875.
Indian Pavilion erected on North Pier (destroyed by fire, 1921).

1875. Primitive Methodist Chapel, Chapel Street (29th August). Previously the members had met in a mission room in Foxhall Road.
Unitarian Chapel, Dickson Road (August).
Wm. H. Cocker's residence "Bank Hey", Coronation Street, purchased by Winter Gardens Company.

1876. Blackpool received its Charter of Incorporation, and became a borough. (Mayor, 6 Aldermen and 18 Councillors.) Elections 11th April and 1st November. Wm. Henry Cocker, Esq., first Mayor (1876-9 and 1884-7).

1877. "Blackpool Times" made its appearance. Joint editors Rev. James Wayman (Congregational) and Rev. Samuel Pilling (Baptist).

1878. Lord Mayor of London, his Sheriffs and more than 60 Mayors and Mayoresses attended the opening of the Winter Gardens Pavilion.

1879. Steamboat "Bickerstaffe".
Start of electric lighting.
Prince of Wales Theatre and New Market.

NOTABLE EVENTS IN THE 1880s

1880. Wreck of the "Bessie Jones".
First Free Public Library opened by Lord Derby, K.G., with 1,600 books in Octagon Room, Talbot Road (Yates' Wine Lodge).

1885. Electric trams, first in the country (29th September), operated by Blackpool Tramway Company. Track 2 miles long.
Death of Rev. Wm. Thornber.
Rigby Road Refuse Destructor (re-constructed 1903, closed 1930).
New lifeboat "Samuel Fletcher".

1886. "Mexico" disaster in Ribble Estuary. St. Annes lifeboat crew lost, and Southport's all but two. "Mexico's" crew rescued by Lytham lifeboat.

1887. Blackpool Borough Police Force established (1st July).
Famous Winter Gardens ballets inaugurated by Mr. "Bill" Holland.
Coxswain Robert Bickerstaffe retired from lifeboat service. Presented with a life-size portrait, silver salver, an additional clasp to his R.N.L.I. medal, and souvenir from the crew, at a public dinner at the Palatine Hotel (5th December).

1888. South Shore Church rebuilt (previous building 1836).
Rawcliffe Street (Ebenezer) Methodist Chapel rebuilt.
53 livery stable keepers and coach proprietors in Blackpool.

1889. Opera House opened.
Standard Debenture Company acquire site for the building of the Tower.

NOTABLE EVENTS IN THE 1890s

1891. Blackpool Tower Company registered. First Chairman, Ald. John Bickerstaffe. Foundation stone laid (21st September).

1892. "Sirene" wrecked by North Pier. Cargo of furs and cheap jewellery. Crew saved by climbing up ropes on to the pier.
Blackpool Tramway Company bought out by Corporation.

1893. Victoria (South) Pier opened.
Samuel Laycock died at Blackpool (buried at Layton).

1894. Tower opened on Whit Monday (14th May).
Grand Theatre opened, and Victoria Hospital.
"Abana" wrecked off Norbreck in a 135 m.p.h. hurricane. Blackpool lifeboat transported by road up promenade and Talbot Road to Bispham. Launched from sandhills. "Abana's" sails torn to shreds. Crew of 17 saved and taken to Red Lion, Bispham.

1895. Empire (Hippodrome) opened.
Death of Mr. "Bill" Holland of the Winter Gardens.
Blackpool Town Hall commenced (completed 1900).

1896. Empress Ballroom opened.
Raikes Hall Estate sold to a local syndicate.
Blackpool—Lytham Tramways opened (11th July).
Big Wheel opened (22nd August).
Big boom year for building.
Blackpool Football Club becomes a limited liability company.
Spiritualist Church, Charnley Road.
Disastrous storms, high tides and floods (October). Fleetwood sea wall breached, town flooded. Blackpool promenade lashed by heavy seas, waves higher than Central Pier. Gynn slade demolished; granite hulkings breached opposite Park and Imperial Hotels.
Fairhaven Golf Links (now Fairhaven Lake area) submerged.

1897. Queen Victoria's Diamond Jubilee celebrations at Raikes Hall and all places of entertainment (June).
Nelson's flag ship "Foudroyant" wrecked near North Pier (June).
Top of Tower on fire (July). Damage to stalls and platform estimated at £1,000. No-one seriously hurt but 7 sudden deaths occurred in the borough following the event.
Freedom of the borough conferred on Wm. Henry Cocker, Esq., J.P.
"Anna" salvage vessel wrecked, coming to take loose timbers from "Foudroyant" (29th July).
Her successor "Aurora" shared the same fate, at North Shore.

1898. Council enlarged from 6 Aldermen and 18 Councillors to 12 Aldermen and 36 Councillors.
Keir Hardie lectured at Blackpool on "Socialism & Character" (March).
The Winter Gardens Company agreed to remove an obstructing wall in Church Street after its widening by Corporation (May).

93

St. Paul's Church, North Shore, replaces former "tin tabernacle".
Welcome Inn, Marton, sold for £2,640 (9th June).
Blackpool—Fleetwood trams commenced (14th July).
Barnum & Bailey's Circus visits Blackpool (August).
Lady visitor killed by flying timber from "Foudroyant" during blasting (17th August).
Raikes Hall Gardens become derelict.

1899. New Central Station.
Alhambra (now Palace) opened.
Blackpool School Board formed.
Claremont Park toll abolished.
Blackpool Liberal Club opened (17th October).

NOTABLE EVENTS IN THE 20th CENTURY, 1900-1919

1900. Blackpool Town Hall completed.
New Bethesda Chapel.
South Shore Unitarian Church.
"Ebenezer" Primitive Methodist Chapel, Egerton Road.
Conservative Club opened by Lord Derby, K.G.

1901. First Musical Festival held at Blackpool.
Blackpool Amateur Operatic Society formed. President, Mr. W. J. Read of South Shore. (First performance, "Mikado", 1902.)

1902. Blackpool Seawater Works taken over by Corporation.
Revoe Board School.
Wesleyan Chapel at Bispham (August).
Airship flight from a site near Blackpool Gasworks. Stanley Spencer reached height of 1,000 feet and flew 26 miles in an airship 75 feet long driven by a petrol motor. (20th October).
Promenade widening begins.

1903. 87 m.p.h. hurricane (27th February). Squires Gate tramshed wrecked.
General Lord Roberts visits Blackpool (July).
Baptist Chapel, Abingdon Street, sold for site of G.P.O. (October).
Alhambra bought by the Tower Company.

1904. Blackpool becomes a County Borough (1st October).
All Saints' Church under construction.
Motor Races at Blackpool, speed trials on South Shore promenade (October).

1905. Great promenade undertaking completed, Victoria Pier to North Pier.
Cemetery enlarged.
More motor racing at Blackpool (July).
Blackpool Lyric Society's first performance, "The Geisha".
Lytham Road bridge rebuilt at a cost of £8,000.
Colosseum, Blackpool's first cinema (formerly the Niagara building at Raikes Hall park).
Mr. Andrew Carnegie offers £15,000 to provide new public library.
Blackpool Secondary School (February).

1907. Blackpool Glee & Madrigal Society perform before Queen Alexandra.
Waterloo Bowling Tournament.
Channel Fleet anchored off Blackpool (August).
New Fylde Workhouse (March).

1908. North Shore Wesleyan School.

1909. Raikes Parade Methodist Church under construction.
North Shore Baths bought by Corporation.
Consecration of Marton New Church.
United Methodist Church, Shaw Road, South Shore, opened (June).

First British Flying Meeting held at Squire's Gate.

1910. Second Blackpool Flying Meeting held at Squire's Gate.
South Shore gypsies' encampment moved from the sandhills on grounds of sanitation (February).
Promenade extensions beyond North Pier commenced.
Formation of Pleasure Beach Company.
Baptist Church, South Shore.

1911. Dedication of St. Mark's Church, Layton.
Death of Wm. Henry Cocker, Blackpool's first Mayor.
Carnegie Library and Grundy Art Gallery opened by Lord Shuttleworth (October).
Coronation of King George V and Queen Mary; youngsters given the "freedom" of Blackpool; free tram rides, Gala and Sports, Bonfire near Revoe, Central Drive; Ox-roasting; Illuminations, etc.

1912. H.R.H. the Princess Louise opened Princess Parade (1st May).
Honorary Freedom of the borough conferred on Ald John Bicker-staffe, J.P. and Ald. J. Fish, J.P. (6th February).
Waterloo Cinema.

1913. Royal visit to the Fylde. Their Majesties King George V and Queen Mary visited Kirkham, Lytham-St. Annes and Blackpool (8th July). Great rejoicings. Blackpool profusely decorated. Vast crowds.
North Shore Primitive Methodist Church.

1914. Claremont Conservative Club, opened by Lord Derby, K.G.
The First World War. H.Q. of the R.A.M.C. established here. Thousands of soldiers billeted in boarding houses. Troops from all over England brought to Blackpool for training.

1915. Honorary Freedom of the borough conferred on Ald. John Grime, J.P. (3rd November), and Ald. James Heyes, J.P.
Sunken Gardens at Gynn completed.

1916. Waterloo Road Station opened.

1917. Bispham becomes part of the borough of Blackpool, 1 new Alder-man, 3 new Councillors.
Blackpool becomes Parliamentary Borough.

1918. Ald. A. Lindsay Parkinson elected M.P. for Blackpool.
Prime Minister the Rt. Hon. David Lloyd George made Honorary Freeman of Blackpool (award collected personally by him in 1922).

1919. Corporation buys Blackpool—Fleetwood trams.

What they remember

FOR sheer enchantment, listen to the old folk recalling memories of the Blackpool of their youth. Pleasures then had a homely and robust simplicity, but a generation which had come up the hard way, with little schooling, much toil, and scant expectations, generally erupted a few outstanding characters worthy of mention. They will tell you of the Olde Curiosity Shoppe in Elizabeth Street, run by Old Percival, a cheerful, jocular character who wore a neb cap and watches for waistcoat buttons. Not for him the stilted phrases of our modern advertisements. Here are some gems culled from his public announcements:

E. PERCIVAL ... Financial Physician who helps lame dogs over the stile. He buys anything and sells everything. Safety matches 2d. per doz. After the Leaning Tower of Pisa, our shop, established in the Year 1 when Adam and Eve swopped me a barrel of apples for their first suits, comes next on the list of the World's Wonders ! ...

You will find everything at my place ... but hung well out of your reach! If you are heavy laden or in pecuniary tribulation, come to me and I will assist you all I can.
PERCIVAL would sooner take all you've got than cheat! (1910).
The Empire Exhibition is fine, with its many models of mill and mine,
... And yet, although it's such a treat,
There are things that it cannot beat
At Percival's in Elizabeth Street ...
Just you call and see for yourselves
What Old Percival's got on his shelves.
Call and have a chat with him, despite his 70 years, full of vim;
He likes to see all gradely folk, to spin 'em a yarn and tell 'em a joke,
And show you round his marvellous store,
The like of which we've ne'er seen before.
And is not equalled the whole world o'er. (1926.)

Eli Percival's home and front garden in South King Street were crammed with ornaments, mottoes, statues, curios and souvenirs of all kinds. The staircase was jammed solid with clocks and his vast stock included old brasses, pots, swords, antiques, knick-knacks, dusty uniforms, items of fancy dress, iron mangles, and everything from delicately carved ivory to a coffin which he occasionally slept in. Visitors, young and old, derived much amusement from these miscellaneous marvels of the one-time Oldham furniture dealer. Eli died in 1937 at the age of 93.

There is an amusing tale recalling Tom Moon who used to take out goods by horse and cart from Talbot Road Station. He had delivered a load of packages and was half-way up the street when he was recalled by an ear-splitting whistle. With some difficulty he turned his horse and vehicle full circle and went back to investigate—only to find himself staring into the solemn eye of the culprit—Old Percival's parrot which was hanging in a cage in the sunshine. Normally Tom Moon delivered out to the South Shore area, taking goods to the shops in Bond Street and hampers of cloth to the tailor's in Bolton Street. In Bolton Street there were three old cobble cottages turned into shops, entered by going down two steps from road level. There was Miss Rossall, the old-fashioned grocer, Mr. Hopwood the ironmonger, and Mr. Jolly the butcher. Mr. Jolly was a far-seeing man who raised money and built three houses and shops which are there now. One day a customer remarked: "By gum, but tha're doing well". "Aye, lad, but just look up there!", remarked Mr. Jolly, glancing up at the smoking chimneys. "They don't feed them monkeys wi' nuts!"

The South Shore gypsies, including Daisy Boswell and her mother, the Smith family and others, came regularly to the Bond Street and Bolton Street area to do their shopping. This was before the encampment had been shifted for sanitary reasons by the authorities in 1910. They always came in with plenty of excuses and no money, but the shopkeepers had long since hardened their hearts to these fascinating but unscrupulous characters whose wattle and blanket tents might have come straight from a biblical scene.

In those days there was a corn mill in Haig Road and the

Premier Garage was a livery stable where the Blackpool Yeomanry were equipped for the Boer War. Indeed, there were as many livery stables in Blackpool as now there are garages and all the traffic was horse drawn. Horse-buses used to run from stables in Church Street along the country road (Whitegate Drive) leading to the Oxford Hotel and Marton. From 1880 onwards visitors used to drive out to the Cherry Tree Gardens which had developed from the Cherry Tree farm and nursery gardens run by the Fisher family. Sir Lindsay Parkinson always claimed that he was the first man in Blackpool to own a private car but there was a counter-claim by Mr. A. Pollard of South Shore who insisted that he was the first, and that his registration number was "FR 1". But these were the days when horses were the thing.

At Read's Baths on Central Beach (Luna Park) the proprietress kept a wary eye on the school boys who would have spent the whole day splashing about in the water and getting full value for their money. When she thought they had had enough she used to chase them out with a long whip.

The Tower Company had a reserve animal depot on Lytham Road on an open space near St. Mary's Church. The keeper lived in one of the still existing cottages close by until, as the tale runs, he entered the lion's cage without caution and was mauled to death. There were no shops in front of the Tower in the early days but the animals were on show behind a surrounding wall with railings on the top.

Old Revoe Farm about 1900 (now the site of the Gymnasium and Library).

Mr. Doidge's Auction Shop in West Street was a tremendous attraction to visitors and it was unthinkable to leave Blackpool without paying this great local character a visit. He sold all manner of beautiful glass, silver, china, leather and ornamental ware and by all accounts there were some rare bargains to be snapped up and taken home with the luggage.

Before the building of the Town Hall, commenced in 1895, there were shops on the site, including Wright's confectioner's shop and licensed restaurant. Across the road was Jenkinson's Café, established before the middle of last century. During the 'eighties it was run by the two Misses Jenkinson who lived over the shop and made a great reputation with their meat and fruit pies. They employed a staff of five or six who started work at 6-30 in the morning. Two hindquarters and two shoulders of prime meat were delivered daily by Masheter's, the butchers in Market Street, and cut from the bone. The succulent pies became famous throughout the Fylde and at lunchtime customers used to sit and eat them in the shop. By a nice distinction, bank managers and important businessmen were invited to step into the Misses Jenkinson's room and eat in privacy. Until late in the evening the younger members of the staff went out delivering pies to hotels and private houses at North Shore. Some lived in, going home only at weekends. They put in long hours, worked hard and had little freedom, but for a few minutes in the evenings they used to hang around the doors of the Theatre Royal (Tivoli) hoping that their young colleague, a spare-time page boy, would slip them in without payment to see such old-time tear jerkers as "East Lynn" and other Victorian melodramas.

In the late 'eighties, Mayor James Fish, after a visit to the south of France, instituted a similar "Battle of Flowers" at Blackpool. For a year or two this was a highly successful event, but the rowdy element crept in and put a stop to these floral carnivals.

The area around Talbot Road Station has changed considerably since those Victorian times. Beyond the Talbot Hotel (demolished in 1968 for Prudential House Development) there was an earth yard opening to the mews behind. The accommodation there was big enough to house the circus elephants. Horses were led up a wooden ramp and bedded down on the first floor, a sight that always fascinated the children. Beyond the hotel and mews was Talbot Terrace (site of 'bus station), a row of nine houses (three later turned into shops) with gardens at the rear and a back street and saddler's shop overlooking a big field (now St. John's Market). Circus employees lived there in their caravans, including Johnny the Monkeyman who had lived and slept with his chimpanzees for so long that it was difficult, folk said, to tell them apart. The Talbot Terrace houses were not large, but being conveniently situated for the station, some took in visitors for the season. Instead of taxi-cabs there were strings of landaus which entered the station down a ramp opposite Swainson Street.

There was great excitement when the famous tight-rope

walker, Blondin, arrived in Blackpool to perform at the Raikes Hall Gardens in the 'nineties. In actual fact, he stole in quietly a week before his show was due to go on, giving himself enough time to set up his equipment and practise his act. Naturally, no word of this leaked out to the public and on the day that Blondin was due to arrive "from London" and to a great fanfare of publicity, he took a cab to Poulton and hopped on the London train there. A vast reception and a quantity of red carpet awaited him at Talbot Road Station. Rows of little girls in frills were poised ready to shower the hero of Niagara with posies. Hundreds of old uniforms left over from the crowd scenes at the panoramic firework displays had been hauled out of mothballs for the occasion and, to music and cheers and fluttering banners, the great Blondin, heading a mammoth landau procession of judges, soldiers, sailors and heroes of all nations, all looking slightly dusty and tarnished, made a triumphal procession through the streets before going back to the Raikes to commence his performance.

Another scene which drew the crowds was the annual Mayday procession of the Talbot Road Station carters. On that occasion they took an immense amount of trouble trimming up their horses, scrubbing and polishing the leatherwork, plaiting manes and tails, and so forth. But let Tom Moon's daughter, "Janey", take up the tale:

My father used to send me to Harrisons opposite th' Victory Hotel in Conce Street for th' brasses. 'Course, he lent 'em quick enough, for they wur all clayned before they went back. They wur clayned and clayned till they fair shone. My father had a lot of his own but he used to borrow th' extra ones. Belly bands, cockades, bells and a lot o' things. Clip-clop, they went. Sometimes th' noise they med startled th' horses when they wasn't used to it, but they looked nice. We always looked to see which was th' nicest when they wur all trimmed up. My father had been used to horses all his life. He had a grut horse, quiet enough but it seemed like a grut elephant to me. One year he fotched it home into th' yard to dress it up for th' May-day. He med me howd it. I was frittened to death but I dossent let on. Every time it moved, I let go. In th' end my father tied it to th' door. I should like to have seen my sister having to howd it, but there was only me and I couldn't get out of it. That was the only time he fotched it home. We used to set off at five in the morning with all the things loadened up in th' pram and he carried another lot. Th' horses were scrubbed and brushed till they looked lovely. Th' collar was blackened and shiny so you could see your face in it, and as clayn inside as out. My mother used to make ribbon rosettes for it, and then there were bunches of flowers, and brasses, and streamers and suchlike. They looked lovely. There wasn't any prizes for th' best turn-out, or owt like that, but we used to dread it coming round, my father med that much to do. Usually they turned out o' th' yard at six in th' morning but they were always a bit later on May-day. They used to set off in procession from th' station, down Talbot Road to the Promenade and then they split up and went on their rounds. My father was always th' second in th' procession. John Hornby was first and Mr. Seed, as broad as he wur long, was third. They went in rotation, them as had been longest fost.

These were days when people took a pride in keeping themselves respectable and out of debt, though it wasn't always easy when the breadwinner's wage ran to little more than a pound a week. Mothers of large families were obliged to "hutch" up the family into little space and let off every available bed for the season. One family in George Street took in visitors for years at the beginning of the century, and their little daughters were kept hard at it from six in the morning till bedtime, seven days a week, in the season. They charged 2s. 0d. a night for a double bed and 3s. 0d. for two beds if there were children. There was an extra charge of ½d. a day each for milk and 1d. for potatoes. This family did not charge for the cruet though some landladies did. It was a toilsome business, carrying hot water jugs upstairs, cleaning visitors' shoes and cooking, at no extra cost, a massed variety of food items brought in daily by the separate families. One Bank Holiday Monday, when there were eleven beds going, a shake-down on the floor, plus a horde of day trippers, there were 49 for potatoes in a three-bedroom town cottage with no bathroom and oil lamps! To crown all, "it rained as it never rained, wash day an' all". No wonder the mother declared, "Never again!" Nevertheless, these domestic landladies were extremely hospitable and homely and their guests returned to the same digs year after year. These packed households made their own fun and played the usual jokes—apple pie beds, sewn up pyjamas, and so forth. The departing visitor, by tradition, left his photograph to be inserted in the family album and commemorated his happy holiday with a greetings card at Christmas.

An elderly lady recalls how she came, as a child, with her parents to take over a company house sleeping 47 visitors. She passed the "Labour Examination" and was let off school for the summers. The three of them did all the work and Saturdays were a nightmare with as many as 90 to be catered for, what with one party still upstairs sleeping and the new arrivals banging on the front door at seven in the morning. They arrived from East Lancashire as hungry as hunters and their food boxes were lined up in the passage; it was cheaper to bring provisions from home than to pay the seasonal Blackpool prices. Father spent his summer life perched on a slanting stool, washing up till one in the morning; and they were up again at 5-30 a.m., to face another day's toil.

But if there was plenty of excitement and hard work, there was very little at the end of it. A Burnley woman wrote in booking "a bed and a half" for herself, husband and four children. This immediately posed the question ... "Ho yes! And who's going to sleep in th' other half?" Naturally, she was charged for two beds but her curious request gives some indication of the stringency of the times.

Yet there was no lack of thrills in the 1890s, a decade of rough seas, many wrecks, and exciting rescues. In 1961 I listened to Mr. Peter C. Miller, the renowned Fylde artist whose mural depicting St. John the Baptist in the Wilderness had just been completed in the chancel of Whitegate Drive Baptist Church, recalling boyhood memories of that Sunday morning of the 9th October 1892. He was walking along the promenade to Sunday School, along with his brother. There was a great sea running before a driving south-west wind, and a three-masted, square-rigged ship, the Norwegian barque "Sirene", was drifting helplessly towards the shore. It was no secret then to the sailors under canvas that the Irish Sea coast was one of the most dangerous in the world. There was barely time to race to the home of Mr. Miller's grandfather, a retired sea captain, and borrow a telescope, and to scale the drinking fountain which then stood opposite West Street. From this vantage point the two boys witnessed every dramatic detail of the wreck, the men slithering about helplessly on the decks, the masts keeling over, and finally the harsh sound of the vessel grounding on the hulkings in the angle formed by the promenade and North Pier. The bowsprit rammed the decking at the pier entrance and levered the stalls and shops to a crazy angle. Lifeboatmen lowered ropes from the pier and the crew climbed up to safety, and at the recession of the tide, sight-seers and souvenir hunters crowded round the stricken "Sirene", picking up items of cheap jewellery and bedraggled furs which had formed the bulk of her cargo. Not all was handed back to the authorities and when the memory of the wreck had dimmed a little in the minds of the Blackpudlians, a few local ladies removed the tissue paper wrappings and dared to walk about in their "Sirene" furs!

The year 1895 brought other gales and wrecks along the coast from Norbreck to Lytham, and claimed at least ten Fleetwood fishermen whose smacks were driven ashore or capsized off Blackpool. A fund was raised to assist 27 Fleetwood children orphaned by this fiercest storm that brought havoc and mourning to our coast.

The "Foudroyant" wreck was another memorable disaster, though fortunately her company of 28 men and youths, dressed up as Jack Tars, were safely brought to rescue. Nelson's old flagship was sold out of the Service for firewood, an event which stirred a nation's indignation. Eventually this historic vessel was bought by a Mr. Cobb and an associate for £6,000 and a further £20,000 was spent on re-fitting the "Foudroyant" for exhibition to the public, first at Southport, and in 1897 at Blackpool. She lay two miles off the coast, but in a sudden squall on 16th June, 1897, the vessel broke loose, the mizzen mast crashed down, and despite all the efforts of the crew the "Foudroyant" was swept headlong to her doom. Thousands poured into Blackpool to see the wrecked flagship whose timbers were later dismantled and made into souvenirs—walking sticks, jewel boxes, linen chests, newspaper racks, and the like. That wild Silver Jubilee Year storm blew for three days, incurring great damage, endangering our mariners, but bringing in a welcome influx of trade in the usually quiet month of June.

Pioneer flying—Blackpool gets in first

BALLOONING was a popular and exciting sport in Britain by the end of the 18th century and in early Victorian times. In the 'nineties, Percy Pilcher, resembling a king-size bat, was gliding

101

through the air, not always with the greatest of ease, and tearing back to his workshop to think out what went wrong. In 1909 M. Louis Bleriot achieved every man's dream by crossing the Channel in a heavier-than-air-machine and was duly wined and dined at the Savoy Hotel by Lord Northcliffe in honour of the event. Shortly after, in August, 1909, all the pioneer aviators of the time converged upon Rheims for a week-long Flying Meeting which made aviation history. The weather was brilliant. Enthusiasm was running at fever pitch. The Chancellor of the Exchequer, thrilled by everything he saw, declared: "We must do something like this at home". This was to H. Hamilton Fyfe who at that moment was hailed by a friend saying: "I've been looking for you everywhere, I want to introduce you to the Mayor of Blackpool. He has come over to arrange for a Flying Week there!" With less than seven weeks in hand, stands and hangars to be built, and committees, publicity and catering arrangements to be made, Blackpool intended to hold the first English Flying Races of all time.

"Can you do it in the time?", the Mayor was asked.

"Aye, Blackpool can do it", was the reply. "Blackpool will not fail". It was no idle boast. By the 18th October, 1909, it was recorded: "Blackpool has done it ... Already one fresh record has been created at this meeting—a record for rapidity of organisation. Blackpool holds that record beyond doubt!"

All the top talent from the Rheims meeting had been invited to take part and induced to exhibit their prowess by more than £8,000 offered in prize money. There were bi-planes, and monoplanes, all of them looking like fragile kites held together with wire and fitted with pram wheels and skids. Seated at the controls, and looking much more determined than comfortable, were such leather-clad aces as Latham ("the cleverest and most graceful flier in the world"); Henry Farman ("World's distance and time champion"); Paulhan; Rougier, the world's altitude champion; Duffour, Le Blon, A. M. Singer, Moore Brabazon, Frank McLean, A. V. Roe, and Fournier, a racing motorist "with nerves of steel", who were all hoping to make their mark. Everything went well but the weather, which held up flying for at least two days during the week. Eleven huge marquees catered for 200,000 spectators who created another record by their consumption of food and drink, including: 500 hogsheads and 36,000 bottles of beer, 40,000 dozen bottles of minerals, 500 cases of champagne and 600 of whisky; 1,000 hams, 2,000 pork pies and literally millions of sandwiches!

To tell the customers what they might expect, coloured flags were flown from the top of the Tower. According to the handbook: "Red Flag means Flying in Progress; Black Flag means Flying Suspended; White Flag means Flying Probable". In view of the winds it was remarkable that 15 flights were made. Rougier rose up to 300 feet and achieved a top speed of 40 m.p.h. The £2,000 prize was collected by Farman after his epic distance flight of 48 miles and to this was added £400 for his 46 m.p.h. top-speed of the meeting. Bands blared, crowds jostled, and the spectators went almost hysterical with excitement when two machines actually took to the air at the same time. Without doubt, Blackpool had set the lead for future aerial events and opened up a whole new exciting world of experience. 1910 was especially significant. On 27th April, British C. Grahame-White and French Louis Paulhan competed for the "Daily Mail" £10,000 prize for the first-ever flight from London to Manchester. Mr. Grahame-White set out from a field at Wormwood Scrubbs and finished up grounded a few miles from Lichfield. M. Paulhan took off at Hampstead, spent the night in Lichfield, and touched down in a field at Didsbury exactly 12 hours later, having completed the course at an average speed of 47 m.p.h. This great achievement captured the imagination of the nation and the newly air-minded flocked to the 1910 Blackpool Flying Event arranged under the auspices of the Lancashire Aero Club.

Some fine flying was seen at Squire's Gate between 28th July and 20th August, 1910, and once more, in view of the weather, the achievements were all the more remarkable. French pilot, Tetard, flew around Blackpool Tower and cruised over the Fylde countryside; Chavez rose to the height of one mile; and fresh from his glorious failure in the £10,000 London—Manchester competition, G. Grahame-White thrilled all Blackpool by touching down on the sands near South Pier and flying off to such remote places as Barrow-in-Furness and New Brighton. He was also the first man to transport mail by air. During this meeting he carried a bag of mail for seven miles in the teeth of a strong wind. In collections somewhere there must still be preserved some of those letters and postcards, bearing a special mark, in commemoration of the first-ever airmail flight.

There have been many air pageants in Blackpool since those stirring pioneering days. We have seen magnificent performances by the R.A.F., and the daredevil aces of Sir Alan Cobham's Air Circus. Many paid to see those hair-raising stunts, looping the loop, rolling, walking the fabric wings holding on to a rope with one hand, flying upside down or in formation, and breath-taking aerobatics. Many thousands more enjoyed the spectacle for nothing (and in doing so trampled the binding starr grass of the Squire's Gate sand-dunes!).

We have watched flying become not only a popular, but an everyday occurrence, so that to-day one takes a plane as readily as a Corporation 'bus. But those pioneer days had their own magic. The young men who elevated themselves, very sedately, into space, were our national heroes, blazing a trail so that in a few years Mr. Everyman could take a flip round the Tower for a dollar, and loop the loop for a quid! Now we have the whining snarling jets, the shattering thump of the sound barrier being broken at regular intervals, the joy-flights, the regular passenger services, the mercy helicopter trips, the mail planes. We have seen the Isle of Man flying boats come and go, and there was that memorable occasion, a few years ago, when that Empress of the Air, the Bristol Brabazon named after Moore Brabazon (later Lord Brabazon of Tara), one of the competitors in Blackpool's first air races, made her majestic flight over the Fylde. On that occasion, like the spectators of 1909 and 1910, we craned our necks and blinked back tears of pride at man's long and glorious struggle to conquer the air.

Parish Church personalities and olde tyme spring cleaning

THERE have been many tales told of Blackpool's tempestuous Vicar-historian who came to St. John's in 1829. The Rev. Wm. Thornber was born at Poulton on 5th December, 1803, and died under care in a private asylum at Stafford on 8th September, 1885. He was a powerful man, aggressive, strong-featured, suspecting the worst in everybody and bluntly outspoken. Yet he was devoted to English literature, contributed regular articles to the "Preston Pilot", and excelled above all in recording the doings of his times. In seeking the history of Blackpool, he was fortunate to have married the daughter of pioneer-innkeeper, Henry Banks, whose long memories of the growing hamlet inspired much of Thornber's work. By all accounts the marriage was far from happy and the incumbent's drinking habits were well known to the parishioners who had felt the lash of his tongue, the sting of his pen and the potency of his fists. Unfortunately he carried his frailties into the pulpit. On Sunday mornings the old bell-ringer was sent out for supplies which were lowered on the end of a rope through a hole in the floor of the bell chamber. The thirsty Vicar was waiting in the dressing room below and in the same way the empties were hauled up without detection.

He is said to have thrashed an atheist one Sunday night in the middle of Talbot Square after a session in the Clifton, under the impression, presumably, that this was the best way to pound home the gospel of peace and goodwill. On several evenings a week he hired a dilapidated building, Th' Hill Farm, and taught the young bloods of the district how to box. Without doubt, he crossed swords with many a local inhabitant and some of his historical flights of fancy, which may have sprung from a deranged mind, could quite easily have originated in some retaliatory leg-pulling and yarn-spinning on the part of his enemies. The Vicar wanted information and he got it, but one wonders how many sly old faces creased with merriment when his story of Blackpool came into print. His eccentric behaviour caused him to resign in 1845 and from that time Thornber figured prominently in local affairs, especially during elections for the Local Board. Here are some extracts from broadsheets and pamphlets aimed at the ex-Vicar by rival candidates in 1868:

TO THE RATEPAYERS OF LAYTON WITH WARBRECK I have been childish since I have known you—I have gulled you from the year of my residence (1827). I love my glass and appreciate all who pay for it ... I love all who vote for me and if you will only encourage me ... we will go hand-in-hand to improve our properties. Electors, never mind, although in reading this you may miss my usual grunt—I cannot help it,

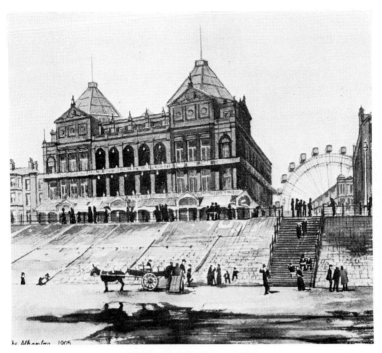

The Alhambra (later The Palace), opened in 1899 (from a monochrome painting by Keith Wood).

The Prince of Wales Market and Theatre.

Winter Gardens Pavillion.

The Big Wheel.

The Grand Theatre, opened in 1894.

Above: Two famous shipwrecks—the "Sirene" in 1892 (top) and the "Foudroyant" in 1897. Opposite:— Top: Blackpool Town Hall, completed in 1900. Bottom: Britain's Henry Farman, the long distance winner, in flight during Aviation Week, October 18th-23rd, 1909.

Above: Marton Moss. Top: Old Shovels Inn, with Folds Row cottages and the white shippons of Folds Farm (extreme right). Bottom: Folds Farm—a cruck structure with later additions—as it was fifty years ago.

Opposite: Blackpool tramcars. Top: A Dreadnought tram in Dixon Road in 1963. Centre: Vambac tram on Whitegate Drive, 1962. Bottom: The last Standard, built 1927, still in service in the 1960s.

111

Marton Moss.   Top: The Old School House, Division Lane. Centre: Blowing Sands Smithy and Cottages, Squires Gate Lane. Bottom: White-washed cottages, once thatched, in Fisher's Lane.

if it is piggish. I say if you will only elect the three of us we will dispense with that great eyesore and nuisance of a slade opposite our own property (promenade cottages near the County Hotel) and remove it to the North Shore at your expense. It will only cost £500 or £600 to do it and I feel sure ... that none of you would object to it.

Ratepayers, all of you give me a vote and I will look after your interests. I will get improvements done to your property and those that don't support me I will take care that their property is not improved, except at their own expense.

WILLIAM OF BLACKPOOL.

Ratepayers, look out! Forty years ago, efforts were made by the ancestors of this same party to stop up the ancient slade and highway near the Albion and Lane End Hotels. And what did the Blackpool people do then? Why, they smashed down the barriers and prevented the public being robbed of their rights and privileges. And now it is for you to "squelch" the attempt to get ... Thornber ... returned to support a movement for the stoppage of the above named public highway which is to this day maintained by the town at the expense of the ratepayers.

O, Reverend William, stick to thy drinking and preaching and retire into obscurity.

A great fuss and commotion, we may think, about a cleft in the cliffs leading down to the sea!

In later years, Thornber showed marked signs of mental disturbance and an order for his detention was sent through to the Blackpool Police. Sergeant Whiteside was detailed to apprehend the ex-Vicar whom he spotted in Talbot Road which at that time was being excavated for the laying of sewers. "Hey, I want to see you", called the officer. "Oh, do you!", retorted Thornber, landing out with an uppercut which left the astonished Sergeant lying flat on his back in the trench. Thornber's was a sorry end to a turbulent career but his graphic history of Blackpool, published in 1837, has made him more friends since his death than the enemies of his lifetime, and we can only think kindly of a character so colourful and diverse.

Another little anecdote concerns the late Canon Jeffrey who was appointed curate of St. John's in 1869 and who resigned the living in 1915. In those early years, the flagged court opposite the Veevers' Arms Hotel in Cookson Street, where the pigeons now swoop down to be fed, was a grass plot surrounded by railings. One night a noisy fight spilled out of the Veevers' Arms and flared up again at this point just as Canon Jeffrey was passing. The venerable old gentleman intervened, tried to restore peace and got the worst of it, and amputation of a leg followed injuries sustained in the brawl.

A well beloved Sexton for 28 years was the late Mr. R. Nickson, a handsome bearded man who died in 1926. He was respected by those who employed him and loved by those whom he employed. He lived for more than 40 years in the same house in Milbourne Street, once set in the midst of open fields. His mother in law, Mrs. Christopher Johnson of the old Whitegate Farm, built the first houses in Milbourne Street and the bricks came from a kiln adjoining the site. Mr. Nickson was born in West Street and baptised at St. John's. His parents had a farm where General Street is now. As a boy he was stricken with diphtheria, a dreaded and often fatal disease. In the last extrem-

113

ity, Dr. Cocker forcibly removed the mucus from the throat and the boy recovered. Years later, when reminded of the episode, the good doctor joked: "Well, has it been a good job, or a bad 'un?"

It was certainly a good job for St. John's Church which Mr. Nickson served with superlative efficiency. In one week between Easter and Whitsuntide, a gang of seven or eight women were engaged for the annual spring cleaning of the building. There were no vacuum cleaners or labour saving devices in those days and every inch of the church was scrubbed with bar soap and soda which left the women's hands cracked and unbearably sore. Carpets were taken out and batted in the sunshine and when the floors and aisles had been scrubbed surgically clean, all the pews and woodwork were polished from end to end. It was hard work from eight in the morning until six at night but the cleaning gang took it all in their stride and even enjoyed the companionship of a shared task. They wore men's cloth caps, with the nebs to the rear, which Mr. Nickson sympathetically allowed them to remove on condition that heads were hastily re-covered if the footsteps of the Misses Jeffrey were heard on the premises. The cleaners lived in fear of these formidable ladies and nudged their caps along with their buckets, ready to put on in the instant. Otherwise there would have been a terrible rumpus! At the end of a gruelling week's work the women were paid the princely sum of 18s. 0d., yet the same gang, often including several members from one family, regularly returned for the annual spring cleaning, and all spoke in kindly terms of the long-serving Sexton.

The 1920s. In the aftermath of a great world war

IN THIS nostalgic era the post-war problems of housing, mass unemployment, trade depressions, coal shortages and surplus women, were overlaid by the almost pathological gaiety of the "Bright Young Things". The young man flaunted his plus-fours and Oxford bags and tore about in the newly popular motor car. The "Flapper" exposed her knees and rammed a curious cloche hat over her eyebrows, and the Bathing Beauty was a regular feature on the beach. After the stringencies of war-time, the re-introduction of cheap railway excursions brought the seaside within the reach of Everyman and his family, and the weight of motor char-a-bancs heading Fylde-coastwards, assumed startling proportions.

Following her most-prosperous-ever season in 1919 Blackpool viewed the dismal situation of the nation somewhat apprehensively and waited for the fears and rumours of the pessimists to be fulfilled. Instead, the 1920 season proved better than anywhere in the kingdom, being cut short only by the coal strike in October. This was the year of the great cotton boom when men retired early on their sudden fortunes and brought their families to live on the coast. Within months they had been beggared as suddenly by the slump and forced to return to the scene of their former activities. This was an era which produced "Love On The Dole" and Walter Greenwood portrayed Blackpool in the 'twenties as the mecca of every working-class couple with a few pounds to spare.

In this decade War Memorial plaques and windows were quietly unveiled in almost every church in the land. Ex-servicemen stood begging at street corners; but the younger set were chiefly concerned with having a "ripping good time". Noise and speed and fancy dress balls were the thing and in 1923 Blackpool held her first Grand Carnival. It was based on the original at Nice. Continental craftsmen supervised the arrangements and at a cost of about £5,500, hundreds of thousands of visitors had been attracted into Blackpool. Miles of paper streamers and tons of confetti were unloosed on the promenade; costumed revellers appeared in their thousands. There were floral tableaux and hydrocephalic figures, dog shows, motor races, sports meetings and international swimming. This was Blackpool in hilarious mood, a week of gaiety unlimited. And on the promenade the obelisk commemorating her fallen heroes was nearing completion.

The gigantic success of the first carnival led to the second in 1924. This time £6,000 had been spent on elaborating and extending the event to ten days. Blackpool enjoyed a fanfare of world-wide publicity. The sun shone. The crowds came. But things got a little out of hand. On every street corner there were pedlars hawking inflated bladders on sticks and it was considered the height of merriment when heads were thwacked, hats dislodged, and children left screaming. The rowdy element which crept into the 1924 Carnival was strongly criticised and there was no attempt to repeat the event. Instead, in 1925, the Autumn Illuminations were revived but on a scale much grander than pre-war. Crowds flocked in to see this fairyland spectacle which extended the season until well on into October and eclipsed the attractions of all other British seaside resorts.

Despite the overall policy of the times, Blackpool in the 'twenties pursued a vigorous policy of building, improvements and extensions. Stanley Park, South Shore Promenade and Open Air Baths, the Miners' Convalescent Home, Devonshire New Road, North Shore Open Air Baths and many other ambitious schemes were products of this decade of contrasts. There were royal visits and big-name celebrities, motor 'buses, fires and floods, and some wonderful flying. The skyline changed when the Big Wheel was demolished and another landmark, the old Gynn Inn, made its exit in the 'twenties.

NOTABLE EVENTS IN THE 1920s

1920. First publication of the amalgamated "Blackpool Gazette & Herald" (1st January).
Sir Arthur Conan Doyle lectures on Spiritualism (20th January). St. Mary's Church, South Shore.
Madame Melba performs at the Opera House (10th October).

1921. Regent Cinema opened (17th January).
Blackpool & Fylde Wireless Society test their apparatus at the top of Blackpool Tower.

Chief Constable H. E. Derham presented with the King Albert
Medal for his services to the Belgians during the war.
Blackpool acquires a motorised road sprinkler and sweeper.
Memorial chancel screen unveiled at St. John's Parish Church
by Dr. Temple, Lord Bishop of Manchester.
Oil substituted for coal at Blackpool Electrical Power Station.
Eclipse of the sun. Thousands on the promenade. Many watch
it through a telescope on Princess Parade (April).
H.R.H. the Prince of Wales visits Blackpool (July).
Ex-servicemen engaged on saving the North Shore cliffs after the
building of the seawall.
Grand Theatre entrance remodelled (April).
First motor-vehicle ice cream stall seen on Blackpool sands (June).
Blackpool Corporation motor 'buses run between Cleveleys Beach
and Thornton Railway Station.
The historic Gynn Inn (original whitewashed buiding) closed in
May and demolished in August, following the auction sale of the
contents. Nostalgic crowds took a last look at this famous land-
mark.
North Pier devastated by a great fire which destroyed the pavilion
(11th September). Salvage sold for £310.
Sod cut for Poor Children's Holiday Camp at Squires Gate, cost-
ing £15,000. Gangs of unemployed set to work on Devonshire
New Road (Warbrick Hill Road end) (November).
North Shore Open Air Bath under construction.

1922. Palace Cinema reconstructed, and Princess Cinema rebuilt.
A. Lindsay Parkinson, Esq., M.P., receives a knighthood (3rd
June).
Lloyd George collects his Freedom of the borough (14th October).

1923. Lifeboat rescues crew of Liverpool steamer "Ophir", aground at
Blackpool; re-floated (30th January).
Fylde Wireless Society's H.Q. opened (Hippodrome 1st February).
Bloomfield Hotel (March).
Sale of Blackpool steamer "Greyhound" for service in Constan-
tinople (17th April).
Squires Gate Poor Children's Camp opened by Lady Mayoress of
Manchester (17th April).
Blackpool Carnival Week (9—16th June) ... "the greatest event
of its kind ever known" ... "an almost embarrassing success."
South Shore Promenade extensions and Open Air Baths opened.
Salvationist "General" Bramwell Booth visits Blackpool (11th
September).
"The Story of Blackpool" by Allen Clarke, published.
Cenotaph unveiled by Brig. General T. E. Topping (10th Novem-
ber). Cost, more than £17,000.

1924. Swedish steamer "Nord" aground at Blackpool (10th January).
Refloated (22nd January).
Miss Peggy O'Neil in Blackpool for Lifeboat Institution Cen-
tenary Celebrations.
Albion Hotel sold for £50,000 (May).
Sir Lindsay Parkinson gives cricket ground to the Corporation
(May).
Carnival (June) marred by rowdyism.
Miss Lucy Morton of Blackpool, won Olympic World's Swimming
Championship, 200 metres breast-stroke (18th July).
85 m.p.h. hurricane, great damage at Blackpool (21st September).

1925. Blackpool Football Supporters' Club formed (28th January).
Albion Hotel's licence transferred to Beach Hotel, S.S. (April).
Rossall School, War Memorial Chapel dedicated by Archbishop
of York (26th June).
Sod cut for St. Stephen's-on-the-Cliffs (27th June).
Part of Stanley Park opened.
Central Drive Independent Methodist Church (24th June).

Bill authorising the removal of the Market passed the House of Commons Committee (9th July).
The Corporation plan to take part of St. John's Churchyard for Church Street widening scheme.
Blackpool Illuminations revived.

1926. St. Mary's Church, Layton, and Whitegate Drive Baptist Church under construction.
JUBILEE YEAR OF BLACKPOOL BOROUGH. (Royal Assent given to the Charter of Incorporation, 21st January, 1876.) "Progress", Jubilee Pictorial Souvenir published. Also Allen Clarke's short "History of Blackpool".
Great gales and sand-storms (March).
Alderman John Bickerstaffe receives a knighthood (3rd July).
Sir Harry Lauder in Blackpool (July).
Victoria Schools, Foxhall Road (now Ministry of Labour, Tyldesley Road) sold to Office of Works for £9,500.
Three new Freemen. Ald. T. Bickerstaffe (Mayor); Sir Lindsay Parkinson; and Ald. W. H. Broadhead (1st September).
Jubilee Illuminations, switched on 25th September. Switched off 28th September, due to General Strike.
New £250,000 promenade at South Shore, and Stanley Park, opened by Lord Derby, K.G. (2nd October).
Kreisler gives a performance at the Winter Gardens (10th October).
First Annual Meeting of Stanley Park Golf Club (29th October).
New Baines Endowed School, Marton (4th November).

1927. H.R.H. the Prince of Wales visits Blackpool and Fylde (28th June) and opens Miners Convalescent Home, Bispham.
Total eclipse of the sun. More than 100,000 spectators at Blackpool (29th June).
Stanley Park Cocker Memorial Clock Tower (in honour of Wm. Henry Cocker, Esq., first Mayor of Blackpool) opened by Ald. Sir John Bickerstaffe (29th June).
Suzanne Lenglen, French tennis ace, plays exhibition match at Bloomfield Road Football Ground (15th July).
Greyhound Racing starts at Blackpool (30th July).
Fleetwood Flood Disaster (28th October). 78 m.p.h. hurricane and high tides hit the coast from Lytham to Fleetwood. Lytham inundated in Dock Road and Preston Road area, main dyke overflowed, houses devastated, railway trains suspended. St. Annes sandhills flooded, water "neck-deep" in places, all double deck tramcars withdrawn. Electricity failure. Blackpool's new South Shore promenade hit as if by an earthquake. Huge concrete slabs, shelters, pillars and gardens in ruins. Star Inn surrounded by a "lake". Bonny Street under several feet of water. Heavy damage to Pleasure Beach, South Shore Baths and North Pier. Tramcar blown over at North Shore. Great damage from Gynn to beyond Bispham. Fleetwood grievously affected, with an estimated £200,000 of damage. Householders marooned. Homes and belongings destroyed. Boys of Rossall School rescued victims by boat. 5 fatalities.

1928. Tower Company and Winter Gardens Company. Proposals for amalgamation approved (9th February).
Sale of Bannister's Bazaar (6th February). Taken over by Feldman's. (Queen's Theatre.)
Death of Squire John Talbot Clifton of Lytham (23rd March).
Death of Charles Noden ("Mr. Blackpool"), aged 81 (15th April).
The Big Wheel. Winter Gardens Co. decide to demolish (31st May).
Great Air Pageant, Squire's Gate (6th—7th July). Civilian Aero Clubs and R.A.F. put on a fine display. The greatest event of its kind ever seen in the north. Fine publicity for Blackpool but financially unsuccessful. (Estimated loss £6,000.)
Death of Jabez S. Doidge (93), famous auctioneer and salesman who established the House of Doidge in West Street in 1880 and

117

later moved to Victoria Street. (He advertised: "DOIDGE'S and Blackpool have been inseparable".)

Waterspout in sea off Blackpool (29th August).

The Big Wheel. Demolition contracts let (12th October). Last trip (20th October). Carriages auctioned (29th October).

"Bickerstaffe", old Blackpool paddle steamer, sold for breaking up (22nd November). 80 m.p.h. gale at Blackpool.

Year of unemployment. Winter Relief Schemes announced (10th December).

1929. H.R.H. the Prince of Wales accepts a book of poems by "Teddy Ashton" (Allen Clarke).

Hippodrome and Princess Cinemas sold.

Big Wheel site. Talks of a £150,000 building scheme, including Olympia.

"The West Lancashire Evening Gazette" appears for the first time (13th May).

Prime Minister Baldwin visits Blackpool (21st May).

Madame Tussaud's Waxworks opened (18th May).

New Tyldesley Senior Boys' School, Condor Grove (28th May).

Prince Paul of Greece visits the Mayor of Blackpool (27th July).

New Municipal Aerodrome, near Stanley Park, opened (22nd August). Licensed for light air traffic.

Sacco, the world famous fasting Dutchman, reaches his 65th day of fast on Blackpool promenade (16th September). He died 3rd November.

Consecration of additional ground at cemetery (27th September).

The 1930s. A period of depressions and great achievements

IN THIS decade of depressions and dole queues, a nation beamed on the romance of Prince George and Princess Marina, cheered the launching of the Queen Mary, mourned the passing of a beloved monarch, lost a good deal of sleep over the abdication of Edward VIII, and laughed uneasily over the antics of Adolf Hitler who, in the middle of it, had swept to supreme power in Germany after the death of President Hindenburg.

As a holiday resort Blackpool was enjoying comfortable, if not prosperous, seasons. Times were not easy, money was scarce; yet in Blackpool hundreds of thousands of pounds were being invested in development schemes to improve the borough and to relieve the desperate plight of the unemployed. New roads, and improvements to those existing, completion of the South Shore promenade, work on the North Shore cliffs, a new Victoria Hospital, and Technical School, a bridge and railway station at Squire's Gate, and the superb new Derby Baths, North Shore, were only a few of the ambitious projects born of the 'thirties. The schemes which did not come to fruition, but which were discussed at length, were gigantic in comparison.

In 1934 experts were called in to advise on the possibilities of building a palatial town hall and civic centre. The first opinion opted in favour of a site which would have necessitated the setting back of Central Station to Chapel Street. Others suggested a North Shore site adjoining the Derby Baths; Stanley Park; the old market site; an area bounded by Abingdon Street, Church Street, Talbot Road and King Street (excluding St. John's Church, the Talbot Hotel and G.P.O.); or the block bounded by Church Street, Regent Road, Albert Road and South King Street. The plans included a magnificent civic building with surrounding gardens and fountains and an underground car park. At the same time Blackpool was toying with the idea of building a £500,000 super sports stadium, the like of which had not been seen in the north, which would set the seal on her fame and which, at the same time, would provide a great deal of employment for a number of years. These were pipe dreams and they came to nothing. In 1935 the Council axed their costly plans in the interests of keeping the rates at 7s. 6d.

At the same time Blackpool was casting acquisitive eyes in the direction of Poulton-le-Fylde. The very mention of amalgamation threw that ancient metropolis of the Fylde into a state of agitation and the proposal was rejected by a large majority at a meeting of the Urban District Council who took prompt steps to treble their size by absorbing parts of Carleton, Hardhorn and Singleton.

On the lighter side, Blackpool saw the comings and goings of the famous and the infamous. The late Earl of Derby was a regular visitor in this decade which made him an Honorary Freeman and gave Blackpool the pleasure of a number of memorable royal visits. Location shots for the film "Sing as we Go" brought Gracie Fields and a midnight premiere to the Winter Gardens. Blackpudlian Anglo-American broadcasting personality Alistair Cooke, was carving a career at the B.B.C. Gertrude Lawrence and Douglas Fairbanks Junior, playing in "Here Lies the Truth" at the Grand Theatre, were mobbed by stage-door crowds and had to be rescued by the police in 1934.

Charles B. Cochrane, Laurel & Hardy, Sir Harry Lauder, Amy Johnson, Jim Mollison, Capt. A. T. Neville Stack, Edgar Wallace, Hannen Swaffer, Kubelik, Sir Malcolm Campbell, Ramsay Macdonald, Stanley Baldwin and Ernest Bevin, all came to Blackpool in the 'thirties, along with millions of British holidaymakers who queued up, paid up and sniggered at some of the lamentable exhibitions staged along the Golden Mile. In July, 1932, following scenes on the promenade, fines were imposed on a "fasting barrel" impresario, but later in the same season the unfrocked Rector of Stiffkey (Rev. H. Davidson), described as a "cocky little man" with a "filthy vocabulary", allowed himself to be exhibited in this manner. After a notorious court case, millions paid good money to gape at this degrading spectacle, the central figure of which, later in his career, appeared at Skegness as Daniel in the Lions' Den. Like Stanley Holloway's "Albert Ramsbottom", he finished up "etten" by his erstwhile companions.

From fasting in barrels, some bright spark thought up the idea of exhibiting starving honeymoon couples, lying in bed and behind glass. Despite vigorous protests by town councillors, irate individuals and the churches, in 1935, a certain peep-show promoter, Luke Gannon, proposed to put on a "Starving and Freezing Brides" show along the Golden Mile. Many of these stunts were arrant frauds, the participants emerging from incarceration during the hours of darkness and treating themselves and their friends to food and drink.

In 1938 Parliament approved the vast scheme to rebuild the Central Station — Central Drive — Golden Mile area under a £2,000,000 re-development scheme (excluding the setting back of the railway station) which would have proved of inestimable benefit to the borough. The project was under contemplation in 1939 but Hitler's evil gang of cut-throats had other plans for the energies and resources of this island. The Odeon Cinema, Pleasure Beach Casino, and Opera House, were already under construction in 1939, but as regards the great re-planning scheme Blackpool had lost the battle against time and her face remained unchanged.

With war on the horizon, the Blackpool Regiment was formed and brought to full strength in less than a fortnight and early in that fateful September of 1939 the nightmarish uncertainty became a reality. We were a nation at war.

NOTABLE EVENTS IN THE 1930s

1930. Lifeboat "Samuel Fletcher" condemned for service, due to badly worn decks. Sold for £70 and later used as a pleasure craft on Stanley Park lake. Her successor installed in the Lifeboat House, Lytham Road (October).
Work on North Shore cliffs and elevator.
Cenotaph floodlit.
Olympia building opened at Winter Gardens.
Squire's Gate railway bridge commenced (October)—£47,000.
Clifton Drive, South Shore (approx. £10,000).
Bispham crossing, new road and railway bridge—£50,000.
New gas main—£5,000.
Proposal to build new hospital and Technical School.
£200,000 expended in schemes to relieve the unemployment situation.
New Refuse Disposal Works.
Revoe, Devonshire Road and Thames Road Schools. (£64,342 including furniture.)

1931. New lifeboat "John Rowson Lingard" launched for inspection (8th January).
Gale (80 m.p.h.) and storm damage at Blackpool (17th January), and again on 12th February. Shop windows blown in.
"Blackpool Times" becomes a weekly paper. First issue 26th March.
Kubelik, world famous violinist, at Opera House (5th April).
Winter Gardens Extensions, Baronial Hall, Spanish Galleon. Tudor Room, Spanish Courtyard, etc. (28th May).
Prime Minister J. Ramsay Macdonald and Miss Ishbel Macdonald open Stanley Park Municipal Aerodrome (2nd June).
Ernest Bevin visits Blackpool (2nd July).
"Fairyland" amusement arcade destroyed by fire (20th July).
Death of "Ohmy", trapeze artist and circus impresario (August).
Squire's Gate railway station opened (14th September).
Old well discovered at Ardwick Hotel, S.S. (21st September).
Amy Johnson, pioneer woman aviator, lectures at Blackpool after her epic flight to Australia (27th September).
Sod cut for Bee Bee biscuit factory (1st October).
Edgar Wallace, thriller writer, adopted as Liberal Parliamentary Candidate.
Hannen Swaffer speaks at Opera House on Spiritualism (22nd November).

1932. Hills' Bazaar (R. H. O. Hills) gutted in greatest fire in Blackpool's history. Damage £150,000 (13th January).
Houses in Cunliffe Road demolished for Park Road to go through (February).
Samuel Rimmer, longest surviving member of the "Robert William", Blackpool's first lifeboat, died aged 90 (14th February).
Coun. Jacob Parkinson resigned the chairmanship of "the intensely disliked municipal aerodrome".
Foam Baths at Cocker Street. Footballer Jimmy Hampson takes the first (6th June).
Air pageant at Stanley Park (26th June).
Graf Zeppelin over Blackpool (3rd July).
Larry Gains, Canadian boxer, Laurel & Hardy, film comedians, and Sir Harry Lauder at Blackpool (July and August).
Capt. A. T. Neville Stack welcomed after his flight in the "Blackpool" from England to India (11th July).
New Norbreck—Anchorsholme Road opened by Mayor.
Fylde Water Board's Hodder Reservoir opened by H.R.H. Prince George (July).
Mr. Stanley Baldwin speaks at Winter Gardens (7th October).
Death of Canon A. W. R. Little, M.A., revered Vicar of Blackpool (15th October).
Sir Malcolm Campbell speaks at Tower Ballroom after achieving land world speed records (12th November).
Blackpool's First Drama Festival, Opera House (14th November).
Demonstration in Talbot Square by Blackpool's unemployed (16th November).

1933. Aviator Jim Mollison visits Blackpool (14th January).
Big freeze-up. Skating on Stanley Park Lake (January).
Bellringers from Holy Trinity, Bolton, rang a peal of 5,000 changes of Little Bob Major at Bispham All Hallows Church (7th January).
New Super Greyhound Track opened at Squire's Gate (7th April).
"The Book of Talbot", award-winning biography of the late Squire of Lytham and Marton, by Mrs. J. T. Clifton, published (11th May).
Lord Derby lays foundation stone of new Whinney Heys (Victoria Hospital) (9th June).
First Quaker Wedding in Blackpool (28th June).
Watch Committee seek legal ruling on the opening of Sunday cinemas (August).
Charles B. Cochrane visits Blackpool (13th September).
Duke of Atholl at Blackpool (20th September).
A year of great unemployment and hardship.

1934. Technical College. Lord Derby lays foundation stone.
Pleasure Beach fire. Chinese theatre and miniature railway destroyed (18th July).
Parts of Hardhorn, Carleton, Marton and Staining amalgamated with Blackpool.
Freedom of Blackpool bestowed on (late) Earl of Derby.

1935. Bond Street, S.S., extended past Pleasure Beach.
Death of Sir Walter de Frece (C.), M.P. for Blackpool 1924-30 (resigned owing to ill-health of his wife, Vesta Tilley). (7th January.)
New Market Building proposed.
£300,000 drainage scheme approved for Anchorsholme and Little Bispham.
New clubhouse, Stanley Park.
Dreadnoughts, last of the old tramcars, withdrawn from service and broken up (February).
Sunday joy-flights abolished at Stanley Park aerodrome (20th February). Ban quickly withdrawn.
Protests against Central Beach (Golden Mile)—"an eyesore ... the happy hunting ground of cheap penny gaffs". Improvement Act contains a clause prohibiting "offensive and objectionable

exhibitions of human persons".
Manchester Hotel—rebuilding plans approved (£30,000).
"Grand National" added to Pleasure Beach.
Road driving tests and 30 m.p.h. limits introduced.
Wurlitzer organ installed at Winter Gardens. First played by Horace Finch (April).
John Roland Robinson, M.A., LL.B. (Barrister-at-law, M.P. for Widnes) adopted as Conservative Parliamentary Candidate for Blackpool and Lytham-St. Annes.
Britain's Cotton Queen, Edna Taylor, of Oldham, elected at Tower Circus finals (29th June).
Sir Alan Cobham's Air Circus. 2 planes collide over town; plane parts fall in Cedar Square and Swainson Street. Pilot and 2 women passengers killed.

1936. Blackpool's Diamond Jubilee Celebrations, commemorating 60 years of incorporation.
Great fire. Municipal Offices and Messrs. Boots, Corporation Street, burned down. Fireman killed (7th October).
Air crash at Stanley Park. Isle of Man plane strikes a hangar in dense mist. Pilot and 1 woman passenger killed.

1937. Freedom of Blackpool conferred on Baron Stamp.
Celebrations on Coronation of King George VI and Queen Elizabeth (8th May).
Last extension of promenade opened by H.R.H. Duke of Kent (late).

1938. Talbot Road 'Bus Station and Car Park. Cost £115,000.
Technical College opened by Earl of Crawford and Balcarres.
North Pier Pavilion burned out for the second time (19th June).
Casino, Pleasure Beach, disaster. Floor under construction collapsed; 4 men killed, 2 injured.
St. John's Market cleared away from Church Street and re-established in King Street.
King George VI and Queen Elizabeth visit the Fylde coast and are given a rousing reception at Lytham-St. Annes and Blackpool. Freedom of Blackpool conferred on Sir Cuthbert Grundy.
Visit of H.R.H. Duke of Kent (late).
Great re-building scheme to remove Gas Works, widen Central Drive to 100 ft., re-build Central Beach and set Central Railway Station back to Chapel Street (an estimated £2,000,000) approved by Parliament.

1939. Poor season at Blackpool due to uneasy international situation.
Pleasure Beach fire. Indian Theatre destroyed (27th September).
Vast building projects in hand, including New Casino, Odeon Cinema, Pavilion on North Pier, Opera House, New Derby Baths, Harrowside Sun Shelter and Lounge; 18 miles of sewers (up to 8 ft. 6 ins. square); widening of Highfield Road to 60 ft. between St. Annes Road and Common Edge Road; St. Walburga's Road widened to 64 ft.; Vicarage Road, Cherry Tree Road and Clifton Road widened to 60 ft.; Talbot Road widened to 65 ft., involving demolition of property between Larkhill Street and Eccleston Road.

The 1940s. Blackpool's war effort and peacetime recovery

UNDER a swift metamorphosis, Blackpool shed her gay, mad, multi-coloured look of peace and almost overnight became a drab reception centre for uniformed men and homesick evacuees. The famous "Lights" had gone out with a vengeance. Over 100,000 evacuees, grey-faced expectant mothers and labelled, bewildered children were accommodated in the Borough, 37,000 of them arriving by the train load within four days. Hotels were taken over for use by thousands of Civil Servants transferred from London. The Vickers-Armstrong factory at Squire's Gate, with 10,000 male and female employees, was operating at full blast making more than 3,400 Wellington bombers (and heaven knows how many signet rings and cigarette lighters!). Hundreds of thousands of servicemen endured weeks of square-bashing along the promenade. The R.A.F. had 45,000 airmen billeted in Blackpool and this figure rose to 70,000 after Dunkirk. But this was a town of many nations, Polish, Dutch, French, Norwegian and American uniforms mingling with our own khaki, navy and air-force blue.

Blackpool emerged unscathed from the ravages of warfare apart from one bomb which fell on Seed Street and North Station, killing 8 and injuring 14. But during the black-out her promenade provided a grandstand view of the vicious Liverpool blitz, with bomb flashes and dockland fires lighting the sky, and an incessant ack-ack accompaniment drifting over the dark waters.

Blackpool entered into the war effort with all her usual gusto, providing hospitality and canteen facilities for the forces, extending a warm welcome to her war-time guests despite shortages of food, fuel, and all the domestic items which were difficult, and often impossible, to replace. Even through the darkest days of the war the cinemas opened their doors to grateful servicemen and in every church the warm hand of friendship was extended to lonely exiles. Towards the end of the war the scene was almost dominated by "The Yanks", breezy American servicemen with a zest for enjoyment, plenty of money, and a great attraction for the local girls, many of whom later went to the States as G.I. brides.

In 1945 the Labour Party held their conference here, and after taking a decision not to support a Coalition Government were shortly afterwards swept into office by a war-weary electorate. Despite the temporary eclipse of the Conservative Party, in 1946 (at the time of the Nuremberg Tribunal when the principal Nazi war criminals were near sentence of death) the Freedom of Blackpool was bestowed on (Sir) Winston Churchill. On 4th October, huge crowds turned out to pay homage to this great statesman whose superb confidence had cheered and heartened a nation, whose unerring leadership had steered our island through the darkest years of war to Victory in Europe. On the route from Lytham, where he was staying, to Blackpool, cries of "Good old Winnie", "Cheerio, Winnie" rang out from grateful people of all parties. He was about to become the 21st, and perhaps the greatest, Freeman of Blackpool.

The winter of 1947 still sticks out in the memory like a sore thumb. There were still plenty of uniforms about, and shivering ex-servicemen reached once more for their discarded great-coats in 24 degrees of frost. If the housing shortage was painfully acute, the fuel cuts imposed by the Labour Government were almost beyond enduring. The war was receding slowly into the background, but its irksome accompaniment, the black-out, was here once more. Electricity was cut off from 9 a.m. until Noon, and in the afternoon from 2 p.m. to 4 p.m. Shops and offices were lit by candles. Shivering clerks and shop-hands worked in their out-door clothes. Skaters worked up a healthy colour—on the ice of Stanley Park lake. The Fylde countryside looked beautiful under a five-inch blanket of snow but 3,000 workers at the Squire's Gate factory had other weighty matters on their minds. Through the fuel crisis, and like the rest of north-western industry, they were grinding to a halt. It was a gloomy time, that winter of 1947. Crime was on the increase. Only a few fortunate women shoppers managed to bag a pair of the precious nylon stockings which trickled into local shops. Fed up with it all, a Blackpudlian party, 24 strong, set off in ex-army trucks in search of a new life in sunny South Africa. They were given a civic send-off at the Town Hall, and pulled out of Blackpool in a flurry of snow.

Despite all, however, Blackpool was steadily gearing up to her old tempo. There was great excitement when the hero of Alamein, Field Marshal Viscount Montgomery, became an Honorary Freeman of the Borough in 1948. The Royal Lancashire Show came here in 1949 and in the autumn of that year the Illuminations were re-introduced on a more lavish scale than ever before. They have gone on ever since, extending the summer season by several weeks, costing something like £400,000 in apparatus, and drawing 8 million visitors every year from the British Isles and overseas.

NOTABLE EVENTS IN THE 1940s

1940. Great Snow-up. Rail and road transport at a standstill, schools closed, funerals held up. Food and fuel supplies halted. Chaos for days (27th January).
Purchase Tax introduced (23rd April). Civilians urged to carry gas masks.
Blackpool's Citizens' Army begins recruiting (20th June).
Seed Street houses demolished by Nazi bombs (12th September). 10 high explosive bombs and 30 incendiaries fall on St. Annes (October).
Double-deck Standard Tram No. 50, en route to Fleetwood, blown over opposite the Grill Bar entrance of Hotel Metropole, just beyond the Princess Cinema, by a gale-force gust of wind. Few passengers aboard at the time, injuries negligible. Badly damaged tram body later scrapped. Line cleared within 2 hours.

1941. Eggs disappear from the shops.
Margarine coupons used for the purchase of clothing—66 allowed for the year. Sugar drastically cut. Visitors bring their own (June).
Blackpool Football team wins the North War League.
Air collision over Blackpool. Two R.A.F. planes involved. One plane crashes on entrance hall of Central Station. 18 killed, 35 injured. Householders in Reads Avenue narrowly escape when an engine falls through a house.

1942. Blackpool Regiment fight the Japanese. Singapore falls (16th February); local families wait anxiously for news.
Donkeys' Charter bans fat persons and adults and ensures proper rest periods.
Coach tours and excursions suspended.

1943. Blackpool Home Guard carry out an anti-invasion exercise on beach (16th May).
"Wings for Victory Week" raises £1,800,000.
3,000 boarding house beds requisitioned by Government at short notice. Visitors ejected. Landladies protest.
Evacuated Civil Servants stage a sit-down strike on tram lines to draw attention to inadequate transport services. The North-Western Regional Traffic Commissioner investigates and authorises more trams.

1944. Amusement Arcade (corner of Temple Street and Church Street) demolished by fire.
Blackpool's adopted cruiser "Penelope" lost at sea.
445 Blackpool men listed as prisoners of war in the Far East.
"Salute the Soldier" Weeks aims for £2,000,000.
Ceiling falls in at Salvation Army Club (over Yates' Wine Lodge); 100 servicemen have a narrow escape.

1945. Labour Party Conference at Blackpool. The Socialists take the vital decision not to support a Coalition Government. Shortly afterwards electorate sweep them into power.
V.E. Day (8th May). Flags, bunting and rosettes everywhere.
Thanksgiving Services in Churches. Evacuees begin the trek home.
Great potato shortage. 4,000 wait for Council houses. Food and coal are scarce and some Blackpool pubs close up when beer supplies run out.
Blackpool is made into 2 Parliamentary Divisions.
Death of Bert Feldman, impresario and music publisher, who ran the "White Blackbirds" Company on Central Pier and song-parlours and other attractions in the town. In 1928 he purchased Bannister's Bazaar (now site of C. & A. Modes) for something like £70,000 and turned it into two theatres, the first floor Feldman's Playhouse devoted to repertory by the Fred D'Albert Players. Converted to one theatre in 1935, modernised in 1938 and bought after Bert Feldman's death by James Brennan for £71,800. (Later re-named the Queen's.)

1946. Victory in the Far East.
(Sir) Winston Churchill becomes the 21st Freeman of the Borough of Blackpool and receives a tumultuous welcome.
First nylon stockings appear in local shops.

1947. Another great freeze up. Coldest winter for years. Coal short-ages, electricity turned off for 5 hours per day to save fuel. 3,000 Squire's Gate factory workers given notice. Industry rumbles to a halt in the North-West.

1948. Freedom of Blackpool conferred on Field Marshal Viscount Montgomery of Alamein.
Closure of Squire's Gate Factory renders thousands jobless.
House waiting list swells to 8,770.
Blackpool beaten 4-2 by Manchester United in Cup Final.

1949. THE LIGHTS GO ON AGAIN. Blackpool's famous Autumn Illuminations are resumed on a larger scale than ever before. Millions come by road and rail for this great post-war spectacle.
Royal Lancashire Show comes to Blackpool.
Pleasure Beach and Icedrome extensively damaged by fire (13th July).
Mereside estate, first houses occupied.

"Up the Pool!"—Seaside Soccer

FOOTBALL has played a prominent part in Blackpool's world of sport since before the borough received its charter of incor-poration. The old South Shore Club was in existence before 1876 and this club eventually amalgamated with the old Blackpool St. John's whose ground was at Raikes Hill. In the early years of this century the Blackpool Club was centred at Bloomfield Road and it was in 1900 that the team was admitted into the Second Division of the League. The colours originally were claret shirts and light blue knickers, and red shirts and white knickers between 1905 and the First World War. Several colours were introduced in the next year or two but in the first half of the 'twenties the team wore black and white, and in the second half, tangerine and black. About 1929 the present famous tangerine and white were adopted, and we hope they will so continue for all time.

The Club has not been without its ups and downs and for many years recorded deficits with almost monotonous regularity. In the season 1924-5 the Club faced a financial crisis which, of a sudden, rallied the support of the town, brought the Football Supporters' Club into existence, and ensured the necessary £3,000 to put the Club's affairs into good order. Sir A. Lindsay Parkinson then relinquished the chairmanship which was taken over by Alderman (Sir) John Bickerstaffe who had been the Club's first President. In 1927-8 the team were struggling to retain their position. £12,000 was spent on new players and during the following year the Club's standard of play had so greatly improved that promotion to the First Division was only missed by a few points. From that time serious efforts were made to secure promotion, and attention was paid to improvement of the grounds. In 1929-30 Blackpool and Chelsea were promoted to the First Division of the League. The Mayor of Blackpool made a public appeal for £20,000 to be spent on ground improvements but only a quarter of this amount trickled in. Nevertheless extra accommodation was provided, making room for 30,000 spectators at Bloomfield Road. A loudspeaker system was also installed during that season.

Far be it from me to enter into any arguments about who were the greatest players ever seen at Bloomfield Road, but I would predict that, so long as football is discussed and wrangled over at Blackpool, they will be harking back to those scintillating years of the late 'forties and early 'fifties. A brilliant team, combining the sturdy dependability of Harry Johnston, the lightning speed and superb headwork of that great favourite, "Morty" (Stan. Mortensen), and the internationally acclaimed wizardry of the one and only Stanley Matthews, who was knighted in 1965, infused Saturday afternoons with an electrifying magic which at times, with the immense roars of acclaim, almost lifted the roofs from the stands. This was the team which battled at Wembley and successfully brought home The Cup in 1953.

The season 1960-1 saw the other side of the coin. Blackpool F.C. slid into the doldrums, barely escaped relegation to the Second Division and actually achieved that somewhat dubious distinction in 1967. The golden era, the great days appeared to be over (temporarily, we hope) and the glamour of Saturday afternoon Soccer was blighted by bad behaviour on pitch and terrace alike. The day of the "Football Hooligans" had arrived. harassed Police strove manfully to cope with the distasteful phenomenon and attendances dropped. Gangs of youths from home and away came before the courts charged with breaching the peace, causing damage, intimidation and inflicting bodily harm. Only the toilet roll manufacturers did well out of this black period of Soccer history as some mindless spectator started a mania for unfurling these missiles, like streamers, on Saturday afternoons. But there are signs in 1975 that the Police and the public have had enough and hopes that, with counter measures and stricter supervision, discipline will return and lapsed supporters will come back to Bloomfield Road and send up the famous cry: "Up the Pool!"

NOTABLE EVENTS OF THE 1950s

1950. "The Blackpool rock racket"—"spivs" caught selling rock without sweet coupons.
Severe gales damage second post-war Lights.

1951. Empty Squire's Gate Factory taken by Hawker Aircraft for the building of Hunter jets.
King George VI and Queen Elizabeth tour the Fylde.
Committee appointed to vet "dirty" postcards flooding the stalls.
Grange Park Extension—100 acres of Poulton land earmarked for Corporation housing.
Blackpool F.C. in the Cup Final. Beaten 2-0 by Newcastle.

1952. Squire's Gate jets necessitate an extension to the runway.
Plans for a ring road (Queensway) approved.
Delivery of the first "Coronation" trams.
Feldman's Theatre sold (re-named Queen's).

1953. Sound barrier broken off the coast by Neville Duke flying a Hawker Hunter jet.
Royal Agricultural Show at Blackpool.
Blackpool murder case. Killing by rat poison. Mrs. Louisa Merrifield executed.

1954. H.R.H. Princess Margaret visits Hawker Aircraft Factory. Arnold Girls' School opened by H.R.H. The Princess Royal. High tides create a full scale emergency at Rossall. Sea wall damaged.

1955. A year dominated by the Royal Variety Show attended by H.M. Queen Elizabeth II and H.R.H. Prince Philip, Duke of Edinburgh. Royal box specially built at the Opera House for the glittering occasion.
Glamorous veteran film star Marlene Dietrich appears at the Opera House.
Illuminations switched on by Jacob Malik, Russian Ambassador.

1956. Gifts Fair held for the first time in Blackpool.
Disastrous fire (13th/14th December) caused by a cigarette end left in a chair results in £500,000's worth of damage to the Tower Ballroom. Blaze described as "a scene out of hell" fought by 50 firemen and 100 Tower Company staff; brought under control in 6 hours.

1957. British Home Stores building completed and opened.
Plans for a £7m. redevelopment scheme for Central Station and Golden Mile area.
Squire's Gate Factory closed.

1958. Trailer-trams introduced (9th April). First double-deck trams run to Fleetwood (Easter).
Gala opening (23rd May) of restored Tower Ballroom, Lounge and Bars, 18 months after the fire.

Chapel Street sub-way opened.

1959. County and Lane End Hotel (requisitioned for war-time Civil Service offices) purchased by Tower Company for £178,000.
Illuminations switched on by Jayne Mansfield, American film star and sex symbol.

The changing face of Blackpool
The 1960s and 1970s

SINCE the first edition of this book appeared in 1961 there have been many and drastic changes in Blackpool. A 19th century pioneer or a Victorian visitor returning to-day would stand aghast at the rushing traffic, super-stores, a pedestrian precinct behind the Tower, miles of double yellow lines, a foot-walk over the Prom and the obliteration of the old Central Station, and the Golden Mile area as they once knew it; and would likely sigh nostalgically for the homely contours, the sights, smells and unsophisticated amusements of yesteryear.

The winds of change which began to blow about 1960 when the Zoo scheme was first talked of had risen to gale force ten years later. The result is a new-look Blackpool swept clean of much of its past and bearing little evidence of its great and glorious history; and resembling, in many aspects, any crowded bustling highly-commercialised concrete and glass city which just happens, accidentally, to have sprung up beside the sea. Nevertheless, the resort is secure in the large number of "loyal" visitors who come back year after year and for whom Blackpool and holidays have been synonymous for a lifetime. This gives grounds for confidence, but not for complacency, about the town's future which will continue to depend on the excellence of its accommodations and, above all, on the quality of its entertainments and the provision of exciting things to do for Mr. Average and his family.

In 1960, the starter-year for major developments, there were hopes that Blackpool might be fortunate enough to attract the proposed new Lancashire university. Several authorities put out feelers but, in the end, Lancaster secured the prize and a site was selected at Bailrigg. That was in 1961 in which year Blackpool purchased Squire's Gate Airport for £193,000 and opened the new Blackpool Grammar School at Highfurlong. The Tower Company sold The Palace and the old County and Lane End Hotel to Lewis's for a site for their new emporium; and the first traffic wardens stalked the streets, eyes cocked, notebooks at the ready.

In 1962 the Layton skyline was altered dramatically by blocks of high-rise flats built after the clearance of old run-down property in the Queenstown area. In that year the A.B.C. Theatre replaced the Hippodrome and the corner of Abingdon Street and Birley Street was cleared; interested crowds watched excavations into the Ice-Age boulder clay of Blackpool prior to the building of Timothy White's (now Boots store). H.R.H. Princess Alexandra came to Blackpool to open a Home for the Blind.

1963 saw the opening of the A.B.C. Theatre, the acquisition of North Pier by Fortes, the commencement of the Mecca Locarno building and proposals to re-develop the Talbot Hotel area. There were two royal visits—Prince Philip attended a golf tournament at North Shore and the Princess Royal opened the Gifts Fair.

Messrs. Lewis's store opened and Central Station closed in 1964—a year of fires, at the Clifton Hotel and the Tivoli Cinema, and at South Pier where the Theatre was destroyed. Lawrence Wright, famous song writer and music publisher known variously as Horatio Nicholls, "Mr. Music" and the "Father of Tin Pan Alley", died in May 1964 at the age of 76 leaving £366,000. One of my treasures is his album "Songs the World Sings" which this giant of show business, stricken in his last years, presented to me during a visit to his home in Carlin Gate. He even managed, with feeble hand and the utmost difficulty, to inscribe the message: "Wishing you success with your wonderful creation. Your book, everyone will love. Sincerely, Lawrence Wright". The memory of our meeting floods back, bringing the wheel full circle, for the first song of which I was ever conscious as an infant was "Wyoming Lullaby" published by Lawrence Wright whose song-plugging parlours in later years I well remember.

Another impresario died in 1964, rags-to-riches bachelor James Brennan who started his career as a scrap merchant behind a handcart in Barrow-in-Furness, bought the Tivoli Theatre there and finished up a half-millionaire owning a chain of cinemas and theatres. He bought Feldman's Theatre, turned it into the Queen's and promoted great summer shows with outstanding talent. George Formby, Paul Robeson, John McCormick, Dora Bryan, Joseph Locke, Charlie Drake, Harry Secombe, Hylda Baker, Jack Douglas, Donald Peers, Ted and Barbara Andrews, with Julie, and many other remembered and half-forgotten stars worked this theatre at one time or another. After 1961 Bingo reigned supreme at the Queen's and at the end of 1972 the demolition men were preparing to bring the house down, for the last time.

In 1965 it became difficult to park in a Blackpool newly decorated with double yellow lines; and Stanley Matthews, the legendary Soccer star, received a knighthood. The remedial section at Derby Baths was opened; and in the following year 1966 Blackpool paid £950,000 for the 23 acre site of Central Station and announced plans to construct new Law Courts at a cost of £1,325,000. A plan for comprehensive education was also adopted.

In 1967 Blackpool was "lit up" in a spectacular way by a fire which destroyed the premises of R. H. O. Hills (second time in 35 years). E.M.I. acquired the Tower Company and Fortes took over the South Pier. Blackpool F.C. was relegated to the Second Division but £½m. extensions at Victoria Hospital were completed and opened by Lord Derby. 1968, a sad year for steam-locomotive fans, saw the last of the steam trains in the Fylde. The passenger line to Fleetwood was closed; the new R. H. O. Hills store, rushed up with sometimes round-the-clock urgency, opened for business. Central Pier celebrated its centenary with a new theatre and show-bar; and plans for the Zoo were approved and put into operation in the following year.

By that time, 1970, it was appropriate to enquire: "Have you been converted?" (to North Sea Gas, but naturally!) and to bid an emotional farewell to Reginald Dixon, M.B.E., the organ maestro, on his retirement after presiding at the Tower Ballroom Wurlitzer for 40 years. His final performance at Easter 1970, backed by the B.B.C. Northern Dance Orchestra and attended by 3,000 admirers, was a great night of music, brilliantly staged and rapturously received. A silver replica of the Wurlitzer was presented by the B.B.C. to the King of the Console whose broadcasts over the years, and his signature tune "I do like to be beside the Seaside" had endeared him to countless listening millions. In the same year H.R.H. Princess Margaret attended a charity ball in aid of Dr. Barnardo's; Blackpool F.C. was promoted (briefly, as it transpired) to the First Division; and a celebrated old pub, The Victoria on the Prom, was offered for sale with vacant possession for £200,000.

The year 1971 stands out like a painfully sore thumb. On the happier side, the Zoo project was well in hand; Blackpool's team won the Euro-televised "It's a Knock-Out" competition; the Victoria Hotel underwent a face-lift and emerged as Ripley's "Odditorium"; the Royal Lancashire Show was held here, but for the last time before transferring to Wrea Green; sea defences were constructed at South Shore at a cost of £160,000; and H.R.H. Princess Anne came to the Gifts Fair. On a darker note, Blackpool F.C. was relegated once more to the Second Division but, blackest event of all, Superintendent Gerald Richardson, a popular police officer in his late thirties and described as "the best copper a town ever had", was shot dead in a back entry off Sherbourne Road after an armed raid at Prestons, the jewellers in the Strand, on the morning of Monday, 23rd August, 1971. After a police chase through the streets of North Shore, the escape vehicle was rammed by two police cars but the villains stole a butcher's van in Cheltenham Road, crashed into a garden wall in Carshalton Road and ran up a back street firing at their pursuers. "Gerry" Richardson was shot in the chest below the heart and died in Victoria Hospital an hour later. Two other police officers, P.C. Carl Walker (37) and P.C. Ian Hampson (27) were shot, but recovered, and Sub-Officer Ronald Gale, a Blackpool fireman who tackled the gunmen in the Strand was coshed over the head with a heavy bar. The tragedy shook the nation and Blackpool was plunged into mourning. Thousands lined the funeral route to St. John's Church on 26th August, 1971, in tribute to a gallant and greatly admired public servant. Four of the gang, all London men, were brought before Blackpool Magistrates on 27th August but the murderer Frederick Joseph Sewell (38), a motor trader, had slipped through the police cordons and made off. He was eventually arrested in London, charged and convicted after a massive nationwide search led by Chief Superintendent Joe Mounsey, head of Lancashire C.I.D. The George Cross was awarded posthumously to Supt. Richardson. Sgt. C. Walker also received the George Cross; Sgt. I. Hampson and three other officers were awarded the George Medal and two further officers received the B.E.M. At the close of that year of sorrowful memory, four of the oldest cottages in South Shore, a row of small cobblestone buildings in Britannia Place, were demolished (site now used as a car park) in December 1971.

The first phase of the Zoo opened in 1972 and a one-and-a-half acre Model Village behind Stanley Park, but the year brought further tragedy to Blackpool. Three child patients at Victoria Hospital were brutally murdered, supposedly by an intruder, though later it was ascertained by a doctor on the staff who was charged but found unfit to plead. A party of nine German businessmen were killed when their light plane took off from Squire's Gate Airport and crashed into the holiday camp nearby. The New Inn and Central Hotel, which stood on the corner of the promenade near Central Station and once featured in thousands of holiday photographs, was demolished in the spring of 1973. On its forecourt once stood a cannon salvaged from a wrecked vessel, beside which little boys in sailor suits were told to "smile for the dicky-bird!" One of the oldest dwellings in Little Marton (twin and near neighbour of the former Old Homestead Preaching House) came under the auctioneer's hammer as a prelude to demolition after the death of Miss Agnes Wade who had been born there more than 80 years earlier; work was proceeding on the new Police Headquarters and, towards the end of the year, the demolition men were busy knocking down Central Methodist Church, the Queen's Theatre, the Palatine Hotel, that "grand old lady of the Prom", and Cocker Street Baths. In October 1973 the death was announced of Sir Alan Cobham, pioneer of the touring "Flying Circus" which was a feature of the 1930s. (At one of these events, two Blackpool sisters in their thirties, Misses Lilian and Doris Barnes of Gloucester Avenue, were killed on 7th September, 1935, when an Avro biplane, in which they were passengers, collided in mid-air with a Wessex airliner and crashed after striking property in Swainson Street.)

Throughout 1974 and 1975 rebuilding has proceeded on so many familiar sites that a visitor returning after an absence of only two or three years will scarcely recognise the old Blackpool. The Golden Mile, that tatty, tasteless and totally fascinating stretch of stalls, booths, dilapidated property, barkers, blaring music, garish signs, gawping crowds and the conglomerate smell of onions, fish and chips, toffee apples, candy floss and holiday-making humanity has almost vanished out of existence. The piers look strangely modern, there are discos everywhere; railway maniacs now have their own personal Mecca on Platform 3 at South Station and, after an incredibly long run, Queen Bingo is still a universal favourite. Even as the text for this revised edition goes off to the printers, the dear old "Dreadnought" tram is back on Blackpool Prom, not running, but collecting funds for her own restoration in preparation for a great event which lies a few months ahead, the centenary of 1976. Blackpool Borough, with a wealth of history and achievement behind her, will be a hundred years old; irrepressible and forward-looking as ever. I present my compliments to the brashest, breeziest, brightest centenarian in the business!

Population and housing

1770. Perhaps 30 primitive hovels along the Blackpool front.

1788. "About 50 houses", says William Hutton, who was there. "About 35", says Porter, who was not.

1800. Again Porter estimates "about 30", but possibly the oldest of the clay huts had been engulfed or abandoned by this time and were therefore excluded.

Census of inhabitants in Layton-cum-Warbreck of which Blackpool was at first a small part.

1801— 473	1851— 2,564
1811— 580	1861— 3,907
1821— 749	1871— 7,092
1831— 943	1881—12,987
1841—1,968	1891—21,970

Blackpool Census

1881— 14,229	
1891— 23,846	
1901— 47,348	
1911— 58,371	
1921— 73,800	
1931—101,553	
1951—147,184	
Mid 1959—143,600	(Registrar General's estimate.)
1961—152,133	(Provisional estimate including all visitors and Conference delegates in Blackpool at the time of the Census.)
1971—150,000	

1876—Gross Rateable Value				£76,838.
1896—	„	„	„	£260,252.
1916—	„	„	„	£592,637.
1936—	„	„	„	£1,574,063.
1961—	„	„	„	Exceeds £3,000,000.
1971—	„	„	„	£17,621,238.

1st April, 1960—Total number of hereditaments in Blackpool Borough—57,898.

Area of Blackpool Borough—8,650 acres.

Foreshore and tidal water—2,068 acres.

Municipal matters

Layton-with-Warbreck became a Local Government District by order of the Local Government Board on 23rd October, 1851. A Local Board of Health was elected. The name of that authority was altered to the Blackpool Local Board of Health in 1868. By an Order in Council it became the Burial Board (under the Burial Act, 1857) on 16th May, 1871. A Charter of Incorporation was granted by Queen Victoria on 21st January, 1876. (Population then approximately 10,000.) In 1879 part of Marton and part of Bispham-with-Norbreck were included in the borough. In 1917-18 the boundaries were again extended to include the urban district of Bispham-with-Norbreck and part of Carleton. In 1934, Marton, Carleton and part of Hardhorn-with-Newton were absorbed into the borough.

Members of the Local Board originally 9, later increased to 18. Council Members at date of incorporation 24; Seats increased from 56 to 68 in 1961.

Blackpool became a County Borough on 1st October, 1904.

The Corporation's Undertakings

Gas, Electricity, Markets, Tramways and Buses, Public Baths, Parks, Cemetery, Public Abattoirs, Public Libraries and Housing Schemes.

Gas

First supplied by private enterprise in 1851. After an unsuccessful start the works were taken over by the Local Board in 1862, leased for 7 years, then re-possessed by the Local Board whose successors administered the undertaking from 1869 until the nationalisation of the industry.

Transport

In October, 1885, the first electric tramcars, operated by an underground conduit system, were put into service by the Blackpool Electric Tramway Co. Ltd. There were 10 cars, each capable of carrying 34 to 52 passengers. Stoppages through blown sand and sea water were frequent and prolonged but as yet no overhead system of traction had been invented in this country. The Company's lease expired in 1892 and the service was then taken over by the Corporation. An overhead traction system was installed in 1898 and in 1919 the Corporation bought out the Blackpool and Fleetwood Tramroad Company's undertaking, taking over on January 1st, 1920.

The trial run of the first Marton tram took place on 20th May, 1901. In 1932 the Marton service operated via Talbot Square, Central Station, Central Drive, Waterloo Road and Whitegate Drive. At midnight on Sunday, 28th October, 1962, in gale force winds, the 61-year-old tram route finally closed down. Two illuminated trams, Nos. 158 and 159 loaded with 100 tram-lovers and well-wishers including Mayor J. S. Richardson, J.P., the Mayoress and Transport Officials, departed from Talbot Square at 11-30 p.m., and proceeded nostalgically to the Whitegate Drive Depot followed by a cavalcade of cars with horns blaring. More than 300 tram-fans watched the doors close on the two double-deckers. It was the end of an era and the buses took over.

The Layton route, opened on 13th June, 1902, was converted to buses in October, 1936, as was the Central Drive route. The Lytham Road track, laid in 1897, was closed, along with Station Road and Squire's Gate Lane, in October, 1961; and the Dickson Road track from the Gyn. to North Station and Bispham Depot, ceased to function in October, 1963.

Trailer-towing tramcars were introduced at Blackpool in 1958. Vintage Blackpool trams, including the "Dreadnought" (which has been transported back in July, 1975, in preparation for the Centenary Celebrations in 1976) can normally be seen at the Crich Tramway Museum, near Matlock, Derbyshire.

Electricity

The Corporation obtained powers to run electric tramways along the promenade in 1884. An Electric Lighting Order was obtained in 1890, and on 13th October, 1893, the newly erected electricity works were opened by Lord Kelvin, a leading scientist of his day. The undertaking which began business with 30 consumers is now nationalised under the auspices of the North Western Electricity Board.

Bispham-with-Norbreck

The mother of Blackpool

TELLING the story of Blackpool before mentioning Bispham is historically the same as putting the cart before the horse. Blackpool is only mentioned by implication ("le pull") in the 15th century and specifically recorded ("blackpoole") in 1602. Bispham, on the other hand, was one of the later Anglian settlements which sprang up between A.D. 700-800. There are two theories as to the origin of the name. "Biscop" and "ham", meaning the settlement or village belonging to a family called Biscop, and "Bishop's ham", meaning the homestead of the Bishop. The latter is more likely to be correct. Bishops of the Celtic church, mobile and vested with the power of ordination, were active amongst their Fylde followers in the centuries following the Roman occupation. It was from Celtic, that is Welsh and Irish, rather than from Roman sources, that Christianity was established in these parts before the Norman Conquest. About the year A.D. 900 boatloads of Norsemen invaded, if one can thus describe a fairly peaceful activity, these western shores and proceeded to set up their communities alongside the Anglian settlements. (Examples: Bispham-with-Norbreck and Layton-with-Warbreck.) The Fylde is an outstanding example of the co-existence of two widely differing peoples who, once the preliminary clashes and skirmishes had died down, would each tend to be influenced and, to some extent, absorbed by the other.

In Domesday Survey, compiled between A.D. 1080-6, "Biscopham" is listed as having 8 carucates of land (a carucate being approximately 120 acres), a greater acreage than any other settlement in the Hundred of Amounderness, while to "Latun" were assigned 6 carucates and to "Lidun" (Lytham) only 2. No mention is made of a place of worship but there is reason to believe that a church or chapel annexed to Poulton was erected in Bispham in the 11th century. There may well have been a Celtic Mission in existence before this time since the church at Poulton was dedicated to the Saxon St. Chad.

A detailed history of Bispham would fill a volume and for specific information the reader might like to consult "The History of Bispham" by Henry Fishwick (Chetham Society publication, 1887. Volume 10 New Series). Briefly, the lands were given by Adam de Biscopham to the Benedictine Abbot and Monastery of St. Peter at Shrewsbury. In the 12th century the Cistercian

Monastery of Dieulacres near Leek in Staffordshire held considerable interests in Bispham and Poulton, and in the 13th century the Abbot of Shrewsbury re-leased Norbrec and Little Biscopham with the tithes of Laton to the Abbot of Dieulacres. At the beginning of the 14th century "a knight's fee in Laton, Warbreke and Great Bispham" was held by William le Botiller whose son, also named William, secured the manors to himself and his wife for life, and thereafter to his son and daughter-in-law, Richard le Botiller and Joan. Until the time of Henry VIII the Butler family continued to hold Bispham, Norbreck and Layton. The estates, along with Marton and others, then passed into the hands of the Fleetwoods who subsequently disposed of their interests to the Cliftons of Lytham.

The vanishing village of Bispham

VERY LITTLE remains of the old world village of Bispham where once charming 17th century cottages were set close to the roadside, their walls as white as fresh snow and their tiny windows shadowed by the overhanging thatch. Picture postcards sent many a Victorian visitor off in search of "the pretty village" not far from Blackpool. The traditionalists revelled in this unspoiled corner of England, where life went on at a steady, unhurried gait, prolonging the atmosphere of an earlier century, long past its time.

Bispham, however, was absorbed by her daughter town in 1917. Her tempo in some measure has been accelerated by her lively offspring and nowadays sites are reckoned in terms of hard cash. The last of the cottages has come down and a little world of long traditions has crumbled out of existence. For this

Bethel Chapel, Bispham.

135

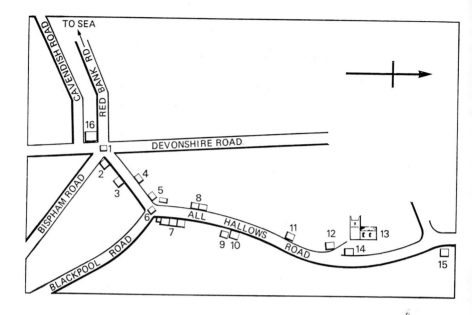

reason it might be interesting to reverse the process by taking an imaginary walk along the route indicated on the map.

(1) BETHEL CHAPEL. Porter (1876) records: "There is a small Nonconformist place of worship in the village, surrounded by a wall, being partially covered with ivy and overshadowed by trees". This was the Bethel Chapel, built in 1834, which stood at a point now covered by traffic islands at the cross roads. The Congregationalists moved out about 1912 when their new church was built in Cavendish Road and the old chapel was demolished around 1914.

(2) An old cobble farm building, no longer in existence.

(3) An old cottage, painted red, with a traditional cobble-stone wall at the rear. (Site now occupied by the Police Station.)

(4) An old cottage, partly built of cobbles, having a tiled roof in place of the earlier thatch. Beside the inglenook chimney was a curious cavity which puzzled antiquarians.

(5) IVY COTTAGE, demolished about 1958. This was Bispham's best known and best loved domestic building and thousands of visitors will recall visiting the Ivy Cottage Tearooms. It was probably in existence long before the Tinckler family placed their initials, E.T.: E.T.: R.T., and the date 1686 on a panel which is now preserved in the Grundy House Museum, and was one of the typical three bay cruck houses which abounded in the Fylde. Those which remain are mostly condemned and will not much longer survive. There were evidences of considerable alterations having been made in the 19th century, but the old fire hood remained, dominating the house. The construction methods employed in the building of Ivy Cottage are made very clear in Mr. R. C. Watson's excellent illustration.

(5) ONE ASH COTTAGE stood on a site near island (6) on the map. This lovely home was destroyed many years ago when an oil lamp was accidentally knocked over and the thatch went up in flames. The last tenant was a photographer, Miss Caton.

136

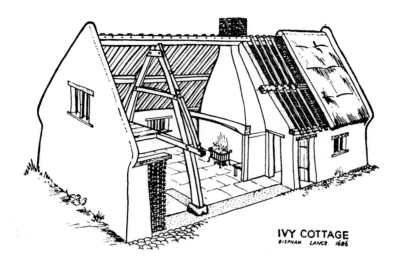

IVY COTTAGE
BISPHAM LANCS. 1686

Ivy Cottage, Bispham. Above:
Section sketch by R. C. Watson.
Right: Date panel bearing the initials
of the Tinkler family (now at
Grundy House Museum).

(6) BISPHAM OLD POST OFFICE.—This was a brick building of
Victorian construction which stood in the centre of the village on the
site of island (6). There were two little cottages adjoining. When the Post
Office was demolished a number of years ago the site was cleared and
eventually the island was laid out.

(7) ROW OF THREE COTTAGES demolished in June, 1961. Originally
built of cobbles and clay, these once presented a picture of dazzling
whiteness until, in fairly recent years, their frontages were faced with
cement. They stood lower than the road level and were often flooded. In
the rainy season the tenants blocked doors and windows with clay to
keep out the water. Rumour hints that all three cottages were once
joined together into a public house. This, however, is not only uncon-
firmed but strongly denied by some of the older inhabitants. Nevertheless,
between two of the cottages there was at least one sketchily sealed com-

Top: One Ash Cottage, Bispham. Bottom: Smithy and wheelwright's (left) and Smithy Cottage, Bispham.

municating door and the rear of the buildings was a crazy patchwork of bricked up windows and doors, suggesting a number of alterations at different periods. There is reason to suspect that there were fire hoods in the principal groundfloor rooms where traces of the old speeres remained.

(?) MOUNTING STEPS.—These are still a great talking point in the village. No two people can agree where they stood, but at least one resident stoutly maintains that they were to be seen outside the above-mentioned three cottages. Others retort "Rubbish" (or words to that effect) and suggest that the steps were near the site of the Old England.

(7) THE BRIG. Earlier in the century this name was applied to a cobble wall, running at the end of the three cottages, where the local parliament used to sit of an evening debating the affairs of the day. On a mid-19th century tithe map a bridge was marked at approximately the same spot and obviously a water course passed the end of the cottages at this point. At times such was the flow that one resident remembers people rowing past the cottages in boats and children being ferried part-way to the Sunday School by the same means. There is no sign of any waterway now, which suggests that the streamlet was some time culverted, though the name of "The Brig" is persistently applied to that locality to this day.

(8) TWO COBBLE AND THATCH COTTAGES which disappeared years ago, without trace. A shop now stands on the site.

(9) SMITHY COTTAGE. I was very familiar with this ancient three-bay cobble and clay cottage and knew it when the interior was beautifully preserved and was a dressmaker's workroom. There was a parlour at one end and from the central portion, "The Housepart", a miniature flight of steps led to a quaintly shaped bedroom over the small kitchen and buttery and immediately under the roof. The thatch had long before been covered with corrugated iron; and it was very easy to imagine the cosiness (and some of the inconveniences) of living in this doll-sized but delightfully attractive little home.

(10) THE SMITHY. This adjoined the cottage, the cobbled gable end being clearly visible from the interior of the smithy which, latterly, was used as an armature winder's shop. Once there was the clatter of horses about the place and the din of the sweating blacksmith busy about his trade. The wheelwright pared his lumps of wood, heated his iron hoops, burned them into the wooden rims and tossed the charring smoking wheels down the well to sizzle and contract. There was a vigour and dexterity about these old brother crafts which fell into a decline with the coming of the new motor car. The smithy was recently demolished.

(11) THE RED LION.—The earlier hostelry was referred to colloquially as "The Red Cat". In his "Lancashire Sketches", Edwin Waugh recalls for us a midsummer storm when Tom Bockin and Rondle o' Dotherin' Johnny's are seated in The Red Cat, watching the rain splashing down the windows and recalling "that dreary time when th' cotton famine wur agate". Three wet travellers rush in to shelter from the storm but their colleague trudges on, refusing an invitation at least to step in for a gill. "Nawe", says he, "it'll not harm me now, for I'm as weet as I con be". "Off witho, then, an' fill thi bally wi' rain-wayter",is the reply, as he plods on his way, leaving his companions to ruminate. "Why, he'll be as weet as a wayter-dog!" ... "Well, he says he likes it" ... "Why, then, let him help his sel'—there's plenty on it ..."
For a short period after the end of the Second World War the Red Lion was occupied by squatters. Shortly after they were evicted the building was demolished. Meantime, the present Red Lion Hotel was under construction.

(12) and (13) THATCHED COTTAGES.—One stood on the site of the lych gate and the other on the left of the Sunday School building.

(14) ALL HALLOWS CHURCH.—The earliest reference to a church in Bispham occurs in the reign of Richard I (A.D. 1189-99) when Theobald Walter quitclaimed his right to the churches of Poulton and Bispham to the Abbey of Sees in Normandy and St. Mary's of Lancaster. During the 13th and 14th centuries it would appear that Bispham was a chapelry attached to Poulton. In 1345 both buildings were in such a state of disrepair that the Archdeacon of Richmond pressed the Rectors of Preston and St. Michael's-on-Wyre to "canonically coerce the Vicar of Poulton and the Abbot of Lancaster to remake and repair the chancel of the church of Poulton and the chapel of Bispham annexed to the same". In 1351 the Archdeacon made a personal visit to assure himself

that his requests had been carried out and later he called upon the brethren of St. Mary's demanding to know by what right they held Poulton Church and Bispham Chapel. They gave reply by "many instruments and muniments and apostolic letters and by witnesses worthy of credit".

The original church was a low red sandstone building with a two-gabled roof supported at the junction by a row of black oak pillars set down the centre of the building. It had a chancel and black oak pews, three lancet windows at the east and a low tower to the west.

In 1773 the roof and pillars were removed and the building, without aisles, or chancel, was heightened. Only the tower and doorway arch were left untouched. The first organ was only installed in 1857. Before that date the "singers" were accompanied by violin, clarinet, 'cello and bassoon. This second church was cold and without comfort, relying only on the warmth from a large central stove. It was entirely demolished in 1883 and the site was used for the building of the present church. During the process, and in addition to an old Saxon piscena and the remains of a three-light window, one of the treasures of Bispham All Hallows came to light. It was only accidentally discovered that some of the stones, whitewashed and plastered over, and haphazardly lying about the premises, were parts of the original Norman sandstone arch with chevron carvings and the twelve signs of the zodiac. More than half were weathered almost beyond recognition, but the Crab, the Bull and the Virgin were still distinct. The stones were cleaned, re-erected and re-tooled and this zodiac arch of Bispham is well worth a visit.

(15) BRIDGE END. The white farmhouse took its name from a dyke or streamlet which flows under a bridge near the site and by culverts and dykes ultimately joins up with the Wyre. This is probably the same stream which flowed under The Brig and wound round the back of the houses before meandering on to Bridge End.

In the old days, when the dyke was full and the frost keen, the lads of the village used to dam up the water near Bridge End and the ice that formed on the flooded fields made it possible to skate as far as Anchorsholme. An elderly resident recently produced an old-fashioned pair of skates which he used for that purpose as a boy.

The story of Bridge End goes back centuries and the first Queen Elizabeth is mentioned in the deeds. The Anyon family lived there in the 17th century and on 22nd November, 1635, "Richard, the sonne of John Anyon of the bridgend" was baptised at Bispham Church. Early in the next century Susannah Veale of Whinney Heys (now the Nurses' Home attached to Victoria Hospital) married John Fayle of The Holmes and afterwards of Bridgend, Bispham. The Fayles are said to have built their home at Bridge End on the model of the original hall at Whinney Heys and a date stone near the kitchen door was inscribed "John and Susannah Fayle, 1711". Possibly some of the older building was merged with the new. Cobbles from the shore were mingled with hand-made bricks. Wooden beams were heavy and hand-wrought. Flag floors once neat became worn and uneven with the passage of time.

In later years Bridge End was cement faced and it is likely that at some period a number of windows had been bricked up. All in all, however, it presented a dignified picture of a farmhouse of substance typical of the early 18th century.

To the right of the house stood a large barn with huge wooden beams, and a number of outbuildings. All these properties were demolished in April, 1961, to accommodate a housing estate.

(16) BISPHAM ENDOWED CHURCH OF ENGLAND SCHOOL. No-one knows exactly when the first free school was founded in Bispham but it is said to have existed as early as 1621 which makes it the parent of all Blackpool Schools. In 1659, Richard Higginson, a Bispham lad who was baptised in the church there in 1603, but who later became a prosperous City Alderman of London, left an annual sum of £30 for the schooling of the children of his native parish. The school was then "a low thatched place, with a master's house at one end ... very small, only 30 feet x 14 feet and 7 feet high, with a flagged floor ar l a stove in the

centre". The endowment came from the rents of the "Black Lion" and the "Golden Bull", two inns close to St. Paul's Cathedral, which were consumed by the Great Fire of London in 1666. After the death of Richard Higginson, his widow, though remarried, fulfilled her late husband's intentions by donating £200 to be invested in lands and the purchase of rents "for the maintenance of a schoolmaster at Bispham". Instead the capital was loaned out at interest, producing sufficient to cover the schoolmaster's miserly salary of £7 per annum which probably precipitated the closure of the school.

For about 100 years, until a new school was built in 1800, the scholars were taught at the Presbyterian Chapel and School, by arrangement between the respective trustees, and in 1827 Mr. Peter Wood was appointed headmaster at a salary of £70 per annum, a position which he held for 59 years. In 1850 there were 30 day scholars and 6 boarders, though during the 19th century attendance varied between 30 and 60. A school inspector's report of 1869 gives a vivid picture of educational provisions in the old days: "The present school house is in a shocking state. It is an old building, through whose thatched roof the rain can find its way in winter, dripping down among the children and forming pools on the floor. The air is exceedingly foul. I was obliged to keep the door open while examining the children. The master has a cottage . . . and a poor one it is. There were present at the school not more than half the number on the books. A page of writing is done in copy books; all other work is done on slates, each boy having as many as three or four."

It is not surprising that the building was abandoned in 1873 and until the present school was erected in 1878 (buildings, fittings and playground costing £821) the scholars were accommodated in the Temperance Hall in the village.

The hamlet of Norbreck a century ago

"IN Norbreck everything smacks of the sea", wrote Edwin Waugh of this tiny hamlet perched on a green hump sloping down to the cliffs a hundred years ago. "The road, which comes up thither from many a mile of playful meanderings through the green country, as soon as it quits the last house, immediately dives through the cliffs with a sudden impulse as if it had been . . . drawn all that long way solely by its love for the ocean".

A handful of cottages, all but one of them ranged on the same side of the grassy track that called itself a road, were built unpretentiously of sea stones. They turned their backs to the north and their shoulders to the sea. They shone out of their green setting with a startling whiteness, bewitching to the eye in their simplicity and homely charm. The stranger chancing upon the place might think it deserted, for as Waugh says: "There is seldom much stir in Norbreck, except such as the elements make". Callers were a rarity, whatever the season, though there might be some slight activity when a pile of accumulated wreck salvage called for a periodical sale, or when the summer visitor strayed in, glad for a while to be rid of the bustle of Blackpool.

Let us picture the place at full summer, basking in the heat of the sun, heavy with the sweet scent of roses, the stillness only intensified by Nature's own noises—the song of the lark, the seabird's cry, the barking of a dog in the distance, the muted clip-clop of cattle on the grass road, and the strident squawking of poultry. From the shippon drifts over a snatch of the milkmaid's song. The cow-lad clatters his pails and whistles the while. "Owd England", the weather-beaten "Patriarch of Norbreck, may paddle across the road to look after his cattle or, staff in hand, may be going down to the 'low-watter' a-shrimping, with his thin hair playing in the breeze".

They are house-and-garden-proud, these folk of Old Norbreck, the name of whose hamlet descends directly from the Norse. Their flower beds are bordered with sea-shells. Stones of every colour pattern their pathways. Trellis work and rambling roses beautify the low six-room cottage running lengthwise from the sea. The grasses nod, and the fruit trees bend before the wind. "The main body of the hamlet", Waugh tells us, "consists of a great irregular range of buildings, formerly the residence of a wealthy family" but now divided into small dwellings, the end-most having a small enclosed lawn. From these a broad field separates the only other place of habitation, a picturesque hotch-potch of varying heights and periods. The lowest portion has been turned into one-storey cottages with "an air of order and tasteful rusticity". The highest portion rises to two storeys, with attics, and with great bow windows commanding a fine view of the ocean.

Autumn becomes a season of noble solitude and glorious sun-sets and presently harsh winter hurls her fury on a wild and lonely Norbreck which by springtime, looks "moulty and ragged to the eye" and ready for a fresh lick of whitewash. It is not surprising that the Lancashire poet returned again and again to this miniature village with the scent of the sea in its nostrils, the boom of the breakers in its ears, and the desperate cry of the doomed mariner ever on its mind, nor that this isolated community inspired some of his finest descriptive writing.

By 1876, Porter tells us, five elegant marine residences had been built for neighbouring wealthy families. These formed the spearhead of an invasion by the modern builder whose activities in comparatively short years rubbed Old Norbreck out of existence.

142

Marton

Marton Moss and Mere

IN some far off century before the Romans set their mark upon this island the coastal region of the Fylde was a wild and marshy woodland. Giant trees, fir, oak and yew, cast sombre shadows over bog and standing pool. Animals of the forest roamed at will, the wild boar, the wolf, the red deer, Urus the great horned ox, extinct in Britain before the landing of the Romans, and all the lesser creatures of the woodland. In prehistoric times the sea rose up with a violence unparalleled and, driven by a hurricane wind, boiled over the low-lying lands, felling the forest giants in its path and leaving behind a devastation too fearful to imagine. Venerable oaks, so large that in later centuries a labourer might not grasp the hand of his colleague stretched over the trunk, had kneeled over like straws before a great wind. They lay sprawled and intertangled on their bed of greasy clay, obstructing drainage and encouraging the kind of plant life which flourishes in stagnation.

This was the beginning of a long process of decomposition. Bark and foliage rotted down into peat and each year's growth of plant life, falling to decay, was assimilated into the slowly forming moss. Thornber tells us that the trees of Marton Moss forest were felled in a south-easterly direction from the shore and that sea shells and marine silt had been turned up in the peat bed overlying the original clay. Even to this day the farmer's plough will occasionally hit an obstruction and another "bog oak" will have to be prised from its prehistoric bed, perhaps to be made into furniture or, more likely, to litter the farmyard.

Thus, by the sudden wrath of the sea and Nature's own process of annual growth and decay, was the great Moss of Marton formed, extending more than one mile in width and six miles from north to south. The same storm which ripped down the forest may have formed Marton Mere, once a lake of considerable extent, lying between two ridges of high ground, and having at one time a valuable fishery and three watercourses emptying into Lytham Pool, Skip Pool and the Black Pool. Until the Skippool watercourse was cleared in the 18th century, reducing the level of Marton Mere by many feet, flooding from this source was a regular hazard.

Reclamation of the Marton area, however, was proceeding

143

satisfactorily by 1780, though only after many years of discussion and delay. Efficient drainage and an accretion of sediment gradually reduced the size of the Mere, once several miles in length and one and a half in width, to its present insignificant proportions. Yet such was the extent of this present-day haunt of the angler, the bird-watcher and the wild fowler, that in earlier centuries the outfall from Marton Mere turned the wheel of a water mill near to Great Marton.

Until the 18th century Marton was the place of many waters. Cursedmere, mentioned in the 12th century foundation charter of the Lytham Benedictine Priory, was situated on the borders of the Lytham manor, not far from Peel. It was so named, some said, in memory of a horrid murder, but others declared it to have been merely a watery grave for unwary cattle. Cursedmere disappeared with the reclamation of the mosses but Porter tells us that beneath the boggy surface of land then known as The Tarns, "a husbandman discovered the remains of a small open boat which had doubtless been used in earlier days on the waters of Cursedmere". The remains of two coracles, small boats made of skins stretched over wooden frames, were also unearthed from the old bed of Marton Mere, and at Mythop a few years ago a farmer ploughing where once was deep water hooked up an old anchor which had lain undetected for years in its bed of peat.

The natives of this area before the coming of the Romans were an offshoot tribe of the Brigantes, known as Setantii. They were wise to the ways of their waters and their marshes where a stranger might not travel without danger. The aboriginals neither built, nor planned, but lived tribally in crude shelters made of branches or mud, supporting themselves on the fruits of hunting and fishing, paddling their frail skin-craft over a series of streams and lakelets, and relying on their dark forest and the treacherous nature of their boglands for protection. Theirs was the desperate struggle to continue the thread of life and to survive the on-slaughts of sea, storm and flood, and the ever present menace of the enemy, whether human or animal. Small wonder it is that the highly civilised Romans found this waterlogged terrain little to their liking and delayed the subjugation of this north-western pocket of resistance until late in their campaign.

Of early man in this area but little has come to light to reveal his way of life. A couple of stone age hammers, a stone celt or cutting implement, some 8 ins. long, a bronze axe, a coracle or two, cairns of uncertain date located at South Shore, and an anchor, are all that emerged from those far-off times. But it is obvious that this rich and fruitful moss land, bordered by the hawes and a ridge of star-grassed dunes composed of accumu-lated particles of blown sand, has supported human life through countless centuries.

"Meretun" of the Domesday Survey to Marton of the 17th century

TO "Meretun", the town of the Mere, Domesday Survey assigned six carucates of arable land of which shortly afterwards Sir Adam de Merton held half in return for military service when necessary. Before A.D. 1206 lands at Meretun were held by Theobald Walter whose descendants assumed the name of le Botiler, or Butler, and in that family they continued until the time of Henry VIII when Sir Thomas Butler sold his manor of Great Layton, and Marton, once separate but then annexed to it, to John Brown, Citizen and Mercer of London. John Brown flits fleetingly through the story for within brief time his holdings were purchased by Thomas Fleetwood, Esq., who established the family seat at Rossall Hall. The Fleetwood family continued to hold considerable possessions in the Fylde coast area, including Bispham-cum-Norbreck and Layton-cum-Warbreck, and Marton, until 1841 when the Lord of the Manor, Sir Peter Hesketh Fleetwood, disposed of his possessions to Thomas Clifton, Esq., of Lytham. Until modern times Marton was in no way influenced by the popularity and phenomenal growth of neighbouring Blackpool, and within living memory she still retained a pace and a simplicity all her own.

At the time of the Great Survey, "Meretun" was composed of three separate communities set on rising ground above the Mere, the sand-dunes, and the swamps. They were Great Marton, Little Marton and the "Peel", a place of refuge in time of trouble and, says Porter, an "ancient turreted manorial mansion" having a moat and drawbridge. Geographically isolated, limited of outlook, the Martonians placed at a far distance from their parish church of Poulton, and tied for ever to the land, retained their mediaeval traditions for centuries after they had fallen away in other districts. They held their fairs and markets and saw to their own hangings. They paid suit and service to the Manor Court summoned by the Squire, which obliged them to scour their ditches and dykes, to "repaire their parte in the highway", under forfeit, to see "that the pin fould shall be maintained kept sufficient, every one their part", and discouraged them from squabbling with their neighbours. (1670: "We present Richard Ryley for his wife abuseing of Agnes Fisher and taking her goods forciblie from her, in 00.06.08d.".)

In the 16th century these country folk had more than their share of excitement. In 1530 "over 100 riotous persons" from Layton, Marton and the Moss rose up in support of Dame Margaret and her son, Thomas Butler, and advanced upon the Lytham border armed with fierce expressions and weapons probably of a domestic or agricultural nature. Their first target was the house of Lawrence Billington on Layton Hawes but belonging to the Priory of Lytham. The Butlers considered this to have been set up within their domain and accordingly their supporters pulled it down and in doing so "cast out valuable goods ... and cut the timber into pieces". One hundred loads of rushes, valuable for thatching and making into rushlights, were carried off in the skirmish and much damage was occasioned to ditches, fences and growing crops, which impoverished the Priory so "that they were unable to keep up the hospitality of the place, as had been their wont". After this vigorous uprising the terrified Prior fled for his life, "the defendants having threatened to pull his house down over his head". The Butlers were bidden to "refrain from meddling in the land of the Hawes" but a temporary truce led to a second engagement when 200 Butler supporters of both sexes "advanced upon the land under dispute" (known locally ever since as "Mad Nook") and in attacks spread over three days in May, 1532, uprooted hundreds of fence poles, demolished a boundary cross and drove out 154 Priory cattle. The case was investigated by the Chancellor of the Duchy of Lancaster who listened to many a garbled tale and exaggerated account before finally finding in favour of the Lytham Priory. If the Butlers accepted their defeat with grace, a deep hostility had been implanted between the "sandgrown 'uns" of Lytham and the "mossogs" of Marton, and in some old native families it still lingers, though inevitably softened by time.

In 1583 William Fleetwood lodged a complaint against John Massie of Whinney Heys, and other persons, to the effect that his manor house at Layton, let to John Massie, had been allowed to fall into decay and had "become so ruinous that it is ready to fall down"; that enclosures, ditches and fences had been destroyed; and that the complainant's servant, having been sent quietly to drive Massie's cattle off the premises, was assaulted and kept at bay with long piked staves.

In the closing years of that century the five sons of Edmund Fleetwood commenced a suit against John Massie and Anthony Veale, alleging riotous behaviour and unlawful assemblies, the destruction of turves and brickstones, the uttering of threatening words, taking the liberty of fishing "to the hinderance of the complainants", influencing 80 tenants to absent themselves from the manor court, hindering brickmakers at their work, and the malicious cutting of mares' manes and tails. James Massie answered that, after taking legal opinion, he had discovered himself to be "discharged and freed" from attending the Manor Court, and therefore did not appear; that an unknown number of inhabitants had conferred together at the house of Emlinge Hull; that the Squire's turves had been trampled, and his mares barbered, but by persons unknown; and that the brickmakers, for taking clay from ground other than that belonging to the Squire, had been warned to continue at their peril. All these crises, though trivial and domestic, would enliven conversation on the Moss for many a long year and would undoubtedly gather colour in the telling.

About 1625 the Martonians, petitioning that some five waterlogged miles divided them from their parish church at Poulton, requested that their township, together with "Layton, Layton Rakes and Blackpool" might be constituted a separate parish. The parliamentary commissioners were apparently unsympathetic to this reasonable request and more than 150 years elapsed before the claim received practical acknowledgment.

Old customs and superstitions
Nonconformity, bad roads and the Preaching House

"LITTLE less than a scene of moral destitution" is how Thornber sums up Marton in the days before James Baines of Poulton erected and endowed a charity school there in 1717, and by doing so, dispelled "the mists of ignorance and superstition which", he says, "to a lamentable extent overshadowed it". The pronouncement is somewhat lacking in charity for basically the people of the Moss were tough, hardworking and decent. Life was a continuing battle against disease, floods, the raging of the elements, and the need to wrest sufficient from the land to cram into hungry young mouths. Man and woman alike, they toiled in the fields. Their tiny houses were neatly maintained, with trim "thack", fresh white walls, and stone floors newly sanded. True enough, they used their Sundays on Layton Hawes for frolic and fun-making. Their pastimes had all the vigour of unenlightened rusticity. Cockfighting, bull baiting and bear baiting, foot racing and trials of strength, were favourite diversions.

Christmas was the time of Yule loaves, mince pies, card-playing through the night, and the warming of the hob-penny in readiness for the first Christmas singers. On Christmas Eve housewives from all the remote Fylde hamlets flocked into Poulton market place to buy their Christmas beef. The village lads amused themselves with rough-and-tumble games, knur-and-spell, tripstick and football (without rules) along the village lanes, and at this season the gun could be used by all.

Easter revived the old-time custom of "pace-egging". Even until recent years there was always a sharp drop in school attendance as children profitably spent their time knocking at cottage doors demanding gifts of coins or fresh eggs which were boiled hard and dyed with the skins of onions or the yellow broom blossom. At Easter, too, the Waits strode unceremoniously into cottage kitchens and commenced their mumming. Cockfighting and pancakes were traditional on Shrove Tuesday. Candlemas was hiring time when farm servants and labourers lined up looking for new masters. On "Booning" days the Squire summoned his tenants to assist with the work on his estate.

Weddings always drew idle crowds to the church door, waiting to scramble for the new bridegroom's scattering of halfpence. Burials, as often as not, degenerated into bouts of drinking, tobacco smoking and loud laughter at the home of the departed, and were often disgraced, says Thornber, "by pugilistic encounters between the rival townships of Thornton and Marton". With the marriage ceremony the Moss folk were not unduly concerned and those who were disposed to tie the legal knot were often discouraged, and sometimes debarred, by the miles of flooded fields and muddy lanes which separated them from their church. Even into the present century good hard-working and respectable couples dispensed with the ceremony, yet lived together in amity for a lifetime, bringing up large families and being thought no worse of for their attitude of sturdy independence. These informal partnerships were not entered into lightly or promiscuously, but were permanent and often more felicitous than legalised unions.

The folk of the Moss were, by inclination and circumstances, static. Footslogging along the lamentably rut-ridden and mud-strewn Fylde lanes was no pleasurable pastime and to travel on wheels was only to court certain disaster. In October, 1655, the inhabitants of Great and Little Marton petitioned Quarter Sessions for permission to erect a bridge over the outlet from Marton Mere to the sea, having been "many tymes in the winter debarred from the benefitt of the Marquett at Preston at the most beneficiall and usual tymes of commerce", the highway being "in the winter so soft by reason of the slitch and water that it is not passable but with great danger of losse or spoilinge theire goods". Within living memory it was still customary to carry market garden produce into Preston by means of horse panniers.

Despite Thornber's allegations of widespread laxness and immorality there is evidence of a small puritan element existing in Marton in the 18th century and particularly at Little Marton, once a picturesque community of bonny clustered cottages and solitary farmsteads and plenty of whitewash and thatch. There were always artists heading for Little Marton which had its own tiny school (later used as library-cum-clinic) and field ponds

The Old Homestead Preaching House, Little Marton.

glistening like living mirrors in wide emerald green fields. (The whole area is now dominated by the Mereside housing estate.)

On the left of Clifton Road proceeding inland, until recent months there survived a 17th century or even earlier cottage of great charm, despite the asbestos roof in place of thatch. Beyond it, past Brindle Lodge (one of the country's largest homes for the elderly, purpose-built on the site of Moss Edge Farm of the Johnsons, and opened in 1964 by Miss Gracie Fields) and past the modern flats, once stood its twin, "The Old Homestead", before the bungalow "Otter Bank". Catherine Johnson from the farm married into the Fisher family whose ancestor, Robert Fisher, in 1762 helped to establish nonconformity in this part of the Fylde. It was a formidable proposition. The Fylde folk were notoriously rigid, passionately opposed to new ideas. Yet, the Rev. Benjamin Ingham, who was labouring about the same time as the Wesleys, sent his Inghamite preachers to Little Marton and even wrote to Mr. and Mrs. Fisher at "The Old Homestead".

13th March 1762.

Dear Friends,
Though unknown, I have received your kind and loving letter wherein you express your thanks to God and also to unworthy me for the benefit you have received by the preaching and conversation of my brethren and fellow labourers who have been amongst you. All thanks are due to God alone because all the good that is done upon earth the Lord doth it Himself. ... May He give you to know Him. I am your servant and well-wisher in the Lord.
BENJAMIN INGHAM.

The angry Vicar of Poulton threatened to prosecute the open air preachers for their intrusion, whereupon Robert Fisher trudged the 20 miles to Preston on 8th October, 1762, and got his house licensed for preaching. Shortly afterwards, a few converts met regularly in the cottage-chapel and received the Sacrament from the Inghamites. After a brief ministry, they withdrew to more fruitful pastures and the Martonians stoically trekked nine miles over flooded fields and terrible Fylde tracks to attend the Congregational Church at Elswick. But the licence still held and the thatched white cottage, so low that a tall man could not straighten up without a painful reminder from the beams, was used periodically for divine worship by the Independents. A letter from Phoebe Fisher to her son on 1st November, 1797, makes reference to that effect: "We have the Lord's Supper here again and meetings on Sabbath days. I am in good health, the Lord be thanked".

In 1890 Benjamin Nightingale described the place internally as being "even more quaint and ancient looking than it is without ... The floor, now covered with red tiles, was formerly made of clay into which hollows of considerable depth had been worn in course of time. The fireplace has been modernised but a huge oak beam across this part of the building hangs low and proclaims its antiquity. Some letters have been cut into it but they cannot be deciphered".

In 1962 Mrs. Catherine Fisher, then aged 89, recalled memories

149

of the family going back to "Richard Filius Johis ffisher de M'ton" who was baptised on "ffebruarie xvj 1592". A few years later they built "The Old Homestead" of cobbles and clay, with low ceilings plastered on rushes, clay floors and a firehood sweeping down like a canopy and supported by a stout timber beam. There was a hook for rushlights and an iron bar served as a fireguard. An extra ring was slotted on to it for each child born into the family. Built in clay and attached to the cottage were a large shippon and barn but these were demolished about 1905. Until late in Mrs. Fisher's life, the family retained the oak and redwood early 18th century pulpit-chair which the preachers used as a lectern, anchoring the leaves of the Bible with two leather straps. It was often used in the open air in front of "The Old Homestead" in the presence of a few curious villagers and onlookers.

From the 1760s, Church of England services were held in the schoolhouse endowed by Baines' Charity. Marton's Church of St. Paul was erected by subscription and licensed in the year 1800 and consecrated in 1804.

It was a simple structure, without chancel or tower, which were added later, having front and side galleries and accommodation for 400 worshippers. For years the musical accompaniment was provided by three wind instruments but some time after 1846, in which year our barrister-journalist "J.B." commented somewhat tartly on the vocal performances, a barrel organ was installed. This was later substituted by a modern organ and there have been many alterations and improvements since that time.

Methodism comes to Marton

THE Wesleyan Society attracted its first convert from Preston about the year 1755. Martha Thompson (born c. 1731) left home after her father's second marriage and went up to London to work as a domestic servant in a gentleman's household. She was 19 at the time. Five years later, whilst performing an errand for her mistress, she hovered at the edge of the hymn-singing crowds congregating at Moorfields to hear the great John Wesley. The power of his message stirred her soul and filled her with such gladness that her fellow-servants and her employer's physician declared her quite mad. She was hustled off to a lunatic asylum where she might have languished life-long but for the intervention of John Wesley himself who secured her freedom, satisfied himself that she was capable of supporting herself by millinery and mantle-making if she could only make it back to Preston, and even gave her a lift, part-way, on the sociable pillion. The journey was completed in a carrier's cart and, in her native town, Martha made good. Devoted to the Methodist cause, she sought converts, the first being an ale-house keeper of Church Street, a Mrs. Walmsley whose son William was presently drawn into the Society. On Sundays they walked six miles

to Brimicroft, then included in the Haworth Circuit, and wor-
shipped with a small group of converts; but every six weeks a
travelling preacher came to Preston and meetings were held in
Mrs. Walmsley's alehouse. Martha Thompson (later Mrs. J. B.
Whitehead) toiled valiantly in the field until her death at Preston,
at the age of 88, in 1820.

During the 1780s, three young Methodist evangelists were
striding through the Fylde countryside seeking converts. Roger
Crane, born at Preston in 1758, was an educated man of means,
descended from a line of staunch Presbyterians. He was to enjoy
the personal friendship of John Wesley and entertained the great
preacher during two of his Preston visits in the 1780s. William
Bramwell was a country lad born in 1759 in a thatched cottage
between Elswick and Copp Church. He gave himself whole-
heartedly to Methodism after hearing Wesley preaching at
Preston in 1780. Michael Emmett, also born in 1759, was the
son of the landlord of the "Ram's Head" up Gin Bow Entry
near the Market Place, Preston, a dingy quarter of the old town
noted for its ancient and ramshackle buildings, narrow entries,
yards, warehouses, slaughter houses and shops. The "Ram's
Head" was an orderly house affording clean beds and wholesome
fare to the stage coach travellers passing through the town.
Landlord Emmett was mightily displeased when his son took
on the Methodist mantle in the late 1770s and they were
estranged for many years. In 1779, Crane, Bramwell and Emmett
joined forces and stepped out bravely towards the coast. Theirs
was a hostile reception. The Fylde natives were already divided
into three bigoted and exclusive groups—Anglicans drawn from
the yeomanry, farmers and tradesmen; Roman Catholics descended from ancient landed families and their tenants who had
never swerved in their allegiance to Rome; and nonconformists
and puritans who held stiffly aloof from other denominations.

New ideas were not welcomed in the Fylde. Inaccessibility had
rendered her natives clannish and hostile to change. Methodism
had made little impact here until Moses Holden, at the Conference of 1810, was urged once more to open up the territory
of the Fylde. In his Journal of 1811 he records his modest suc-
cesses. "Poulton 11, Kirkham 8, Thornton 17, Freckleton 12 ...
Marton 7". (Only at Lytham was he forced to admit to complete
failure. "They received me kindly and heard me gladly, but that
was all".) Dating from Holden's campaign, a small band of
Methodists in Marton and Blowing Sands met in the home of a
Mr. John Hall. From 1835 the Marton Society was included in,
and served by, the Garstang Circuit, and so continued until 1855
when Blackpool became head of a new Circuit, drawing in all the
small societies in its neighbourhood.

Meantime, the Moss-folk met together in members' houses,
receiving with joy a Mr. Richardson who walked from Newton
(17 miles the round journey) to conduct quarterly Love Feasts
adapted from the Agapé of the early church when persecuted
Christians met by stealth to eat bread together "with gladness
and singleness of heart". Love Feasts were conducted with

simple fervour by an honoured local preacher and without resort to consecrated elements or sacrificial offerings. They continued into late Victorian times, when young and old met together for prayers and hymns and the passing round of the water jug and pieces of bread or plain cake.

In 1847 a small plain brick Methodist Chapel was built in Squire's Gate Lane between the little village smithy and a cluster of thatched and whitewashed cottages reaching to the corner of Common Edge Lane. It was a simple building with pulpit and benches and an inscribed stone tablet over the entrance. The folk of the Moss were then widely scattered, living in isolated holdings dotted thinly over rich agricultural acres. Farmers from Mythop and Marton and beyond rolled up in their shandrays to Sunday services at the Blowing Sands Chapel and stabled their horses behind the cottage of Mrs. Singleton. In 1872 the present Moss Side Wesleyan Chapel was built by subscription at a cost of £610 5s. 9d., and opened with a membership of 20. The abandoned chapel was offered for sale—the following is a notice of the event—and realised the sum of £64 8s. 0d.

TO BE SOLD
BY TENDER

A FREEHOLD CHAPEL

SITUATE AT BLOWING SANDS, about two miles from Blackpool. The pulpit and benches will be moved to the new Chapel at Moss Side. Tenders may be sent in until the 31st May to Mr. JAS. HARGREAVES, Moss Side, or to Mr. WM. BUTCHER, Blowing Sands.

W. Porter & Sons, Printers by Steam power, Blackpool.

The chapel was bought by the local blacksmith who demolished it and used the materials in the erection of two cottages which still occupy the site. Many years later it was accidentally discovered that the under-side of the stone draining board in the kitchen of one of the cottages had a roughened surface and it turned out that this was the stone bearing the date, 1847, from the original Blowing Sands Chapel. The tablet was moved from its humble setting to one of prominence over the doorway of the new church.

From 1872 a harmonium provided the musical accompaniment but in 1946, a pipe organ was installed through the generosity of a well-known Moss couple, Mr. and Mrs. J. E. Cardwell. Just to show how things have changed, a lady octogenarian who still lived on the Moss in the 1960s, remembered how she and her father used to tend the coke stove, trim the oil lamps, lay the coal fires for the minister and keep the place spotlessly clean for 2s. 6d. per week!

This year (1975) reaches another milestone in the history of Marton Moss Methodism. A new Marton Methodist Church, across the road from the old one, is under construction and is due to open in September and the existing church which has celebrated two centenaries (its own in 1972 and a previous one in 1947 in commemoration of the founding of the Blowing Sands Chapel 100 years earlier) is likely to be demolished and cleared for redevelopment.

The Saddle Inn, Marton, and the old "No. 3" at Layton

IT HAS been claimed that The Saddle dates back to the time of Cromwell. The earliest deed, however, bears the date 1776, coinciding with the estimated date of the present building which was very likely erected on the site of an earlier cobble hostelry. In 1776 it is described as a Brew House owned by Richard Hall, a saddler of Little Marton, who conveyed the property to Thomas Crookall, Maltster of Great Marton, in 1814. By this time it was known as the Roundabout House for the simple reason that customers coming along Whitegate Lane had to walk "roundabout" the premises to get in the front door which was at the back, looking up Preston Old Road. On the death of Thomas Crookall in 1839 the property was vested in his son, George Milner Crookall of the Blue School, Newton-with-Scales. In 1844 the Executors of Thomas Crookall sold the property, named for the first time The Saddle Inn, to William Parkinson of the No. 3 Hotel in Layton-with-Warbreck.

The Saddle Inn still retains a quaint country atmosphere and has a fine picture gallery of old time music hall artistes, British and foreign royalty, sportsmen, and naval engagements from the 17th century onwards. The "House of Lords" is a room reserved for men only. The "House of Commons", a typical old-fashioned parlour, is open for mixed company. A third room is referred to jocularly as "The Division Lobby".

The No. 3, a whitewashed cobble-and-thatch building when William Hutton came to Blackpool in 1788, was rebuilt, probably in the mid-19th century. Much of the original cobble remains in the cellars, along with sturdy wooden beams of a great age. When the inn was rebuilt the cellars were extended in brick. The first deed, being the conveyance from the Executors of Daniel Hornby, deceased, to The Raikes Hall Park Gardens and Aquarium Company Ltd., is dated 1872. The landlord in 1873 was Robert Wilson of Halifax and in 1877 the property was conveyed to Sarah Hawks, being described for the first time as the No. 3 and Didsbury Hotel.

By this time the hotel had a bowling green, a cab rank and drinking trough for horses, strawberry and pleasure gardens, stables and other outbuildings, and a commodious concert hall (now a refrigerator depot) where non-stop variety was laid on from 9-30 in the morning until 11-0 at night. A band played for dancing and for an admission fee of 4d. customers could spend all day in the theatre and ballroom, getting their entertainment on the cheap, and having their refreshments brought in on trays from the hotel. All the lads of the village must have spent many a happy hour there, rubbing shoulders with the visitors and making sure that the waiters were run off their feet. The licence of the No. 3 still extends to the old theatre premises of which the stage door, into the back yard of the hotel, still bears the number "13".

A tattered playbill which came to light when Feldman's Theatre was being rebuilt many years ago speaks of a "Grand Variety Combination Company" being specially engaged for Messrs. Banks' and Wood's Theatre adjoining the No. 3, commencing on Whit Monday. Performers included "Tom Barry, Negro Comedian, Eccentric Song and Dance Artiste; Miss Blanche, Serio-Comic Song and Dance Artiste; Harry Garrett, the London Star Vocalist and Character Comedian; and Mr. Tom Wilde, The Infant Leybourne".

At the back of the main bar in the hotel is a cosy room where, in Edwardian days, all the town's outstanding personalities called in, and where many a thousand pounds' worth of business was transacted over a glass. The Directors of the Raikes Hall Gardens, the two Blackpudlian knights, Sir John Bickerstaffe and Sir Lindsay Parkinson, and all the influential business magnates of the district gravitated to this room which they made exclusively their own. No local lad, however daring, ever intruded upon the privacy of this august set, whose old meeting place is nowadays reserved strictly for gentlemen only.

The No. 3 was once a country pub, set in the countryside amongst rolling green fields and sheltered by the trees of the Raikes Hall estate. The interior now is as modern as anyone could wish, but an atmosphere of Victorianism still remains in the Vaults.

The nick-names of Marton Moss

IN THE old days, when the Moss was an inter-married and close-knit community, a wide area produced only a handful of surnames. Trying to identify one of the many individuals bearing the same name might have led to hopeless confusion, but the Moss dwellers were ingenious in devising nick-names by which their bearers, and probably their descendants, were afterwards known. These by-names stuck for life and were recognised by all, and after a generation or two it was often difficult for anyone to recall the proper surname of his neighbour.

Some of these curious titles were rooted in physical peculiarities—Dapper, Littlethick, Lanky-Panky, Smiler, Blinker, Whitey, Owd Boco (a rag gatherer from Blowing Sands); others are too pointed to be kind and a few are too outspoken to be printed.

Many defy recognition or interpretation but it is obvious why the Websters were always called Duck, and why James Cardwell from Big Marton, was known as Jem Dayson ("he wur a dayson chap").

THRODKIN	Will Harrison. (When stopped by the law, one time, he announced: "William Harrison. Forty-two thousand". He died worth that amount.)
TOSSIES	The Harrison family.
CHICKIN	The Eaves family. Sons inherited the name—JACK CHICKIN, ALBERT CHICKIN.
OWD BONK	Properly named Wade. He lived in the old (demolished) Fold Row cottages beside the Shovels Inn and was the father of Will Wade who played the fiddle for the Leach Lodge Barn Dances at St. Annes.
SHADY WADE	Will Wade, son of BONK.
GOOD YOLLERS	The Division Lane Websters who were noted for making good yellow (yoller) butter.
DOUBLE YOO	Will Webster, i.e., DOUBLE YOO DUCK.
OWD KNOCK	Will Cardwell from Milkersgate Farm, Highfield Road. (Highfield Road known for years as Milkersgate Lane, and Waterloo Road as Cowgap Lane—pronounced "looan").
DOCKSWITCH	Walter Webster, i.e. DOCKSWITCH DUCK.
SCOTS, KNOBBY & GYPPO	Brothers of the Carr family.
FLEET	The Parkinson family—RALPH FLEET, WILL FLEET, etc.
KELLY	Albert Hesketh.
ALIDA	Wilkins, an undersized Clifton game-beater, who used a jumping pole to clear the dykes.
BARNEY	Jimmy Fern.
JIGGER	Jack Pearson.
SPRIGGS	The Sanderson family.
FLIMMINS	———
SHIGGLES	Tom Braithwaite, a great practical joker in his time. When there was mischief a-foot, gates lifted off, and so on, they would grin and say: " 'Ello! Shiggles musta bin up th' looan!" His son is still known as JIMMY SHIGGLES.
FLATTENER	"Owd Gillett" from Cross Slack Farm, just over the border. He was a good boxer.
TANNER, CHEESE, BUMP & BERRY	Members of the Cartmell family.
PODS	Henry Atkinson. (There is a "Pod's Nook" on the Moss.)
DUKE, FACK, WHITE, CLEGGY & MIDGE	The Ball family.
COAL JACK	A Cardwell.
SHANK	Jack Boardman. His son Richard — DICKY SHANK.
BILLY BRANDY	Wm. Cardwell.
OWD SLUD	One of the Wades from Stanley Road.
MAGGIE POG	Properly called Fisher.
JOE PENNY	Properly called Singleton.
CHAMP	Properly called Westhead.
OWD DOLLY	Properly called Lear or Leah.
TOMMY TODDLES	Properly called Webster.
FLACKIT	Properly called Fisher.
BELLE BUZZER	"A servant from next door to th' Afe-way" (Halfway Hotel).
JEMMY DOWK	James Bagot, who once lived in a tiny cottage, two steps below road level, near the old Church of England School at Marton.

155

Some curious old words are still in use on the Moss. "Prater wysies" are dried off potato tops. A cradle rocker is still a "cather trow". They speak of the "squab" (sofa), of the "jaum" (cosy hearth corner) and the fireside is still known as "t'hob". After an evening beside the "gleed" (red-hot) fire, the housewife will kneel and "scale" out the "ess-hoil" (ash-hole). Quaint expressions puzzle the newcomer, like "Enk!", or "Here's ta-bod!"—"Enk! I'll do id now" ... or "Here's ta-bod! Wod's this weather gooin ta do?" The farmer will pick up his hoe and set forth to "lowkthem tormuts" (weed those turnips), or rid his fields of "kelter" (weeds, rubbish or litter, in field or house). Years ago a Moss native died in a tiny cottage near Old School-house Farm. They found the place jammed solid with old bed-steads, bicycle parts, tin cans, miscellaneous debris and the raked out ashes from the fires of past years; and only a few inches of space remained clear round the table in the centre. "Th' place wur aw keltered up!"

Old Moss memories of schooldays, cottage life, brick-making and practical jokes

Marton amalgamates with Blackpool

FROM 1717 only the more determined children of the more enlightened parents on the Moss took the trouble to avail themselves of the education provided at James Baines' Charity School at Marton. Apart from the long walk involved many of the Moss folk did not hold with this new-fangled schooling. In 1854 another school was founded which was no more conveniently situated. Great Marton Church of England Infant School, a modest seat of learning, had to be enlarged in 1877, closed by order of the Board of Education on 31st August, 1925, and demolished to make way for the building of a new parochial hall. The scholars were then transferred to Baines' Endowed School.

Long before trams or 'buses were thought of, many a Moss child struggled on foot through bitter wintry weather to be taught the 3 R's for 3d. a week, paying 2d. a week extra for learning how to sew and an annual contribution of 1s. 0d. towards the winter's fuel. The mistress was Mrs. Fisher who had married into The Old Homestead family at Little Marton. She taught all subjects to all classes, detailing the older children to take charge of the smaller ones when she was otherwise engaged, a signal honour which was always striven after by the older girls. Mrs. Fisher was an accomplished needlewoman and at a time when women spent many hours over their sewing most of the girls paid to learn this subject as an "extra". The school stood surrounded by green fields along Whitegate Lane. From the Saddle Inn there was the Boar's Head a little way up Preston Old Road, then the school, and the Lord Nelson which was later turned into a fish-and-chip shop.

Opposite the Saddle Inn, on Whitegate Lane, was Hill's Farm, with Green's Farm a little further south, then vacant land as far as the Mill Inn, now called the Oxford. There was once a duck pond in the fields behind Hill's Farm. A thunder storm broke out, many years ago, and the farmer's wife went up the field to bring the ducks down to safety, but a thunderbolt beat her to it and ducks, pond and all, vanished in the instant before her eyes. The windmill adjoining the inn was built in the late 18th century and was above 100 years old when it was demolished around 1900. It stood guard over a quiet country lane. Nowadays traffic thunders by incessantly where passers-by were so rare that two people out walking at the same time gave cause for comment. and a passing thought would accurately determine the object of every errand.

Sanitary conditions among the countryfolk a century ago were a matter of concern to the Fylde Rural Authority. The Annual Report of the Medical Officer of Health for the year 1876 takes a critical look at the realities lurking behind charming scenes of innocent rusticity. "Much has been done throughout the district in the matter of improvement of cottage property", declares J. Davidson Walker. "Closet accommodation has been provided in all houses which the Inspector has found at all deficient in this matter, so that now it has become the exception and not the rule to find a cottage unprovided with proper accommodation in this respect". This happy state of affairs was achieved after 128 notices had been served requiring dwelling-houses to be closed, lime-washed or improved; back-yard, ditches and cellars to be drained; new closets to be built; petties to be removed; repairs to be effected to roofs, ash-pits, cess-pools, tanks and sewers; homes (5) to be cleared of poultry; removals (10) of pig-styes and contents; clearing of manure heaps (17) and three prosecutions for over-crowding.

The relation which existed between bad drinking water and preventable disease was beginning to be recognised by the Sanitary Authority but "many portions of Marton are still sadly in want of a proper water supply, having to depend for the scanty supplies which are afforded by the ditches and ponds in the neighbourhood of the houses, a source of supply which ... is exposed to all sorts of contamination." Yet, despite the excellent water available from the Fylde Waterworks Company (and probably on account of the expense) country-folk were vigorously opposed to abandoning their ancient and badly polluted wells "the contents of which, on analysis ... were proved to contain organic matter equal to one-third and one-half of average London sewage respectively". An inhabitant of Revoe, described as "a small village in the outskirts of Blackpool" (Gymnasium—Central Drive area) declared, after his well had been closed on a Magistrates' Order, that "sooner than drink Fylde Waterworks water he would drink his own urine!"

The serious problem of overcrowding in Marton, Staining and Poulton was aggravated in the summer months by the influx of Irish farm labourers and seasonal workers in Blackpool who were

157

compelled to seek cheap lodgings in the outlying rural communities. Bad ventilation and overcrowding pre-disposed the Fylde folk to infections and fevers. A typical case was cited of a family living in a small cottage with two tiny sleeping apartments, one of which was let to two adult lodgers. In the other slept father, mother, grandmother and four children aged 6, 5, 2 and 1 years, "with the only means of ventilation at hand, the chimney, stuffed up with old rags under the mistaken idea of keeping out the cold". Scarlet fever, then often unrecognised and dismissed as "only a bit of a cold" was raging at the school. The older children picked it up and brought it home to infect the whole family and within six weks, the four children were dead. Diphtheria was another killer and typhoid flared up periodically through contamination of well-water, though the death rate of the Fylde countryfolk compared favourably with many other districts and infant mortality was on the decline. In 1876 the greatest single killer listed in the Table of Causes of Death was "Old Age". One dedicated tippler came to an untimely end through "intemperance and delirium tremens"; and no verdicts were returned of homicide or suicide. Illegitimate births in the district formed 7·8% of the total recorded.

Schoolchildren a hundred years ago had a disciplined look which one rarely sees in their counterparts to-day. There was no slouching at desks during lessons. Straight backs and pens held in the correct position were the order of the day. The girls wore their long hair scraped back severely from their foreheads and tightly held in two plaits. Their serviceable stuff frocks were protected with cotton pinafores, and they wore clogs or boots, woollen stockings and demure expressions. The boys wore calf-length breeches and little Dickensian pork-pie caps. If school years were short, at least the scholars emerged well grounded in the basic subjects, being adept at mental arithmetic and capable of the beautiful hand-writing, acquired from hours of practice on slates and copy-books, which seems to be a lost art in these speed-ridden days.

Fortunately for the children of the Moss, a cottage was eventually made over into a school in Division Lane, though with accommodation for only a handful of the potential scholars. This was provided by the beneficent Lady Eleanor Cecily Clifton of Lytham Hall who cared greatly for the poor folk of the two manors and took a matriarchal interest in all their affairs. "Come to the hall on Tuesday at 2-30", she writes to Mr. Fair, the Clifton Agent, "and drive me in your pony carriage to the Moss School. I want to see about the work there" ... and again ... "I was at Mrs. Butcher's Moss School yesterday—she is having a school tea party and will be grateful for a few evergreens which I told her she should have—also at the same time send her 5s. 0d. from me towards the expenses of the tea fight".

About 1870 the Old Schoolhouse, now an ivy covered farmstead, was succeeded by a larger building in School Lane, which has been extended several times since that early date. On Sundays the building was also used as a church, being served from South Shore.

Brickmaking on the Moss was still carried on in the traditional manner of the ancient Egyptians until well in this century. Clay holes were everywhere and there were three brick crofts between Mad Nook (Division Lane) and the Oxford Hotel. Clay was made into a puddle during the winter and the bricks were made in the summer. The clay was thrown into moulds—it was a skilled job to see that all the corners were filled—and schoolchildren made many a copper by carrying the moulds to a prepared piece of ground, to dry in the wind and the summer sun. When quite dried out the bricks were fired in a coal heated kiln and sold at 12s. 6d. per 1,000, compared with present-day prices of more than £40. Hand-made bricks were produced on Marton Moss until about 1910 when modern methods were beginning to take over.

The sophistication of the towns was slow in influencing the folk of Marton Moss who made their living from the land, "stood" the markets, and rose at impossibly early hours of the morning to catch the first trade. They went everywhere on foot, produced most of the requisites of life, and yet still had sufficient zest to make their own amusements and to entertain themselves and each other with practical jokes.

Blocking up chimneys and smoking out the tenants, up-tipping water butts, removing the gates from all the gardens along the lane, blackening the bedroom windows of the newly married so that fingers could be pointed when the couple overslept, tripping up the pedestrian, or unseating the cyclist, by tying a rope across the road in the dark hours, were hoary old pranks which were always good for a laugh at the expense of the victims. One of the favourite jokes was played down Moss House on a hawker with a donkey cart who popped into a cottage to collect his order. Mischievous lads unhitched the ass and put it back in the shafts —after they had slotted it through a five-barred gate. "Na, how th' eck 'sta getten through theer!!!", muttered the flummoxed hawker, hurrying off to borrow a saw, whilst the culprits, doubled up with laughter, hid in a hedge bottom.

The old Moss folk had a dry sense of humour, with a tinge of malice softened by a grin. Visiting football teams always departed in a shower of turf clods. It was all part of the fun. And a neighbour's recital of woes—"Th' owd fellah's brokken his leg ... th' Missis is a' stiff as a gatepooast wi' th' rewmaticks ... th' watter's dried up i' th' well, an' to crown all, th' hoss 'as gone lame ..." was as likely as not to draw the laconic retort: "Aye, things is bad, aw' reet. Ar Margrit went to th' markut wi' a looad o' praters, an' hu ne'er sowd a god-damn yod 'un".

In the days before street lighting, evening visits to relatives and friends in neighbouring hamlets were always timed for full moon, and one octogenarian recalls how, full often, he trailed on foot from Mad Nook to Ballam hanging on to his mother's skirt and, if he were fortunate, returned in brilliant moonlight in the same manner, clutching a pillow case full of apples and pears. Even the young women rarely wore anything but black, relying on a well laundered cotton sunbonnet and a long gingham apron, for

159

added brightness.

The old homes of the Moss, though beautifully kept, were humble, low-ceilinged places. Tall clocks in low cottages presented a problem which could only be solved by cutting a hole in the bedroom ceiling or digging a hole in the floor to accommodate a well-loved but incommodious time-piece. In a farmhouse at Mad Nook (long since vanished) where the flag floor had worn so uneven that the grandfather clock stood tipsily askew, the occupant, instead of propping up one end and getting a level, cut a slit in the side of the case for the pendulum to swing through. The tabby cat used to sit by the hour beside the clock case, tapping the swinging pendulum with its paw.

Tall men and low ceilings made poor partners and many a cottager developed a significant stoop from years of painful tuition. Triangular bedrooms under the "thack" were reached by cat ladders where stairs were lacking, and the many children crammed into one bed embraced on both sides by the sloping roof had to climb in and out at the same side. There was no tonguing and grooving of floor boards and it was possible to lie in bed of a morning watching mother frying the breakfast bacon in the kitchen below, through the chinks between the bedroom floor boards. At least one woman's leg went clean through the downstairs ceiling as she was busy dusting the bedrooms overhead. Families were as large as the cottages were small, yet it was the proud boast of many a Moss woman that she had brought a houseful of "babbies" into the world, and "none of 'em cost me more nor afe-a-crown!" Neighbours "did" for each other at such times and assisted with such items as sick-nursing and laying out.

The children of the Moss learned early what life was about and were accustomed to spartan fare, bare comfort, absence of luxuries and shouldering family responsibilities from the moment they could walk. Poaching was rife when a good pheasant might fetch 3s. 6d., and "our only spending money was what we made catching sparrows", an old Moss-man told me. "We used a large net attached to a frame with a long handle. We sneaked up and clapped it against the ivy, hoping someone hadn't beaten us to it, and the sparrows fluttered in. We got a penny for two sparrows' heads, four small chicks or eight eggs from the nest. If we left a small stone in the nest the sparrow came back and laid more. It was paid for out of the Sparrow Tax and you could hand them in at two or three farms". The girls were burdened with babyminding before they learned their A.B.C's and it was not uncommon to see a small school-girl with a babe on her arm and three toddlers dragging at her skirts, or a young school-leaver managing a household with several children for a widowed relative. The alternative was a post in domestic or farm-service on the basis of a twelve-months' contract beginning at Candlemas (2nd February). The pay would be up to £14 a year for 16-hour days of back-breaking toil and only one free day off every month; and no matter how harsh and uncongenial the situation, the contract had to be kept.

Old country customs still prevailed on the mosslands—pace-egging at Easter, boys and girls singing at farm-house doors in the hope of collecting an egg or a small present; and also at Easter, the young men of the village went about in groups "Jolly-Ladding", entering households about to retire for the night to sing their traditional songs with actions, in expectation of reward. Christmas brought the carollers and mummers, and "May Boo-in" was a popular pastime. On May Bough Night (eve of May) young blades scrambled up their neighbours' thatch and stuck a branch down the chimney, and chanted a rhyme which had a barb in its nonsense:—

> A wicking for my dear chicking . . .
> A plum tree in bloom, to be married (and soon!)
> A briar for a liar!
> A thorn for a scorn.
> A willow for a witch, a long-tailed bitch . . .
> and so on.

Angry occupants would sometimes respond by letting fly with an old muzzle loader charged with nails, screws or odd scraps of metal—or with a gunload of "Indy" corn, if there was nothing else handy.

The clattering of clogs was everywhere in the lanes. Young and old were partial to this cheap, comfortable and practical footwear. When irons wore thin, everyone went to Nicholas Cardwell, the clogger, who lived in the cottage next to the Blowing Sands Smithy and plied his trade in an upstairs room. Children on their way home from school, or grown-ups on their way home from work, called at the clogger's and sat in their stocking-feet at the foot of the stairs, waiting for their clogs to be fettled on the spot.

The clogger's children spent many a happy hour leaning out of the bedroom window, watching Tom "Abey" (son of Abraham Cardwell), the blacksmith and wheelwright, busy at his work in the yard below. Horses were ever clattering in to be re-shod by Tom "Abey" the blacksmith, but it was more interesting to watch Tom "Abey" the wheelwright, lighting his fire under an iron rim, sliding it on to a new wheel, hammering it on and cooling it down with water to make firm. Children in those days knew how to extract every ounce of pleasure from every simple event, for all too soon they would be busy in the market garden or greenhouse, and a lifetime's responsibilities would descend upon their shoulders. Meantime there were summer days when the lassies roamed the lanes and picked daisies in the fields, or looked for blackberries, when the lads walked to the beach opposite the Manchester Hotel to bathe, and when an old chap from Moss House trudged to Squire's Gate for his daily dip, afterwards running about in the sandhills to get dry.

Inevitably Marton began to develop as Blackpool rose to great prominence. Better roads, easier communications, and a ready and ever-increasing market on the doorstep, where before trade had relied exclusively on Preston, resulted in rapid expansion of the market gardening industry. Countless acres were put under glass and, with improved road traffic, mounting quantities of horticultural produce were exported to the industrial towns of northern and central England. In addition to the now famous "Blackpool Tomatoes", lettuces by the million, bulbs, forced mint, parsley, cucumbers, mustard and cress, cauliflowers, sweet peas, carnations and chrysanthemum blooms find their way from our mosslands to the markets of England.

For many years Marton was ruled by a Parish Council and the Fylde Rural Council. Their limited powers, and the lack of amenities, turned the eyes of the inhabitants in the direction of Blackpool, with whom, after years of discussion, Marton amalgamated in 1934.

The Moss has changed, and is changing. The old places and the old ways are harder to find. Whitewash is seen but rarely amongst the encroaching red brick. The housewife no longer toils in the fields, batting away the midges and the horse flies with her sun-bonnet. Her life is no longer bounded by the garden gate, nor does she potter about the house from one year's end to another, wrapped in the appetising aroma of homebaked bread. Her sliced-wrapped is delivered at the door. She can hop on a Corporation 'bus at the end of the street. Her interests are many, her entertainment comes into cottage parlour, as into modern lounge, at the touch of a button. The Moss-wife is every bit as wide-awake and well dressed as her town-dwelling sister.

Yet, withal, the Moss is still a place where the dialect, laced with fragments of Norse and Old English, occasionally steals upon the ear like sweet music; a land of open ditches and bending willows, of unspoilt nooks and fresh green hedges; of golden sunshine, of cutting winds, of mists coming up like cotton wool, shoulder high; and of rich soil, black and glistening as lumps of jet!

Dun. Cottage, Common Edge Lane, Marton Moss, demolished in the early 1970s.

Bibliography

Acknowledgments are made to the following works which have been consulted during the preparation of this History and which are recommended to the reader for further study:—

THE HISTORY OF BLACKPOOL AND ITS NEIGHBOURHOOD, by Rev. W. Thornber.

A DESCRIPTION OF BLACKPOOL IN 1788, by Wm. Hutton.

REMINISCENCES OF A GENTLEWOMAN OF THE LAST CENTURY, ed. Catherine Hutton Beale, Birmingham, 1891.

HISTORY OF THE FYLDE OF LANCASHIRE, by John Porter.

THE ENGLISH PARTY'S EXCURSION TO PARIS (including A BLACKPOOL JOURNAL—1846), by J.B., Esq., Barrister-at-Law.

TRADITIONAL FYLDE HOUSES, by R. C. Watson. (Historic Society of Lancashire & Cheshire Transactions, Vol. 109.)

LANCASHIRE SKETCHES, by Edwin Waugh.

HISTORY OF THE COUNTY PALATINE OF LANCASTER, VOL. 1, by Edward Baines.

BLACKPOOL AND MARTON AMALGAMATION SOUVENIR, 1934.

EVOLUTION OF A COASTLINE and THE BATTLE OF LAND AND SEA, by Wm. Ashton.

HISTORY OF THE PARISH OF BISPHAM, by Henry Fishwick, F.S.A. (Chetham Society publication, Vol. 10, New Series.)

THE HISTORY OF BISPHAM PARISH CHURCH, compiled by James Hankinson Swarbrick.

BISPHAM ENDOWED CHURCH OF ENGLAND SCHOOL (pamphlet, 1957).

A HISTORY OF LANCASHIRE WITH MAPS AND PICTURES (New Edition) and LIFE IN MEDIEVAL ENGLAND, by J. J. Bagley, M.A.

DIARY OF THOMAS TYLDESLEY OF FOXHALL.

BLACKPOOL'S PROGRESS, JUBILEE YEAR, 1926 (Pictorial Souvenir).

BLACKPOOL GAZETTE & HERALD and BLACKPOOL TIMES YEAR BOOKS AND PICTORIAL SUPPLEMENTS.

THE STORY OF BLACKPOOL and THE STORY OF THE BLACKPOOL LIFEBOAT, by Allen Clarke (author of THE WINDMILL LAND SERIES).

LANCASHIRE GAZETTEERS AND DIRECTORIES, from the early 19th century.

VARIOUS PAPERS, PAMPHLETS, DOCUMENTS AND MAPS at the Lancashire County Records Office, Preston; Harris Library, Preston; Reference Department of the Central Library, Blackpool; and the Carnegie Library, St. Annes.

LANCASHIRE NONCONFORMITY, by Benjamin Nightingale, 1890.

A SCIENTIFIC SURVEY OF BLACKPOOL & DISTRICT, compiled for the British Association for the Advancement of Science, 1936.

RISE AND GROWTH OF BLACKPOOL, 1592-1792, by C. Roeder. (Historic Society of Lancashire & Cheshire Transactions, Vol. LIV.)

Index

New Promenade & Sea Defence Works
OPENED BY THE MAYOR ALDERMAN J BRODIE J P
July 25th 1905